T.A. Lee
Cash Flow Accounting

T.A. Lee
Corporate Audit Theory

S.P. Lumby
Investment Appraisal and Financial Decisions
(5th edn)
(Also available: *Teachers' Manual*)

T.W. McRae
Personal Financial Planning

M.R. Mathews
Socially Responsible Accounting

R.W. Perks
Accounting and Society

A.G. Puxty and J.C. Dodds
Financial Management: method and meaning
(2nd edn)
(Also available: *Teachers' Guide*)

J.M. Samuels, F.M. Wilkes and R.E. Brayshaw
Management of Company Finance (5th edn)
(Also available: *Students' Manual*)

J.M. Samuels, R.E. Brayshaw and J.M. Craner
Financial Statement Analysis in Europe

C.M.S. Sutcliffe
Stock Index Futures

M. Tanaka, T. Yoshikawa, J. Innes and
F. Mitchell
Contemporary Cost Management

B.C. Williams and B.J. Spaul
IT and Accounting: The impact of information technology

R.M.S. Wilson and Wai Fong Chua
Managerial Accounting: method and meaning
(2nd edn)
(Also available: *Teachers' Guide*)

D. Winstone
Financial Derivatives

Financial Derivatives

Hedging with futures, forwards, options and swaps

David Winstone
Department of Financial Services
The University of Central England Business
School
Birmingham, UK

CHAPMAN & HALL

London · Glasgow · Weinheim · New York · Tokyo · Melbourne · Madras

Published by Chapman & Hall, 2–6 Boundary Row, London SE1 8HN, UK

Chapman & Hall, 2–6 Boundary Row, London SE1 8HN, UK

Blackie Academic & Professional, Wester Cleddens Road, Bishopbriggs, Glasgow G64 2NZ, UK

Chapman & Hall GmbH, Pappelallee 3, 69469 Weinheim, Germany

Chapman & Hall Inc., 115 Fifth Avenue, New York, NY 10003, USA

Chapman & Hall Japan, ITP-Japan, Kyowa Building, 3F, 2–2–1 Hirakawacho, Chiyoda-ku, Tokyo 102, Japan

Chapman & Hall Australia, 102 Dodds Street, South Melbourne, Victoria 3205, Australia

Chapman & Hall India, R. Seshadri, 32 Second Main Road, CIT East, Madras 600 035, India

First edition 1995

© 1995 David Winstone

Typeset in 11/12pt Goudy by EXPO Holdings, Malaysia
Printed in England by Clays Ltd, St Ives plc

ISBN 0 412 62770 1

A catalogue record for this book is available from the British Library

Library of Congress Catalog Card Number: 95-67911

∞ Printed on permanent acid-free text paper, manufactured in accordance with ANSI/NISO Z39.48–1992 and ANSI/NISO Z39.48–1984 (Permanence of Paper).

For my grandmother Laura (1896–1995), who became my first finance teacher by explaining to me how she ran the neighbourhood divi club and by letting me help.

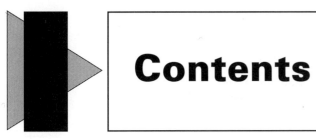

Contents

Acknowledgements

My thanks to the following individuals, groups and organisations who gave help in the preparation of this book:

Tom Burley, UCE, assistance with BSoPM.
Linda Chandler, UCE, word processing, chapters 1, 17–20
Paul Cowdell, reviewer, Sheffield Hallam University.
Jane Carlton, Copy-editor, Tortoiseshell Enterprises.
Sarah Henderson, Commissioning Editor, Chapman & Hall.
Pandora Hancock, introduction to Chapman & Hall.
John Sparrow, UCE, help with diagram software.
Roger Baty, UCE, help with diagram software.
Lynn Mellington, UCE, word processing advice.
Tony Sawyer, UCE with whom I share a staff room.
UCE Business School, Birmingham.
Students taking the Treasury Management option in BA Financial Services at UCE, Birmingham.
CIB Lombard Scheme MBA students at Exeter University.
Chartered Institute of Bankers for permission to use their examination questions.
Securities Institute for permission to use questions from their Futures and Options paper.
LIFFE and CBOT who both gave permission to quote prices, contract specifications and their literature.

1 ▷ Introduction

The intention of this book is to show how financial derivatives work and how they can be used to hedge currency and interest rate risk. Descriptions, diagrams, arithmetic and a little statistics are used, but no calculus is needed.

This introduction only gives an outline, with little supporting explanation for information given. Be assured, full coverage is given in each chapter so that you will be able to understand how derivatives are used to hedge price risk.

Many of the financial derivatives described in the following chapters are relatively new on the scene. Swaps did not really exist in their current form until 1981. FRAs were not developed and used until 1982. Exchange traded financial futures were developed during the late 1970s, but did not really 'take-off' until 1982. Exchange traded financial options were also developed during the early 1980s. However, futures and options on commodities which are not dealt with in detail in the text have a much longer history stretching back to the Middle Ages and beyond, but they would be more recognisable in their contemporary form from 1865 onwards at the Chicago Board of Trade (CBOT). Forward foreign exchange contracts have the oldest history of the instruments described in the text to follow.

The growth in the use of financial derivatives since their inception has been very rapid and now futures and options contracts related to physical commodities such as metals and agricultural products are dwarfed by them. About 40% of all futures are interest rate related, 10% are currency related. It is a similar story for options. These figures do not include futures and options on financial indices such as the FSE100 and 250 or options on individual equities which are not discussed in this book. Most financial centres have a financial futures and options exchange. In London it is LIFFE the London International Financial Futures and Options Exchange. Most of the exchange traded derivative examples used in the book are drawn from LIFFE contracts. The main focus in each chapter is the use of the relevant derivative to hedge financial price risk, be it interest rate/bond price risk or currency risk. Knowledge of the underlying cash market is not assumed and additional information is given where necessary. The opening chapters describe cash markets and establish that price risk does exist and therefore so does the need to hedge.

Hedging with the cash market

The main focus of the book is how to hedge financial price risk using derivatives. Hedgers who use derivatives shift unwanted price risk to others willing to assume risk for a price. In some instances these 'others' will in turn lay off some of the risk they have taken on by hedging themselves. Different layers or types of risk can thus be 'laid off' onto others at a price. Think of the principle of re-insurance as an analogy. As described in the chapters on options, insurance can be thought of as a type of option, with pay-offs and features such as excesses or deductibles.

Hedgers are thus individuals or organisations who do not wish to suffer losses due to adverse price movements over a given period of time. Buyers do not want prices to rise and sellers do not want them to fall by the time they actually make the exchange at a later date. Most hedges involve the fixing of a price today that will be used at a later date. These known values are fixed and cannot be improved upon, there can be no windfall gains due to favourable price movement. Options on the other hand fix a price for later use, they limit loss as the other hedges, but they differ in that the fixed price need not be adhered to if it is better to use prices currently available in the spot market. With options, purchasers enjoy no downside risk, but do enjoy upside potential. This facility does not come for free and is reflected in the cost of options.

In most instances it is possible to devise a way of hedging using the cash market. A simple example is as follows: a UK importer has to pay a US dollar invoice for $50,000 in three months' time. The risk is that when the time arrives to pay the invoice, US dollars will be more expensive relative to sterling than they are now, so that fewer per pound can be obtained in exchange at spot. The UK importer can be sure of the cost of the $50,000 in three months' time by exchanging a suitable amount of sterling now into US dollars at the spot rate, then holding dollars on deposit until needed. This way there is a known cost in terms of sterling for the dollars. No exchange occurs in three months' time. The spot rate in three months' time has no bearing on the matter. The sterling value of the dollars has been fixed. It should be noted that although no exchange losses can occur with this hedge, neither can there be any windfall fall gains due to falls in the value of the US dollar relative to sterling.

Using the cash market, the exchange of currency at spot and the depositing of the dollars obtained has its drawbacks. The main one is that it ties up money for three months on deposit which might otherwise be used as working capital in the importer's business. Alternatively there may be no surplus cash to exchange, in which case sterling will have to be borrowed. Again the importer may not wish to do this because it will use up credit lines that are needed for other purposes, or there may be insufficient credit lines to support the borrowing at all. What is needed is a device which will achieve the same result, the same pay-off, but in a different way so that the disadvantages of using the cash market are removed. In this case the same outcome is achieved by the use of a forward exchange contract. As explained in Chapter 6 the forward rate used in the contract is derived from the interest rate differential, in this case between sterling and US dollars for three month maturities.

To repeat, this hedge gives a known outcome which cannot be improved upon, no windfall gains are possible. You cannot, with the benefit of hindsight, undo the hedge outcome. It is only with hindsight that you might be able to say it would have been better not to have hedged. You are always pleased you placed the hedge if the outcome is better than the one where you had not hedged. It is important that you are able to feel comfortable with outcomes where with hindsight you would not have hedged.

Identification of the need to hedge is important as is identification of when the risk begins. A view can be taken to hedge selectively, that is, to hedge only when you believe the spot rate will move against you. However, be aware that if you do this you are really saying you can predict price movements. Cost of hedges can also be reduced when spot rates move in your favour and you decide to lift the hedge before maturity, but always be aware that effectively here you are saying there will be no subsequent adverse price movements prior to maturity.

What is a derivative?

A derivative, sometimes called a derivative security or a contingent claim, is a deferred delivery instrument designed in such a way that its price relates to the price of a particular asset. The price of the derivative is not arbitrary – when the price of the underlying asset changes so does the price of the derivative. Throughout the book arbitrages are described which ensure that this relationship holds. By this process the use of the derivative replicates the pay-off from a cash market hedge. Thus the pay-off from a forward exchange contract is the same as the cash market hedge described on p. 2. The advantage of a forward contract is that it does not use up so large a credit line in comparison with the cash market hedge. The forward contract is only a contingent liability not an absolute one as it is when borrowing is involved. What we have identified here is a property of derivatives, that of leverage. A small outlay enables control of a much larger cash market position. A full explanation occurs in Chapter 6 for forward contracts.

A forward contract is an example of an OTC (over the counter) derivative. It is tailor-made to the hedger's requirements and is individually arranged. Counterparty risk occurs for both participants, there is the risk that either will not honour their obligations when they are obliged to do. A forward contract differs from many other derivatives in that it is a hedging device complete in itself. By this is meant that nothing further need be done other than complete the obligations embedded in the forward contract. This is not the case for all derivative instruments.

An FRA is the interest rate risk equivalent of a forward contract. However, it is constructed differently. The FRA must be used simultaneously with an appropriate cash market position. As you will see in Chapter 9, an FRA allows a hedger to effectively borrow or deposit funds in the future at a given rate. However, you must, as a separate arrangement, actually borrow or deposit funds at the appropriate time, at the prevailing spot rate. The FRA then provides compensation if cash market rates are inferior to the rate contracted in the FRA or requires the hedger to pay compensation if cash market rates are superior.

Thus, when the derivative position is held simultaneously with an appropriate cash position, gains in one market are matched by losses in the other. In this way a fixed price or rate is experienced. The more one market changes the more the other adjusts in the opposite direction.

OTC or exchange traded?

We have seen (p. 3) that an OTC derivative is individually arranged between the counterparties. As a result counterparty default risk occurs. Each arrangement is separately negotiated and agreed. Futures by contrast are exchange traded so that the time taken to negotiate is reduced to a minimum, mainly due to standardisation of terms. The system of open outcry ensures price transparency and price discovery. The exchange, coupled with the role of a clearing house becoming counterparties to all trades, effectively reduces credit risk to (almost) zero. A margin system and daily marking to market ensures that losses and gains are taken incrementally each day, not at expiration/ maturity. Options can be either OTC or exchange traded.

Credit risk and market risk

Exchange traded futures and options are effectively free from counterparty default, i.e. credit risk, due to the role of the clearing house and the margin system. However, participants who use these markets are still subject to market or price risk, by this we mean that the price of a future or option may move more than anticipated and create losses greater or more than anticipated. In the case of futures these losses will be due to basis risk and for options largely due to delta risk. The losses identified here are different to those which might be expected by a hedger. Remember losses in one market, e.g. futures, will match those in the other, cash market, to create a known future cost. The risk identified here is that the futures price or option price will not behave in this exact way. As you would expect, full treatment of these issues occurs in later chapters.

Exchange traded instruments are virtually free from liquidity risk, futures and options can always be traded, except in extreme circumstances where daily price limits have been reached. Operational risk and legal risk are also largely eliminated due to the role of the clearing house.

Hedgers, speculators and arbitrageurs

We have seen that hedgers will use a derivative simultaneously with a cash market position. It is of course possible to use the derivative market on its own, if this is done then you can speculate upon price movements in the derivative as an alternative to speculating upon price movement in the actual underlying.

Speculating upon price movements in the derivative as a proxy for speculation in the underlying commodity is much easier, especially in futures and options. If you buy and sell a commodity you actually have to take delivery of the commodity if you buy and you have to hold it if you wish to sell (ignoring the possibility of shorting the commodity).

If you speculate in the futures market you take delivery of nothing if you buy and need nothing to sell. This may seem a little strange at first, but it's possible. Using the futures market needs very little capital outlay due to the initial margin deposit and because the holding of a futures position requires very little investment, losses and gains are much larger in percentage terms than in the cash market. These magnified gains or losses are due to the principle referred to earlier as leverage. You will see later that a futures position which controls the value of an underlying of £500,000 for example, requires an initial deposit of about £15,000. If the price of the underlying changes to £510,000 this is a gain of 2% if you possess it. The futures price will also change £10,000, giving a gain of 66.6% on the investment of £15,000. Note that if you hold the wrong futures position you will make a loss of 66.6% which will be realised when the position is marked to market each day and variation margin becomes payable.

It is as well to appreciate that in finance we do not give the title 'speculator' any pejorative meaning as it sometimes has in general use. In finance a speculator is an individual who can identify and quantify risk and is prepared to take it on for an appropriate price, as a result they add liquidity to derivative markets with all the benefits this brings.

Speculators use derivatives to take on risk for a price, arbitrageurs are risk adverse, but also take positions in derivatives without an underlying cash market position because they, like speculators, have no interest in the underlying. Arbitrageurs use derivatives and thus add to liquidity, by taking advantage of price imperfections between prices in different markets. All derivatives 'must' be priced consistently against each other, otherwise arbitrage profits can be made. For various reasons price discrepancies can exist for a very short time, therefore we have arbitrageurs.

General points

The arithmetic and calculations in later chapters ignore transactions costs, unless otherwise identified. Tax implications are not addressed. Clearly both these factors should not be ignored in reality as they may completely alter the outcome and rationale for the strategy taken.

2 ▷ The nature of currency exposure

Currency exposure, currency risk, foreign exchange risk and exchange risk are all alternative terms which mean that unexpected losses (or gains) are made over a given period of time due to the chance that foreign currency will change its value in relation to domestic currency.

Spot rates of exchange are being considered here, i.e. where the amount and rate are agreed 'on the spot' for immediate exchange on the value day. Actual monies take two working days to pass through the relevant accounts. The day on which the currencies are actually exchanged is known as the settlement date.

Spot exchange rates change over time for reasons that are not discussed here. Just to give a flavour of these rate movements between sterling and selected foreign currencies see Table 2.1.

Table 2.1 Sterling exchange rates – selected currencies

Currency units per pound, end of December figures

	1960	1970	1980	1988	1990	1991	1992	1993	1994 (19 Sep)
France	13.73	12.66	10.77	10.96	9.82	9.93	8.27	8.74	8.32
Ger	11.69	8.73	4.67	3.21	2.89	2.93	2.43	2.57	2.43
Italy	1740	1491	2219	2362	2177	2184	2152	2533	2463
Japan	1004	856	484	226	262	225	190	165	156
USA	2.80	2.39	2.38	1.81	1.93	1.63	1.53	1.48	1.58

Note: US$ January 1985 $1.05
Source: selected items Barclays Bank Review

Currency exposure exists for companies if, as a result of these changes in spot rates over time, there is an impact upon balance sheet values or profit and loss figures.

Types of currency exposure

Companies can experience currency risk in one of three ways:

- transaction risk
- translation risk
- economic risk.

Transaction risk

Companies can be said to be 'open' to transaction risk when either buying or selling goods or services in a foreign currency if they take the value of such transactions in terms of domestic currency as given by the prevailing spot rates. As these spot rates can and do change over time they leave themselves open to the consequences of such changes in value.

An open position can be **covered** or **hedged** using a variety of techniques which are explained in the course of the book.

When buying goods or services in a foreign currency the exchange risk runs between the time the company agrees to buy and the time payment is actually made. Formally the risk is said to run between **recognition** (agreeing to buy) and **maturity** (making the payment).

To a company selling goods or services they occur as follows:

- recognition – when a quotation is made or a price list is published in currency;
- maturity – when payment is received in cleared funds.

Note that it is common to use the word currency to mean foreign currency, that is, currency other than domestic currency. Therefore the word currency is used in this and subsequent chapters to mean foreign currency.

Other examples of transaction risk would occur when making or receiving payments to cover interest, profit or dividends. A simple arithmetic example will illustrate:

At the beginning of January 1991 the sterling/Dutch guilder rate was

£1 = NLG 3.26

At this time a UK exporter quoted an NLG price to his customer in the Netherlands based on this rate. A costing exercise had shown that to supply the goods concerned would require the sterling equivalent of £5,000 per item to make an acceptable profit, say 15% or £750.

Therefore the NLG price would be

£5,000 × 3.26 = NLG 16,300

The customer agreed to buy and as a result of the delivery and credit terms actually made the payment with cleared funds at the end of April 1991.

At this time the rate had moved to

£1 = NLG 3.33

When the NLG 16,300 per item were received, they realised

NLG 16,300 ÷ 3.33 = £4894.89

Here an unexpected loss of £105.11 per item has been made, representing a 2% fall in revenue. Anticipated profit has fallen by:

$$\frac{£105.11}{£750} \times 100 = 14\%$$

almost certainly an unacceptable position for the exporter. It is the risk of what future spot rates will be that has produced this result.

It could be argued that if a different example were taken then a gain could be experienced. For example,

£/US$ rate: January 1 1991 £1 = $1.93

April   30 1991 £1 = $1.72

The point, however, is that if a company leaves itself in an open position it cannot predict what its profit margins will be. The level of profit will be as a result of chance, hardly a position which makes for good business planning.

Even when there is an unexpected gain it can be argued that this outcome is not necessarily satisfactory. In the US$ example above, the goods will have been over-priced in that they produce sterling revenue greater than actually anticipated. A dollar price has been quoted which may have resulted in the loss of the order in the first place to competitors. It may jeopardise future orders or affect market share. If £5,000 were required and regarded as an acceptable sterling price, why charge more dollars than necessary to achieve this?

Future spot rates cannot be guessed and therefore it is pointless charging prices anticipating future spot rates. It is also pointless charging more 'just in case the value falls'. It might not fall, in which case the goods will be over-priced and result in a lost or reduced order.

The risk with regard to future spot rates needs to be managed and exchanged for a known position. Management techniques suitable for transaction risk are covered in Chapters 3, 4, 6, 12 and 15.

Translation risk

Translation risk is alternatively known as accounting or balance sheet exposure or balance sheet risk.

If a company has assets or liabilities denominated in currency it will be necessary for reporting purposes to translate the currency values of these items into domestic currency values at accounting year ends. As exchange rates change, the sterling value in the case of UK sterling based companies will alter. Therefore adjustments will have to be made for losses or gains either within the profit and loss account or directly in the balance sheet.

Again a simple arithmetic example will illustrate the principle. Imagine a UK sterling based company with assets of £5m supported by share capital to the same value. It decides to acquire a US company costing US$ 1m. The funds for the purchase are raised by sterling borrowing. At the time of the borrowing the rate is £1 = $1.75. This information placed in the balance sheet would appear as follows:

	£		£	
capital	5,000,000.00	assets (£)	5,000,000.00	
loan (£)	571,428.57	assets (US$)	571,428.57	($1m @ 1.75)
	5,571,428.57		5,571,428.57	

If the exchange rate were to rise over the following year to £1 = $1.90 the current sterling value of the dollar asset would be £526,315.79.

The next balance sheet would need to reflect this new asset value.

	£		£
capital	5,000,000.00	assets (£)	5,000,000.00
loan (£)	571,428.57	assets (US$)	526,315.79
translation loss	(45,112.78)		
	5,526,315.79		5,526,315.79

Such losses solely due to changes in currency values are not acceptable to many companies.

As seen when looking at transaction risk, there is of course the possibility of making an unforeseen gain. The point is that such losses or gains are not controllable by the company, unless the risk is removed by a suitable hedging technique.

Economic exposure

Economic exposure or risk can sometimes be alternatively referred to as competitive exposure or risk. Such exposure results from a company's decision to buy from or export to a particular country. The decision will be based upon cost of goods or services when buying and price when selling. Both costs and price will be heavily influenced by the relevant exchange rate at the time the decision was made (and a possible position being taken as to future rates). Should the rate move against the company, then it may well influence its decision as to where to source its raw materials and components or where to locate its manufacturing capacity.

Economic exposure can also arise for a company even when it is completely domestically based, i.e. it neither exports nor imports. In such circumstances, if the value of sterling were to rise, then foreign producers could sell more cheaply in the UK. As a result such a company would lose sales.

The latter example of economic risk can be referred to as passive, whereas the former can be described as active risk.

Hedging or covering transaction risk

It has been shown (pp. 8–9) how being in an open position can cause unexpected losses or gains due to transaction risk. There are a number of techniques available to cover or hedge such risks. Each technique is not always suitable in every situation. The techniques, facilities, instruments which will be considered in later chapters are listed below.

Internal

- selling and buying in one's own currency   Chapter 3
- selling and buying in ECUs   Chapter 3
- leading and lagging   Chapter 3
- matching   Chapter 3
- netting   Chapter 3

External

- currency borrowing/depositing   Chapter 4
- forward exchange contracts   Chapter 6
- currency futures   Chapters 10 and 12
- currency options   Chapters 14 and 15
- currency swaps   Chapter 19

A number of these techniques are suitable for covering translation and economic risk.

Summary

- Transaction risks are those which are perhaps most easily identified by companies because the consequences of such risks impact upon expected income flows and appear quickly in profit and loss accounts.
- It is for this reason that they receive the greatest attention. Translation risks affect the way in which foreign investment is financed.
- Economic risk influences the location of facilities decision.

Key terms

- covered/hedged position (p. 8)
- currency exposure (p. 7)
- exchange risk (p. 7)
- maturity (p. 8)
- open position (p. 8)
- recognition (p. 8)
- spot rates (p. 7)
- transaction, translation, economic risk (p. 8)

Questions

2.1   Give alternative terms for currency exposure.
2.2   Name the three types of currency exposure normally identified.
2.3   Explain what currency risk is in general terms.

2.4 When buying goods, at what point does the risk begin and end? What type of risk is involved here?

2.5 When selling goods, when does recognition and maturity of risk occur?

2.6 Give the alternative terms or names for translation risk.

2.7 Explain the need to deal with translation risk within a company's balance sheet.

2.8 Explain active economic exposure.

Internal hedging techniques

Selling and buying in one's own currency

If a company were to buy or sell always in its own currency then of course it would never be exposed to transaction risk. It would always pay or receive that which had been agreed in terms of value.

However, by trading in this way it would be transferring risk to the other party to the transaction, who may of course not wish to accept it. In so doing the other company will be required to hedge in some way – all of which will impose additional costs. The bargaining strength of the parties will determine whether this strategy can be adopted and whether or not it will enable competitiveness to be retained. For example, it might mean that to get the selling price accepted in the seller's own currency, a lower price has to be quoted. In some instances the commodity being traded may only be traded in a particular currency, typically US$, in which case, if this is not the domestic currency of either party, both will be exposed to transaction risk.

When the sale or purchase is within a group of companies, then exchange risk will exist within the group. Which company in the group pays or receives foreign currency will determine where the risk occurs. There may also be other considerations. It may be advantageous to place the currency exposure with its subsequent losses and gains where there is the maximum tax advantage, or with the company which can manage the risk the most effectively due to expertise, access to facilities or absence of exchange control problems.

Arguably, selling in your own currency is not a way of hedging risk, but avoiding it and transferring it elsewhere. Such transfer may not be acceptable and sensible in competitive markets where those who do not trade in this way will be able to capture business.

Selling and buying in ECUs (or other basket currencies)

Because the ECU (European Currency Unit) has a value determined by a weighted basket of currencies, its value is less volatile than a given constituent currency only when that currency is more volatile than the weighted average volatility of all currencies in the basket.

- For stable currencies in the basket, the ECU is more volatile than they are.
- For volatile currencies in the basket, the ECU is less volatile than they are.

As a result, trade denominated in ECUs poses less transaction risk when one or both parties has a volatile currency. Such a tactic is really only suitable for trade within the EU.

ECUs are traded on the foreign exchange markets like any other currency and can be borrowed and held on deposit. We will consider their use in Chapter 4.

Leading and lagging

Leading and lagging is a technique which entails either delaying (lagging) or bringing forward (leading) the time when payment or conversion of currency is made. The idea is to delay payment of weak currencies and bring forward payment of strong currencies.

An illustration:

Suppose the US$ is weakening against sterling and a UK importer has to make a dollar payment, the higher the exchange rate (the weaker the US$) the cheaper it becomes in sterling terms for the UK importer. As the rate falls more and more US$ are obtained for the same amount of sterling. Thus less sterling is required to obtain a given number of invoiced US$.

If the payment is for $50,000 and the rate is £1 = $1.75 the sterling cost is

$$\$50,000 \div 1.75 = £28,571.43$$

If US$ are weakening (therefore requiring lagging) then as the rate rises the cheaper in terms of sterling the payment becomes.

If the rate were to rise to £1 = $1.80 sterling cost is

$$\$50,000 \div 1.80 = £27,777.78$$

Leading and lagging always involves taking a view as to the movement in spot rates in the future and therefore to this extent it does involve an element of risk. If the guess had been to delay payment in the above example, anticipating a fall to £1 = $1.80 and the rate had in fact moved down instead of up, then an unanticipated exchange loss would have occurred.

When lagging payment to an independent third party there is always the possibility of upsetting the trading relationship, with possible loss of credit facilities or having your prices increased to compensate for the delay in the receipt of funds. There is also the possibility of damage to the lagging company's external credit rating.

Matching

Matching uses the facility of a currency account. If a company both buys and sells in the same foreign currency it will be possible to match receipts and payments. Receipts can be used to make payments obviating the need for any conversion and thus avoiding any exchange risk.

Any unmatched amounts can be hedged by using, for example, forward contracts (Chapter 6). When the payment has to be made before the receipt then currency can be borrowed (Chapter 4). If the receipt is some time before the payment becomes due, the balance can be left on deposit in a currency account. There may be benefits in leading and lagging unmatched amounts.

It is also possible to use currency receipts where a suitable match is not available to obtain other foreign currency, thus avoiding coming back into the domestic currency. This minimises dealing costs.

Netting

Netting can be used where two companies, either independent of each other or within the same group of companies, make and receive frequent payments to and from each other.

Instead of making each payment, incurring transmission costs, the net position between the two companies can be ascertained say every three months and one payment only be made by the company which is in the net debtor position.

For example the following payment schedule may apply between the two companies X and Y:

Company X	Company Y
payments to company Y ($)	payments to company X ($)
5,000	8,000
10,000	10,000
15,000	5,000
20,000	23,000
50,000	46,000

A single net payment by Company Y to Company X of $4,000 will be all that is required.

It is possible to have such netting arrangements with any number of companies within a single netting arrangement. All that is necessary is for there to be sufficient payments and receipts between them to make it all worthwhile.

The system is perhaps best used where the companies are part of the same group. In this way credit risk is reduced. It is also possible to have multi-currency netting arrangements provided suitable exchange rates can be agreed.

Summary

A number of internal hedging techniques can be used to cover exchange risk, they are:
- sell/buy in your own, domestic, currency – arguably this is transferring risk
- sell/buy in ECUs
- leading and lagging
- matching
- netting.

Key terms

- internal hedging (p. 13)
- leading (p. 14)
- lagging (p. 14)
- matching (p. 15)
- netting (p. 15)

Questions

3.1 Is selling or buying always in your own domestic currency a hedging technique?

3.2 Is leading and lagging truly a hedging technique?

Currency borrowing or currency deposits

Currency borrowing

Currency borrowing is only suitable where a company has a flow of income in the same currency as that borrowed so that the income is sufficient to repay the sum borrowed plus the accrued interest.

To borrow currency without such a currency income is to create a condition of exchange risk exposure. If currency is borrowed, usually attracted by lower interest rates available than in the domestic currency, then exchanged into sterling, there is always the danger that, when the time comes to repay the loan, the exchange rate will have moved against the borrower. Because the borrower has no currency income to repay the loan, currency can only be obtained in exchange for the domestic currency. If the exchange rate is now inferior it will mean that more currency has to be obtained to repay the currency borrowed.

Example $50,000 borrowed for 12 months at 5% interest p.a.
Exchange rate £1 = $1.70 at spot when borrowing occurs
£ interest rate = 10% p.a.

The $50,000 when exchanged at spot realises £29,411.76. Ignoring the interest accrued, if six months later the rate is £1 = $1.65, then the sterling necessary to obtain $50,000 will now be £30,303.03. The extra amount of sterling is necessary due to the outcome of exchange risk.

If this is contrasted with the correct use of currency borrowing, it can be seen that no such risk occurs and that in fact it is a method to cover exchange risk.

If a UK exporter expects to receive $50,000 in one year's time, an amount sufficient to equal this figure (less interest, e.g. at 5%) can be borrowed.

$50,000 ÷ 1.05 = $47,619.05 = sum borrowed
($47,619.05 ÷ 1.70 = £28,011.20)

The sterling sum of £28,011.20 realised can replace the same sum if actually borrowed in sterling at, for example, 10% p.a. When the year has elapsed, $50,000 becomes payable and is repaid by the proceeds of $50,000.

Note that in this way it is possible for UK exporters to remain competitive by borrowing money at advantageous rates, i.e. below sterling rates, if they apply, as enjoyed in the market by the domestic producers with whom they are competing. The same effect is achieved if a forward contract is entered into as an alternative (Chapter 6). It will be constructive to consider any disadvantages of currency borrowing. It is these disadvantages which lead to the use of forward contracts as substitutes.

The above scenario effectively fixed the exchange value of the dollars. No matter how the spot rate changes during the 12 months, the sterling value of the proceeds will always remain a known sum.

In fact it is possible to derive an exchange rate equivalent to a forward rate as seen below. (Forward rates are used and explained in Chapter 6.) It is different from the spot of $1.70 because it must be remembered that although $50,000 is actually being received as payment, a lesser sum, $47,619.05 is actually borrowed and exchanged at the spot of $1.70 to give the £28,011.20.

Here is the way in which a forward rate can be derived:

borrow	$47,619.05	@£1 = $1.70 =	£28,011.20
$ interest @ 5% p.a.	$2,380.95	£ interest @ 10% p.a.	£ 2,801.12
	$50,000.00		£30,812.32

The dollar and sterling amounts are comparable at these figures, so that:

$$\$50,000 \div £30,812.32$$

gives an effective forward rate of £1 = $1.6227.

This effective forward rate will be very similar to an actual forward rate quoted by a bank had the company used this facility instead of borrowing. The effective and actual forward rates will not be identical due to the fact that the bank will be using inter-bank rates when making its calculation of the forward rate.

In addition the bank will also quote a spread against what is essentially a central rate here of 1.6227, to enable it to make a profit when it buys and sells currency forward.

There now follows an example of currency borrowing/depositing which would apply to a company having an obligation to make a payment in the future in currency.

If a UK importer has to make a payment of $100,000 in 12 months' time, it may be the case that it has sufficient funds on deposit in sterling to obviate the need to borrow in sterling. If this is the case it will exchange sufficient sterling to realise a dollar sum, which, when left on deposit for 12 months, will amount to the required sum of $100,000 when the deposit interest has been added.

Alternatively, it may need to borrow this sterling sum. (You should be able to decide for yourself why dollars should not be borrowed. If you are unsure, look back at the first two paragraphs of this chapter.) In either event a sterling sum will now be available.

$100,000 has to be available in 12 months' time. If US$ deposit interest rates are 4.5% p.a. then $95,693.78 deposited now will give $100,000 in 12 months' time.

$$\$100,000 \div 1.045 = \$95,693.78 \text{ (interest} = \$4,306.22)$$

$100,000 is available to make the required payment in 12 months' time when the deposit is received back.

Again an effective forward rate can be determined.

Borrow, if necessary, sterling sufficient to realise $95,693.78.

If spot rate is £1 = $1.68 (bank selling) then

$$\text{sterling} = £56,960.58$$

If sterling interest is 10% p.a. then the cost of borrowing this sum for 12 months is £5,696.06. Therefore there is a cost of this sum with a gain of $4,306.

Borrow	£56,960.58	@ £1 = $1.68 =	$95,693.78
£ interest @ 10% p.a. =	5,696.06	$ interest @ 4.5 % p.a.=	4,306.22
	£62,656.54		$100,000

$100,000 ÷ £62,656.64 gives an effective forward rate of £1 = $1.5960.

Because, in the importer example given, sterling has been borrowed to enable a dollar deposit, the interest spread will make a forward contract a better proposition for the importer. This is discussed further in Chapter 6.

There is also the psychological difficulty in this case of borrowing sterling at a higher rate than the deposit rate available on the currency. Importers will see this as a loss, a cost. In fact it equates to the cost incurred in covering forward anyway, but, as explained in the previous paragraph, the loss is not so great with forward cover. It does represent a cost nevertheless (pp. 35–6).

Disadvantages of currency borrowing/depositing

Where receipt or payment of currency is delayed, borrowing or depositing as appropriate for the extended period will continue the hedge. Where the payment or receipt is not made at all, then the extra cost or saving incurred will approximate to the cost or gain in close out (discussed in on pp. 31–2) which would have been necessary had a forward contract been used as an alternative.

Clearly borrowing takes up the appropriate part of an agreed banking facility and appears on the company's balance sheet as an increase in liabilities.

A further problem is that when the company's balance sheet is produced, inevitably there will be some currency loans outstanding. There will be no currency fixed assets to off-set any gains or losses in translation of these balance sheet liabilities, only currency current assets (the anticipated receipt). This means that large translation adjustments might be necessary should the spot rate have moved adversely. These adjustments might therefore impact adversely on the balance sheet. It may also be that a potential borrower does not have the credit facility to borrow the sum required.

A derivative

It is for these reasons that a hedger, importer or exporter, may prefer to use a facility 'derived' from that of borrowing/depositing. Such a derivative in this case will be a forward contract (Chapter 6). It will be seen later that if a forward rate (one which will be used at a time in the future, but quoted today) is used, this gives the same effect as borrowing/depositing, but without some of the disadvantages.

Summary

Transaction risk can be hedged by appropriate currency borrowing or depositing in the cash market. Those who have future currency liabilities such as importers, will deposit sums of currency, so that when the deposit is repaid currency can be paid away without the need to make exchanges at uncertain spot rates. Exporters will borrow currency sums, so that when the loans mature they can be repaid by currency proceeds from the sale of their goods or services. It is important that currency sums borrowed are exchanged immediately at spot into domestic currency.

Using the cash market to hedge has disadvantages. The principle problem is that sums of money have to be borrowed to finance the hedge position. This uses up bank facilities which may be needed for other financing purposes. For this reason other hedges may be preferable, using instruments whose pay-off profile is a derivative of a cash market position.

Now that you have completed this chapter you should be able to:

- identify and explain the nature of currency exposure with its consequent losses and gains;
- identify the types of currency risk which exist;
- be familiar with and be able to suggest the correct use of internal techniques for managing transaction risk;
- understand the benefits and drawbacks for each internal technique for managing transaction risk;
- list external techniques for managing transaction risk.

Key terms

- cash market hedge (p. 20)
- derivative (p. 20)

Questions

4.1 List internal techniques which can be used to cover transaction risk.

4.2 List external techniques which can be used to cover transaction risk.

4.3 What are the drawbacks of invoicing in domestic currency?

4.4 If you were a UK importer buying in US$ and the dollar were strengthening against sterling, would you lead or lag?

4.5 How do you deal with unmatched amounts of currency when using the matching technique?

4.6 Under what circumstances would it be incorrect to borrow currency?

4.7 When is it correct to borrow currency?

4.8 Briefly explain the nature of transaction risk.

4.9 Briefly explain translation risk.

4.10 Briefly explain economic risk.

4.11 A sterling based importer expects to make a payment in six months' time of $50,000. The current interest rate for sterling is 10% p.a. and, for US$, 7% p.a. Show how transaction risk can be hedged by appropriate currency borrowing or depositing. Illustrate your answer with relevant figures.

4.12 Derive an effective forward rate the importer would achieve in Question 4.11.

4.13 Recognition of exchange risk occurs for an importer when:
   a) domestic currency is exchanged into foreign currency and the foreign currency amount is less than originally anticipated;
   b) when a firm order is received from the overseas buyer;
   c) when a tender is submitted to the potential buyer.

4.14 Translation exposure occurs when:
   a) a company's liabilities are greater than its assets;
   b) when it is highly geared;
   c) when it has assets valued in currency greater than its currency liabilities;
   d) when it has no currency income.

4.15 Passive economic risk occurs when:
   a) a company is completely domestically based and when all its activities are in the home currency;
   b) a company keeps an open position and does not hedge in any way;
   c) exchange rates change outside the control of the company and the consequences of such change are recorded in the company accounts.

4.16 X Company is a Swiss registered multinational which generates considerable regular US$ inflows to Switzerland from its sales. As its general experience has been that the Swiss Franc (SwFr) has consistently strengthened against the US$, X has suffered from its resultant, unhedged currency transaction exposure. It has strong SwFr liquidity and does not have any US$ liabilities to service. This particular trading pattern is expected to continue and, as the company takes the view that SwFr will continue to strengthen against the US$, you are required to:
   a) list different internal strategies the company could follow to reduce the impact of the currency exposure on its cash flow and profits: [5] and
   b) explain THREE of these strategies. [15]
   (CIB, International Finance and Investment, May 1990, adapted.)

5 ▷ The foreign exchange market

Survey of the foreign exchange market

During April 1992 twenty-six central banks, including the Bank of England, surveyed the turnover conducted in their foreign exchange markets. A similar exercise had been carried out in March 1986 and April 1989. Some of the results are given below for the spot and forward markets.

London is the largest centre for foreign exchange dealings in the world. It has increased its lead a little since April 1989. Table 5.1 summarises the situation.

The most traded currency pairs world-wide are USD/DEM (23%) and GBP/USD (19%). Their total has fallen from its previous figure of 49%. London is involved in actively trading more currencies than any other centre, largely due to the location of a number of foreign banks in London

Table 5.1   Major currency centres: average net daily turnover

Centre	1989 $bn per day	1992 $bn per day	% growth 1989–1992
London	187[1]	300	60
Tokyo	115[2]	128	11
New York	129	192	49
Singapore	55[3]	74	34
Switzerland	57	68	19
Hong Kong	49	61	24
Germany	N/A[4]	57	–
France	26	35	35

Source: (turnover figures) Bank of England Quarterly Bulletin (BEQB), November 1992.

[1] Not included in the above London figures are those where London brokers were involved in transactions and both principals were abroad. This accounts for an additional US$12bn per day.

[2] Tokyo is losing market share, although the third largest centre.

[3] Singapore has now overtaken Switzerland to become the fourth largest centre.

[4] Germany did not take part in earlier surveys.

becoming market makers for their domestic currency against the major currencies.

About half the turnover world-wide is in forward business. Spot activity has declined by 14% between 1989 and 1992. Total turnover has increased by a larger percentage than growth in world trade over the same period.

Forward business would be, for example, where 'a dollar deposit can be converted into a sterling deposit by doing a sterling/US dollar *swap* in effect simultaneously lending sterling and borrowing dollars for a specified period of time by selling sterling, for instance spot, to buy dollars and agreeing to reverse the deal at a later date.' (BEQB Nov. 1992:411).

USD/DEM trading dominates the spot market. GBP/USD trading dominates forward trading, 90% of which is swaps. The term swap should not be confused with swaps as covered in Chapters 18 and 19 and the term swap as used in the currency futures market, dealt with in Chapter 12. Here the term swap is used in a different way, so you have to be careful how you use the word. Swaps in this context are as described above.

Most currency trades are against the US dollar. So-called cross rates, like Malawi Kwacha/Thailand Baht are achieved by deriving a rate from exchanges of Kwacha/US$, then US$/Baht.

Inter-bank trading, 77%, accounts for the majority of the market activity, down from 86% in 1989. As a result the share of business with 'other financial institutions' and 'non-financial institutions' both rose, that of 'non-financial' customers rose to 9% in 1992.

Market concentration in London is 'quite well dispersed' according to the survey. Twenty-five of the 352 principals surveyed account for more than 1% each of gross turnover, 14 of which have a share greater than 2%. The ten largest principals have a combined market share of 43%. This is an increase on 1989 at 35%. The top twenty account for 63% (50% in 1989).

In London foreign-owned institutions account for 80% of principals' aggregate turnover. UK principals' share is 20%.

The spot market

The **spot market** or **cash market** as it is sometimes called, is where prices are settled for exchange of stated amounts of domestic (base or counter) currency for stated amounts of foreign (underlying) currency. However, if the dollar is in the quote, it is always taken to be the base currency. The agreement to buy or sell is made on the spot for immediate settlement (therefore cash market). In the foreign exchange markets, in reality, the actual exchange of currencies (i.e. payment, settlement) takes place two bank working days later.

Once the deal is made, on the spot, it is firm and binding, there can be no change of mind. To reverse a position a further spot deal must be struck, by which time the rate will have changed.

Spot market quotation conventions

In the UK we are used to writing exchange rates in a particular way. (We have been using it in previous chapters.) It is known as an indirect quote. It relates one unit of domestic currency to a given number of units of foreign currency. An exchange rate is the value of one currency in terms of another.

In the UK and Republic of Ireland rates are written for example:

£1 = DM 2.50 (indirect)

An alternative quotation method is the direct quote as used almost everywhere else. In Germany a USD/DEM rate would be written:

$1 = DM 1.60

i.e. one unit of foreign currency related to a given number of units of domestic currency.

Note, however, that in Germany the sterling/deutschmark rate would be written as:

£1 = DM 2.50

i.e. the 'same' as in the UK, but different from a German perspective, being one unit of foreign currency related to the relevant number of units of domestic currency.

In the US, the indirect quote is always used except in relation to sterling, the Irish punt and the ECU. Thus the quote of the dollar against sterling is always given as £1 = $1.50, the same as in the UK as written, but the opposite (direct) method from the US perspective.

As with all commodities, there will be a buying price and a selling price. In previous chapters we have largely ignored this and have quoted single rates. It will be useful, perhaps, to have considered them as middle or central rates.

Using the indirect method as in the UK, examples of rates become

£1 = $ 1.5070 – 1.5155
or £1 = DM 2.5550 – 2.5675

Notice that quotes are often to four decimal places. As an alternative the sterling/DM rate could be quoted as:

£1 = DM 2.55 ½ – 2.56 ¾

The question arises which rate is which? Which is the buying rate and which is the selling rate?

The convention is always to look at the exchange from a bank's point of view in relation to what is happening to the foreign currency. Is it being sold or bought by the bank?

After consideration it can be seen that a bank, when selling currency, will sell at the low rate and buy currency at the high rate. The selling (ask/offer) rate is always quoted on the left, the buying (bid) rate on the right. It gives rise to the rule of

SELL LOW/BUY HIGH

which also applies when a direct quote is given.

A numerical example will demonstrate that the rule is correct.

Suppose an individual were to buy $1000 from the bank, using the rate

£1 = $1.5070–1.5155

the bank will sell $1000 at 1.5070, cost = £663.57. Were the individual then to sell the dollars back to the bank, the bank will buy at $1.5155, giving £659.85, a net cost to the individual of £3.72 and a profit to the bank of the same sum. Had the bank used the rates the wrong way around, a loss would have been taken by the bank.

Thus the bank will quote rates to sell low/buy high, to ensure a profit on its trades.

Self-evidently, the difference between the two rates gives the bank its trading profit. The difference between the two rates is known as the margin or spread. The wider the spread or margin, the larger the profit margin to the bank on any given deal. Thus, for larger amounts being exchanged, the spread will tend to narrow. A narrowing of spread makes the exchange more attractive to the bank's counterparty, its customer. Large purchases or sales of any commodity usually attract better prices.

A numerical example will illustrate:

If the counterparty to the bank is buying (bank selling) a narrowing of the margin will give a better rate to the counterparty.

Original rates £1 = $1.5555 – 1.6555

Narrowed spread gives, for instance,

£1 = $1.5855 – 1.6255

To the counterparty, buying currency at $1.5855 is better than at $1.555. Clearly, more dollars are received for every pound given in exchange.

Key terms

- currency pairs (p. 23)
- direct/indirect quotes (p. 24)
- domestic/base/counter currency (p. 24)
- foreign/underlying currency (p. 24)
- forward (p. 24)
- inter-bank trading (p. 24)
- swap (p. 24)
- spot/cash market (p. 24)
- settlement (p. 24)
- sell low/buy high (p. 25)

Questions

5.1 £1 = FFr 8.4414 – 8.4478
Which rate would a UK exporter use to exchange French francs received from a sale into sterling?

5.2 In Question 5.1, which currency is the underlying currency and which is the base?

6 Forward exchange contracts

Forward exchange contracts – an outline

Forward exchange contracts are a popular way for exporters and importers to hedge transaction risk.

A forward exchange contract has been defined as: an immediately firm and binding agreement between bank and customer to buy or sell an agreed amount of currency at a rate of exchange fixed at the time when the contract is made for performance by delivery of and payment for the stated amounts on or between two specified future dates.

Note that some forward contracts are in fact inter-bank, whereby both parties to the contract are banks.

From the definition it can be seen that the key elements of a forward contract are:

- a forward rate;
- an amount of currency to be either bought or sold;
- an exchange of currency agreed to be made at some point or period of time in the future.

If a UK exporter enters into a forward contract there is certainty as to the sterling value of the currency anticipated in payment for goods or services supplied. If a UK importer enters into such a contract there is certainty as to the sterling value of the currency being paid out.

A UK exporter expecting to receive $50,000 in three months' time would enter into a forward contract to sell (bank buy) $50,000 in three months' time. As the rate to be used in three months' time is fixed on the day the contract is entered into, the exporter can be certain of the sterling value of the proceeds. Whatever happens to the spot exchange rate over the next three months will not affect the anticipated value of these proceeds.

No advantage can be taken of a favourable movement in spot rates due to the nature of a forward contract, it being 'an immediately firm and binding agreement'. The forward rate must always be used.

Exchange risk as discussed in Chapter 2 occurs for an importer from the time they agree to buy until the time payment is made in cleared funds. For an exporter the risk runs from the time the price list is published or a tender price is quoted until cleared funds are received. Forward cover should therefore be taken out when exchange risk first begins, i.e. at recognition, and should cover the period until maturity.

Forward rates, it should be emphasised, are not an estimation or prediction of what spot rates will be in the short-term future. In brief, forward rates are determined by the interest rate differential between the two currencies concerned. Further explanation is given later in this chapter and has already been alluded to in Chapter 4.

How to quote a forward rate

A bank will quote a forward rate from a set of information such as:

spot	£1 = DM 2.9510–2.9550
1 month	0.0350–0.0325
or 1 month	3½–3¼ pf pm

The one-month margins illustrate the two ways of expressing the same thing.

These figures will be taken for the moment as given and returned to later in this chapter when it will be explained how the values are what they are.

In addition to the spot rates, forward margins are given. In this instance they are one-month margins. Margins are usually available in monthly intervals. A one-month margin applied to the current spot will give a one-month forward rate. A two-month margin applied to the current spot will give a two-month forward rate, and so on.

The spot on the day the contract is entered into is taken and the forward margin is applied to it. If we take it that the bank is buying, spot will be 2.9550, selling it would be 2.9510. (Apply the sell low buy high rule throughout.)

Now we need to look at the forward margins. There are two ways of quoting them. In the second method above note the term 'pm', this is an abbreviation for premium. On occasion the margin can be 'dis', meaning discount. A premium makes something more expensive, a discount cheaper. In order to make the currency more expensive at a forward rate than at spot, the rate will need to fall. To make it cheaper forward compared with spot, the rate will have to rise.

This gives a new rule:

- premiums are taken away from the spot;
- discounts are added to the spot.

Bank buying spot was 2.9550, therefore in this instance the forward margin of 3¼ pf (pfennigs) must be deducted from the spot. It can be noted that the margin on the buying side is applied to the spot rate. Were the bank to be selling, the figures would have been 2.9510 minus 3½ pf.

To summarise, the forward rate quote becomes:

	Bank selling	Bank buying
spot	2.9510	2.9550
minus	0.0350	0.0325
forward rate	2.9160	2.9225

The forward rate is often called the outright forward rate.

It is evident that $3\frac{1}{2}$ pfennigs can be written as DM 0.0350 and $3\frac{1}{4}$ pfennigs as DM 0.0325.

It will be further noted that when the margins are written

  0.0350–0.0325

there is no written indication as to whether the margins are at a premium or a discount. However, the positioning of the numbers to each other does indicate this.

- When the larger number is on the left, selling side, it is a premium and should be deducted from the spot.
- When the larger number is on the right, buying side, it is a discount and should be added.

Explanation Something at a premium is more expensive. Making the cost of the deutschmarks more expensive in the forward market than at spot to an importer is achieved by giving the importer fewer deutschmarks to every pound. Given the choice of two numbers 0.0350 and 0.0325 a lower figure is achieved by deducting the larger figure available, 0.0350, rather than deducting the smaller, 0.0325, to remain consistent with the sell low/buy high principle.

Had the deutschmarks been quoted at a discount in the forward market, then the rates would have been quoted as follows:

spot	2.9510–2.9550
1 month	0.0325–0.0350

Explanation Something at a discount is cheaper. To make deutschmarks cheaper in the forward market than at spot to an importer would necessitate the bank giving more deutschmarks for every pound. Therefore the forward margins need to be added to the spot.

A higher figure is achieved by adding the discount. Adding on the smaller figure available from the choice of 0.0325–0.0350 gives a higher figure, but consistent with the sell low/buy high principle.

It should therefore be evident that when figures only are quoted as margins, that it is their relationship to each other which indicated whether they are premiums or discounts. Figures only is the method used to quote margins on bank screens. Think of the margins as a spread from a central rate, determination of which is given later in this chapter. Therefore spread is necessary either side in the appropriate direction to enable premiums and discounts to be quoted for buy/sell deals and a bank profit to be made.

Rates quoted before November 1993 in the *Financial Times* used the 'old' notation.

Using the rates given as figures only and translating them into the FT method gives

spot	2.9510–2.9550
or spot	$2.95\frac{1}{10}$–$2.95\frac{1}{2}$
1 month	$3\frac{1}{2}$–$3\frac{1}{4}$ pf pm

or if at a discount

$$3\frac{1}{4}\text{–}3\frac{1}{2} \text{ pf dis}$$

Care needs to be taken with the FT notation that decimal points are positioned correctly. This applies especially to US$ rates.

Note that since November 1993 the FT has been quoting forward rates outright, without margins.

Fixed and option forward contracts

There are two types of forward contract in relation to maturity, i.e. the date on which the agreed exchange is made.

- Fixed – the customer knows that payment or receipt will be on a particular date. The rate is determined as in the previous examples, by applying the appropriate forward margins to the appropriate spot rate to give the outright forward rate which is incorporated into the forward contract. Exchange of currency occurs on this agreed date as fixed.
- Option – the option here is not whether to perform the contract (as with a currency or pure option, Chapters 14 and 15) but when to perform it. A forward contract is always 'immediately firm and binding'. Exchange of currency can be made between two agreed dates with a forward option, but exchange must occur!

The time over which the forward option contract runs should be selected. Invariably it applies when payment or receipt of funds falls between dates, rather than on a particular date, as with a fixed. It can also be used when an option rate is better than a fixed rate from the customer's point of view.

Option nomenclature:

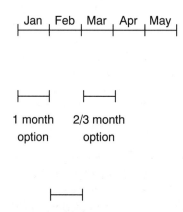

Example A 1/2-month forward option is required by a UK importer to buy currency from the bank.

During February, rates are:
spot $ 1.7050–1.7075
1m   1.05–1.02 c pm
2m   2.15–2.05 c pm

(Note that we are now using dollars for variety and practice at using different currencies.) Here two rates need to be determined initially, the rate at the beginning of the option period and the rate at the end of the option period.

- Bank selling, apply sell low/buy high rule, spot therefore = 1.7050.
- Deduct 1 month premium from spot 1.7050 – 0.0105 = outright forward rate for 1 month = 1.6945.
- Deduct 2 months' premium from spot 1.7050 – 0.0215 = 1.6835.
- Apply the sell low/buy high principle to the two forward rates calculated, as the bank is selling it will quote the lower of the two rates, 1.6835 (not 1.6945).

With practice it will be evident that only one forward rate need be calculated as it becomes obvious which gives the option rate. Other circumstances will of course need perhaps a higher rate to be 'chosen'. In this example this would be required if the bank were quoting an exporter, or alternatively if we return to the importer and the forward margins had been quoted at a discount. Just remember the basic rule of sell low/buy high.

Having quoted the rate of 1.6835 the bank will have to deliver the stated amount of US dollars at any time during February at the request of its customer. A one-month option over January would require a 'comparison' of the spot rate with the one-month forward rate. The rate at the beginning of the option period is of course the spot rate.

It might be useful to see why the sell low/buy high principle is maintained in relation to the rates at the beginning and end of the option period.

Consider that had the bank quoted 1.6945, it would then have been possible for the customer to tell the bank that it wished to take delivery of the currency at the end of February, using this rate. This is at a time when a fixed would have given a rate of 1.6835. In quoting 1.6835, a less favourable rate from the customer's point of view, the bank would have made at least its minimum required profit on the exchange at any time during February. Had it quoted 1.6945, it would only have made its minimum profit had the customer opted to make the exchange at the beginning of February. At any other time than this the bank would have made less than its minimum required profit. ✓

Forward contract close-outs

The question naturally arises, what if the customer in the above does not wish to take delivery of the currency after all? Perhaps the goods ordered will never need paying for due to non-delivery. As the forward contract is 'immediately firm and binding' it must be performed. The bank has made its own arrangements to cover its own exchange risk position having quoted a forward rate. For the customer now not to perform the contract might involve it in additional costs (or savings). In either event these must be passed onto the customer via the close-out procedure.

Suppose on February 20 the importer tells the bank that the currency is no longer required. A close-out will be necessary. (Amount of currency involved = $20,000.)

Procedure:

Feb 20 spot	1.6980–1.6990
1m	1.15–1.08 c pm
2m	2.55–2.35 c pm

Customer buys (bank sells) $20,000 @ agreed forward rate 1.6835.

$20,000 @ 1.6835 = £11,880.01 dr

Bank buys back $20,000 @ Feb 20 spot = 1.6990.

$20,000 @ 1.6990 = £11,771.63 cr

Net cost to customer, difference between cost of $20,000 and proceeds from selling it back:

net = £108.38 dr

Had the spot rate on February 20 been lower than the forward rate there would have been a net gain. This too would have been passed to the customer. Of course, if only part of the value of the contract is needed, the unused portion can be closed out.

Forward contract extensions

If the customer, instead of saying that the currency was not required, had said that payment need not be made until April, due for instance to a delay in delivery, the forward contract could be extended. Again, due to its binding nature, the contract must first be closed out. The contract is extended rather than a new contract being initiated, because this gives a more favourable rate to the customer. It is more favourable in that the close-out rate, not the spot rate, is adjusted by the forward margin. The close-out is in fact, in this case, the buying rate, not the selling rate, and the bank is actually selling here. Not to extend would mean that the customer might go elsewhere in the future for more favourable treatment.

Example Method to extend contract – using previous figures, say customer subsequently requires currency April 20 (i.e. fixed).

Close out $20,000.
Bank sells $20,000 @ 1.6835 = £11,880.01 dr.
Bank buys $20,000 @1.6990 = £11,771.63 cr.
1/2-month forward rate from Feb 20 = 1.6990–0.0255 pm = 1.6735.

Note that this is a more favourable rate to the customer. Had a new contract been taken out the rate would have been 1.6980 – 0.0255 = 1.6725.

April 20 bank sells $20,000 @ 1.6735 = £11,951.00 dr.
Net amount debited to customer as a result of extension = £12,059.38 dr.

Part only of the contract can of course be extended and extensions can be either fixed or option. An alternative to extending might be for the customer to deposit $20,000 to have available for use in April, thus preserving the hedge as seen on pp. 18, 19.

This demonstrates that the correct use of a currency deposit, as here, is an alternative to using a forward contract. A contract can be seen as a derivative of such a deposit – it can be used as an alternative for a cash market activity. This is more fully covered later (pp. 36–9)

Forward contracts – a contingent liability

It is due to the possibility of close-outs and that a debit to the customer's account may result, that forward contracts represent a contingent liability to the bank and its customer. The customer has to be sufficiently creditworthy to be able to accept this potential charge to the account.

As a result banks typically take between 5% and 20% of the value of the contract amount and write it against the customer's agreed banking facility. In this way the bank is not exposed to any risk greater than they wish to incur.

It can be seen that the use of a number of forward contracts can soon erode a customer's facility so as to reduce it to zero. In this way further contracts may not be possible if the facility is all used up. It will also of course affect direct borrowing. This can clearly be a disadvantage to the customer. However, forward contracts are 'off-balancesheet' as far as the customer is concerned. A note in the annual accounts should, however, indicate their existence.

Forward rate margin determination

The question arises, how does the bank arrive at the forward rate it quotes to the customer? How is the forward rate determined? Why are some currencies quoted at a premium and others at a discount and why is the margin the actual size as quoted?

Firstly, it is as well to remind ourselves that it is not a guess or estimate of what the spot rate will be at the agreed time in the future when the currency is to be exchanged. Were this so, then the bank would be exposing itself to exchange risk. It conducts its affairs such that it too hedges the risk that it incurs by quoting a forward rate. Where a bank is uncovered and does not cover forward by use of a contract elsewhere, or the use of other hedging devices, for example futures, it will act as in the following example:

A bank agrees to sell $1m one-year forward fixed and
a bank agrees to buy $2m one-year forward fixed.
It can match $1m of the $2m it agrees to buy with the $1m it has agreed to sell. This leaves $1m bank buy unmatched.

If the bank were now to borrow $1m on the Eurocurrency market the day it agrees to enter into the relevant forward contracts and exchange this $1m into sterling at today's spot rate, it will now have a sum of sterling available effectively borrowed at a dollar rate of interest. This can be compared with the alternative of borrowing (i.e. taking a deposit) in sterling at a sterling rate of interest. A comparison in the dollar and sterling rates of interest can now be made.

Assume the following rates: spot £1 = $1.6695–1.6705.
Sterling one-year interest rate $11\frac{7}{16}$% p.a.
US$ one-year interest rate 6% p.a.
Bank borrows $1m for 1 year @ 6% p.a.
Exchanges $1m into sterling @ 1.6705 = £598,623.16.

Therefore the bank is effectively borrowing £598,623.16 @ 6% p.a. compared with actually borrowing the same sterling sum at a cost of $11\frac{7}{16}$ p.a.

To the bank this is a cost saving which has to be passed on to its customer (competition with other banks ensures that it does, otherwise it will be quoting an uncompetitive rate).

The cost saving is the interest rate differential, strictly the **interest agio**

$$= \frac{i^\$ - i^£}{1 + i^£}$$

$$\frac{0.06 - 0.114375}{1.114375} = -0.0487941 = -4.88\%$$

Note that this differs from calculating the differential by making a straight deduction of

$$6 - 11.4375 = -5.44\%$$

Compare this with the calculation made on pp. 17–19. It would be useful to refer to it at this point. You will see that the derived rate of 1.6227 does not equal 10%–5% = 5%. Were this to be the case then the rate would have to be 1.6150. (5% of 1.70 = 0.085 and 1.70–0.085 = 1.6150).

The benefit of 4.88% p.a. over 12 months has to be passed to the bank's customer by an appropriate adjustment to the rate. As the bank is buying currency from the customer the reduction in cost can be passed on by reducing the rate. Reducing the rate makes the US dollars more expensive in relation to sterling and these are therefore quoted forward at a premium.

The annual forward premium has to adjust the spot by enough to pass to the customer the saving of 4.88% p.a. This can be calculated as

$$\frac{\text{forward rate} - \text{spot rate}}{\text{spot rate}} = \text{saving (cost) p.a.}$$

Plugging in the relevant figures gives:

$$\frac{\text{forward rate} - 1.6705}{1.6705} = -0.0488$$

forward rate − 1.6705 = −0.0815
forward rate = 1.5890

The difference between the forward rate and spot will give the forward margin:

$$1.5890 - 1.6705 = 0.0815 \text{ or } 8.15 \text{ c pm}$$

A more direct way would be to calculate on a per annum basis the necessary adjustment to the spot. In this case 4.88% of 1.6705 = 0.0815.

This exercise also demonstrates that borrowing currency and repaying with currency proceeds equals, in terms of cost or benefit, that of covering forward. If this were not the case, then it would be possible to make a profit without exchange risk from the mismatch between the cash market, derived forward rate and the actual forward rate quoted. It should show why the forward rate is indeed derived from the cash market derived rate. (The issue is fully covered on pp. 36–9.)

If the forward margins and interest differentials do get out of line, then actions of market operators will soon ensure that they come back into alignment. Such opportunities are known as **covered interest arbitrage**. Increases or decreases in borrowing in pursuit of such advantage alters interest rates and forward margins so that there is a movement in rates and margins back towards alignment.

The lesson here is that forward rates are determined by interest rate differentials in the Eurocurrency markets.

- When the currency is at lower interest rates than the base currency, then currency will be quoted at a premium in the forward market.
- When currency is at a higher rate of interest than the base currency, currency will be quoted at a discount in the forward market.

Cost/gain of forward cover

An alternative way of looking at the matters discussed above is to take the spot and forward rates/forward margins and calculate what is often referred to as 'cost of forward cover'. As will soon be seen, this term can be a little misleading.

'Cost of forward cover' can be calculated using the formula:

$$\frac{\text{pm or dis} \times 12/n \times 100}{\text{outright forward rate}} = \% \text{ p.a.}$$

If the forward margins (i.e. dis or pm) are quoted in months then n = number of months in the forward contract. If the contract is in days then $360/n$ should be substituted in the formula.

The reason 360 days per year, rather than 365, are used is because Eurocurrency calculations are made on a 360-day year basis.

Taking the original rates

spot	1.6695–1.6705
12 months	–8.15 c pm

and putting them into the formula gives:

$$\frac{0.0815 \times 12/12 \times 100}{1.5890} = 5.13\% \text{ p.a.}$$

The different answer is due to the fact that in this formula the premium is being compared with the forward rate, rather than the spot rate which was used to calculate the premium in the first instance. Which is correct to use causes much debate. However, practice seems to favour using the forward rate. Note that it looks quite similar to the 5.44% obtained earlier to obtain the interest differential by simple subtraction ($6\% - 11^7/_{16} = 5.44\%$).

The fact that it is similar leads some to suppose this to be the correct method to use when conducting exercises using figures quoted daily in the FT, as they too seem to use this latter technique.

But note:

$$\frac{0.0815 \times 12/12 \times 100}{1.6705} = 4.88\% \text{ (of course!)}$$

(Refer back to the calculations which were made to determine the forward margin.)

The term 'cost of forward cover' is also somewhat misleading in that it can also represent a saving or benefit in covering forward. Some examples should illustrate this.

Exporters prefer the rate to be as low as possible, it gives them more sterling for a given amount of currency received in payment.

$1,000 @ 1.50 = £666.67

$1,000 @ 1.40 = £714.29

Importers prefer the rate to be as high as possible, it gives them more currency to make a payment for a given amount of sterling.

£1,000 @ 1.70 = $1,700

£1,000 @ 1.80 = $1,800

When the forward rate is at a premium this gives a lower rate and therefore gives a saving, rather than a cost, to an exporter. A premium, giving a lower rate, gives a cost to an importer. The technique enables the customer to lock into a forward rate and this gives a rate which is either better or worse than the spot, enabling a saving or cost respectively.

The following table summarises the situation:

exporter sells currency	bank buy	pm	saving
exporter sells currency	bank buy	dis	cost
importer buys currency	bank sell	pm	cost
importer buys currency	bank sell	dis	saving

Forward contracts – a derivative

It should now be clear that a forward contract is an alternative to using a spot market/money market/cash market hedge. It has been shown in Chapter 4 how appropriate depositing and borrowing can hedge exchange risk. In this chapter it has now been demonstrated that forward rates are determined by interest rate differentials. Therefore gains/costs in using either technique will be the same.

The disadvantage of a spot market hedge is that in borrowing or depositing money the full value of the borrowing/deposit is using up a banking facility. A forward contract, however, instead of being a full, actual liability, is a contingent one, which as a matter of practice only uses up between 5% and 20% of a banking facility to cover the potential cost of a close-out.

The potential cost of close-out still exists of course, in effect, if the cash market is used to hedge. If an exporter, for example, borrows currency, changes into domestic currency at spot, and uses the anticipated proceeds of the export sale to repay the currency borrowing, in the now familiar way, there is still a risk that the proceeds arrive either not in time or not at all.

In either event it would incur the equivalent of a close-out cost or gain. If the money were not going to arrive at all to repay the borrowing, then currency would have to be bought at spot to repay. If the spot rate, in this case, is lower than the rate at which it was originally exchanged into sterling, then the equivalent of a close-out cost will be incurred. If the rate had been higher in comparison, then a close-out equivalent gain would have been incurred.

A worked example:

$20,000 exchanged into sterling at $1.50 = £13,333.33
Ignore any interest, if the dollars had to be repaid by exchanging at $1.40, the cost would be £14,285.71.

The equivalent of an extension is the need to borrow for a longer period of time than originally intended. This may result in either interest gains or losses, equivalent to such gains or losses as would have been made had a forward contract been used as an alternative when an extension would have been needed.

Refamiliarise yourself with the material in Chapter 4 where currency borrowing was considered as a cash market hedge. The example used is reproduced here for the sake of clarity. For simplification, interest rates quoted are central rates, i.e. borrowing or depositing is possible at these rates.

Situation – a UK exporter expects to receive $50,000 in one year's time. Borrowing $47,619.05 at 5% p.a. interest gives a repayment of $50,000 in one year.

Take the $47,619.05 and exchange into sterling at £1 = $1.70 spot
= £28,011.20

$ interest	£ interest
(add) 5% = $\dfrac{2,380.95}{\$50,000.00}$	(add) 10% = $\dfrac{2,801.12}{£30,812.32}$

$50,000 divided by £30,812.32 gives an effective forward rate of £1 = $1.6227.

Now, consider if a bank were to quote a forward rate of £1 = $1.80, it would be possible to arbitrage this mismatch between $1.6227 and $1.80.

It would work this way:

Borrow as above, i.e $47,619.05, repayment in one year of $50,000.

At the same time enter into a forward contract to buy (bank to sell) $50,000 at $1.80.

In one year's time take delivery of the $50,000 under the forward contract at $1.80, cost = £27,777.78.

In the meantime, the £28,011.20 would have been placed on deposit at 10% p.a. to realise a figure in one year of £30,812.32. The difference between the £30,812.32 realised at the end of the year from this deposit and the known cost of the dollars of £27,777.78 under the forward contract, allows a riskless, covered arbitrage profit of £30,812.32 − £27,777.78 = £3034.54 to be made.

Had the forward rate been below the effective cash market forward rate, then cash market dollar lending/depositing would be needed with sterling borrowing to fund the deposit and a forward contract to sell (bank buy) dollars. Because the rates we have used as an example are central rates, necessarily there will be a spread either side of this, which will reduce the potential profit. Clearly there will never be such a large arbitrage opportunity such as this in reality. The rates have been quoted to illustrate the principle involved.

In reality if there is an arbitrage opportunity, it may not be worthwhile because of the transaction cost due to the spread across the deposit and lending rates. It should now be clear that the forward rate must equal the true interest differential – interest agio, as discussed earlier (p. 34). An additional reason which may help the understanding of this issue is as follows:

If an arbitrage opportunity exists at all, it will occur for a very short period of time. Arbitrageurs will alter the demand and supply of funds in the cash market as they take positions to arbitrage. They will alter their borrowing/depositing of domestic and foreign currency. As a result rates will alter and alter the interest differential, and therefore the effective rate. In the last example dollar rates will rise and sterling rates will fall.

Finally consider the position of a bank entering into forward contracts, it will need to hedge its position. On a daily basis it will keep a position sheet of its forward deals. Imagine that today it has agreed to the following in one year's time:

- bank sell $1m
- bank buy $2m.

In one year it will receive $2m, $1m of which it will use to sell, making a profit across the spread it will quote on the rates. How will it hedge the unmatched $1m it has agreed to buy?

It will borrow dollars for one year, exchange dollars immediately into sterling and repay the dollar sum owed in one year's time by the anticipated net receipt of $1m. From this action it should be self-evident that the rate it will quote in a forward contract will be the derived rate from the cash market activity.

Fundamentally the forward rate equals the interest rate differential between the two currencies concerned. The possibility of arbitrage ensures that it is so. In reality exchange risk incurred by a bank may be hedged by the use of a currency future, for example, in which case the hedge achieved will again equal the interest rate differential. (See pp. 120–2 for an explanation.)

Range forward contracts

A further variation seen in relation to forward contracts is a **range forward contract** or **flexible forward contract.** Here, instead of a single forward rate, a range of rates is quoted. For example, £1 = $1.50–$1.60. If spot at maturity of the contract is between these rates, then spot is used. If spot is above $1.60, £1.60 is used. If spot is below $1.50, $1.50 is used. In this example the bank would be selling and the customer buying dollars. Other normal forward contract variables (time, amount) apply. You will be able to recognise this in later chapters as a true option.

Summary

- Forward contracts and forward rates are a derivative of cash market borrowing/depositing hedges. Their advantage is that they only use up a relatively small amount of a bank facility, being a contingent, rather than an absolute liability.
- Forward contracts can be fixed or option, in both cases contracts are firm and binding and must be performed. Were this not so, then parties would renege upon their obligations to make exchanges if spot rates were more favourable. Close-outs become necessary if the facility is not needed. Extensions can alter the time when obligations are to be performed.
- Parties cannot take advantage of favourable movements in rates. Forward contracts hedge currency risk because they provide certain, known, fixed values when currency is exchanged at a later date.
- Forward rates are determined by interest rate differentials between the two currencies concerned. Depending upon the relationship, forward rates will be either at a premium or a discount to the spot rate and give rise to costs or gains.

Questions

6.1 Define a forward contract in your own words.

6.2 When would a fixed forward contract be used and when would an option forward contract be used?

6.3 When might a close-out of a forward contract be necessary?

6.4 When might an extension of a forward contract be necessary?

6.5 Why does a forward contract represent a contingent liability to the bank and its customer?

6.6 If a currency is quoted in the forward market at a discount does this represent a cost or gain to an exporter wishing to cover exchange risk by use of a forward contract?

6.7 Comment upon the validity of the following statements:

You should only borrow foreign currency as a hedging device if you have a matching income to repay and the interest on the currency is lower than sterling, if interest is higher you would be better off using a forward contract to hedge.

If interest rates to borrow a foreign currency are lower than to borrow sterling, borrow it and hedge the exchange risk by use of a forward contract.

6.8 a) A US company manufacturing small electrical tools generates an annual turnover of US$2bn and normally makes profits of US$200m. It sources and sells 100% of its turnover in the USA. However, at the latest year end, sales and profits are significantly down and the managing director realises this decline is due entirely to currency exposure.

Explain:

i)   how this decline could be due entirely to currency exposure. [7]

ii) what action could be taken to protect the company from similar exposures in the future. [4]

b) A German company has carefully analysed its costs and regularly makes profits (at a 30% margin) from its domestic sales. However, since it started to export three years ago, the profits generated from its foreign sales have fluctuated widely despite the fact that costs in Germany have continued to be level and tightly controlled. Export sales have been at a consistent level over this period.

Explain why the profit fluctuations have occurred and what services a bank would provide to minimise these fluctuations. (NOTE: the mechanics of any specific instruments need NOT be explained.) [9]
(Total marks for question – [20])

(CIOB Multinational Corporate Banking, Finance and Investment, Spring 1992.)

6.9 a) Explain what is meant by a currency being 'at a premium' or 'at a discount'. [5]

b) Your dealer has obtained the following quotations for current interest and exchange rates:

3-month sterling deposits	$10-10\frac{1}{8}\%$
3-month US dollar deposits	$4\frac{3}{8}\%-4\frac{1}{2}\%$
US dollar/sterling spot	1.5000–1.5010
3-month forward dollar/sterling	0.0330–0.0310 premium

Demonstrate how this combination of rates offers an opportunity to make a profit free of all position risk. (Assume that the 3-month period consists of 90 days.) [10]

(CIOB Banking Operations Regulation, Market Practice & Treasury Management, Spring 1993.)

7 ▷ Interest rate risk exposure

Interest rate volatility

Over the past two decades there have been considerable fluctuations in interest rates caused by the authorities' response to changes in the rate of inflation. In turn fluctuations in exchange rates have encouraged monetary authorities to try to influence exchange rates by movements in interest rates. Table 7.1 shows movements in UK bank base rates from January 1977 to January 1993. Similar charts for US$ rates or other OECD currencies would show the same kind of volatility.

Corporate treasurers therefore may wish to remove risk with regard to interest rate changes by various hedging techniques. Not to hedge is of course always an option, but leaves the company's profit and loss account exposed to the effects of such changes. Equally should rates move favourably, then of course by hedging the company will not necessarily experience the total benefit of such a change. As always though the benefit is certainty. Uncertainty as to rates can be hedged in a number of ways.

In order to hedge successfully the corporate treasurer must:

- Be aware of current and future commitments;
- take a view as to the future level of interest rates;
- decide whether to hedge and which method to use.

Perhaps sensitivity analysis could be used to see if there is a rate of interest below or above which would cause the company to fail. A hedge could be put into place to ensure that adverse movements do not impact upon the company. Various hedging techniques gain the company certainty and with varying degrees.

The various hedging instruments gain the company certainty and in some case still allow a gain to be made.

Table 7.1 UK bank base rates Jan 1977–Dec 1994

1977	Jan 25 13	Feb 4 12.5	Feb 18 12.5	Mar 11 10.5	Mar 31 9.5	Apr 26 9	May 3 8.5	Aug 9 8	Sep 13 7	Oct 17 6	Dec 2 7.5
1978	Jan 9 6.5	Apr 20 7.6	May 10 9	Jun 12 10	Nov 3 11.6	Nov 14 12.6					
1979	Feb 13 13.5	Mar 6 13	Apr 6 12	Jun 16 14	Nov 16 17						
1980	Jul 4 16	Nov 25 14									
1981	Mar 11 12	Sep 16 14	Oct 1 16	Oct 14 15.5	Nov 9 15	Dec 4 14.5					
1982	Jan 25 13	Feb 25 13.5	Mar 12 13	Jun 8 12.5	Jul 14 12	Aug 2 11.5	Aug 18 11	Aug 31 10.5	Oct 7 10	Oct 14 9.5	Nov 5 10
1983	Jan 12 11	Mar 15 10.5	Apr 15 10	Jun 15 9.5	Oct 4 9						
1984	Mar 7 8.75	May 10 9.25	Jul 6 10	Jul 11 12	Aug 9 11.75	Aug 10 11					
1985	Jan 11 10.5	Jan 14 12	Jan 28 14	Mar 20 13.5	Apr 3 13.25	Apr 12 12.75	Jun 12 12.5	Jul 29 11.5			
1986	Jan 9 12.5	Mar 19 11.5	Apr 8 11								
1987	Mar 10 10.5	Mar 18 10	Apr 29 9.5	May 11 9	Aug 7 10	Oct 28 9.5	Nov 5 9	Dec 4 8.5			
1988	Feb 2 9	Mar 17 8.5	Apr 11 8	May 18 7.5	Jun 3 8	Jun 6 8.5	Jun 22 9	Jun 28 9.5	Jul 4 10	Aug 8 9	Aug 25 12
1988	Nov 25 13										
1989	May 24 14	Oct 5 15									
1990	Oct 8 14										
1991	Feb 13 13.5	Feb 27 13	Mar 22 12.5								
1992	Apr 12 12	May 5 10	Sep 16 12	Sep 16 15	Sep 17 10	Sep 22 9	Oct 16 8	Nov 12 7			
1993	Jan 26 6	Nov 23 5.5									
1994	Feb 8 5.25	Sep 12 5.75	Dec 17 6.25								
1995	Feb 2 6.75										

The hedges discussed in this book are as follows:

● forward/forwards	Chapter 8
● forward rate agreements (FRAs)	Chapter 9
● interest rate futures	Chapters 10, 11, 13
● interest rate options	Chapter 16
● interest rate swaps	Chapter 18.

Forward/forwards

Forward/forwards are a cash market activity. They represent a cash market position which could be taken to hedge interest rate risk. However, they are rarely used now for hedging purposes due to the inherent disadvantages they contain. They are described here to illustrate the principle and to show how forward/forward interest rates can be calculated. Such rates are used in the FRA and futures markets, both being a derivative of forward/forwards.

Companies will often be in the position of knowing that they will need to borrow a certain sum of money for a known period of time in the future. They may wish to fix, i.e. hedge, the cost of this borrowing. They can do this as seen in the following example:

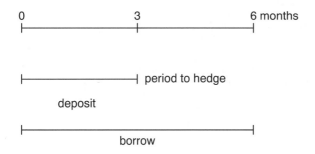

The real need is to borrow between three and six months. By borrowing for the whole six months and lending for the first three only, it is possible to fix the rate of interest on borrowing for the three to six month period immediately.

The idea is to make funds available (borrow) over the three to six month period at a known rate. This is achieved by borrowing for six months and placing the funds realised on deposit for three months. When the nought to three month deposit matures funds are then available for use over the three to six month period as required. At six months the sum borrowed at the outset can be repaid.

As an alternative a company may have a known sum that they wish to lend, i.e. deposit, in the future. A cash market forward/forward position can be taken as follows:

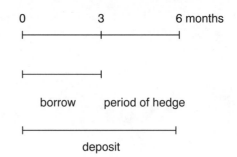

The real, underlying need, is to lend (deposit) funds over the three to six month period, due to an anticipated surplus at this time. Funds are therefore borrowed for three months and immediately placed on deposit for nought to six months. At three months funds are then available to repay the borrowing, being the funds which are the anticipated cash surplus for which the hedge is intended. As a result funds have been deposited for a known future return over the three to six month period required.

Forward/forwards are not too popular because:

- The borrowing uses up banking facilities for six months instead of the three actually required.
- The borrowing increases balancesheet liabilities.
- A cost is incurred due to the interest spread on the borrowing and deposit rates.
- A company may not have the credit facility to undertake any necessary borrowing.

Determination of forward/forward rates

Imagine that the following rates apply:

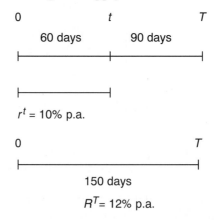

Imagine that the 10% and 12% are central rates and that money can be either lent or borrowed at these rates. There is a formula which will give a rate for the period of time in the future (t–T, i.e. 90 days here) implied by the current rates for 60 and 150 days.

The general formula for the forward/forward rate applicable at time t with maturity at time T is known alternatively as: t against T; t versus T; $t^R T$; t v T or t on T. t is pronounced 'little t' and T as 'big T'.

Using the time period notation of t, T and $T-t$ the rate for

time period $t = r^t$
time period $T = R^T$
time period $T-t = R^{T-t}$
$(1 + r^t \times t/360) \times (1 + R^{T-t} \times T-t/360) = (1 + R^T \times T/360)$

Therefore:

$$1 + (R^{T-t} \times T - t/360) = \frac{[1 + (R^T \times T/360)]}{[1 + (r^t \times t/360)]}$$

and therefore:

$$R^{T-t} = \frac{[1 + (R^T \times T/360)]}{[1 + (r^t \times t/360)]} - 1 \times 360/T - t$$

For sterling the relevant fractions used should be the actual number of days divided by 365.

January 29 1993 to April 29 1993 is 90 days and thus becomes 90/365. Rates described this way are described as Actual/365 fixed. In leap years (not 1993) February 29 would need to be included. Some three-month periods will be for more than 90 days, especially if the three months matures on a non-banking day such as a weekend or holiday. This base is used for all sterling and Belgian Franc rates. Eurocurrency LIBOR base rates are all Actual/360.

Returning to the numerical example and plugging the rates of 10% and 12% with the relevant time periods into the formula gives:

$$\frac{[1 + (0.12 \times 150/365)]}{[1 + (0.10 \times 60/365)]} - 1 \times 365/90 = 0.1311769 = 13.12\% \text{ p.a.}$$

The 13.12% is the forward/forward rate. It is the rate implied in this example in two months' time by the current rates over maturities of two and five months.

If the 13.12% is taken as a central rate, then a spread on this, for example of 1/8% could be made, so that market bid and offer quotes could be:

13.058%–13.183%

If central rates are not quoted, but the actual rates across the spread, then you must be careful to use the correct borrowing and lending rates as appropriate in the formula.

The forward/forward rate will be the rate quoted for an FRA and will represent the 'cost of carry' in the interest rate futures market.

Summary

- Implicit in current rates of interest over differing time periods is the forward rate of interest. The calculation involves depositing/borrowing or borrowing/depositing over different maturities and is known as a forward/forward. They are little used because the borrowing naturally uses up borrowing capacity. The formula for calculating the forward/forward rate is known as t on T.

- The forward/forward rate is the contract rate quoted in an FRA and represents the 'cost of carry' in the interest rate futures market.

Key terms

- forward/forward rate (p. 45)   • t on T (p. 46)

Questions

8.1 Calculate the bid and offer price you would quote for a 3 v 6 FRA using the following information:

r^t = 5.25–5.35% p.a.
R^T = 6.00–6.30% p.a.

(3 v 6 describes the period of time as illustrated in the figures on pp. 45–6.)

8.2 The 6-month Eurodollar rate is 6% and the 9-month rate is 6.5%. What is the 3-month implied forward rate 6 months hence?

(Securities Institute, Financial Futures and Options, December 1992.)

Forward or future rate agreements (FRAs)

FRA definition

An FRA is an agreement between bank and customer that gives a customer a guaranteed future rate of interest to cover a specified sum of money over a specified period of time in the future.

The FRA market has developed since 1983 and in London it is mostly the banks active in the money, inter-bank and Eurocurrency markets which are active in the FRA market.

Contract terms

- The day the agreement is entered into is the deal or transaction day.
- The period covered by the notional lending or deposit is the contract period, running from the settlement date to the maturity date.
- The settlement day is the day two days before the beginning of the contract period and is the day on which the settlement sum is paid. Because it takes two working days for a sum of money to be transferred, if money is paid on the settlement day, it will actually be received by the recipient on the day required, i.e. value/spot day.
- The maturity day is the last day of the contract period.
- Settlement sum is the amount of money either paid or received in compensation as described later.

These descriptions are summarised diagrammatically below:

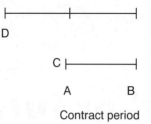

Contract period

A = value day/spot day

B = maturity day

C = settlement day, two business days before value/spot day

D = deal/transaction day

Most FRAs cover a period of time of less than one year into the future and almost all end within two years. The most common and standard contract periods are three or six months.

An FRA covering a three-month contract period beginning in three months' time

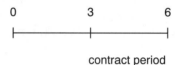

contract period

would be described variously as: 3 v 6, 3 versus 6, 3 against 6, or 3 on 6.

Non-standard FRAs are possible and found, e.g. 4 v 7 over 20th. This means that the contract period begins on the 20th of the month, it begins in four months' time and covers a contract period of three months. Such FRAs are known as broken date FRAs.

If today is January 29 1993, then the contract period (value day) will begin April 20 1993 and end (maturity date) on July 20 1993 (91 days).

Creating a hedge with an FRA

The FRA does not involve actual lending or borrowing of sums of money in the cash market. It is merely an agreement about predetermined rates of interest. As a separate transaction, the FRA holder will need to actually borrow the sum required (this example) in the cash market at spot rates prevailing at the time in the future that the sum is required.

Parties are compensated when the actual rate in the cash market deviates from the predetermined rate (i.e. forward/forward) as agreed in the FRA. The bank will guarantee a (predetermined) lending rate of interest of, for instance, 15% p.a. If actual cash market rates turn out to be 16% p.a., it will pay the client the difference based on the sum actually agreed in the FRA for the relevant contract period.

Taking a small temporary liberty here, for reasons covered later (pp. 53–4), the compensation payable by the bank on a sum of, for instance, £1m for a contract period of three months would be £2500. This would match the extra actually paid to borrow in the cash market above the FRA agreed rate. Thus a hedge is achieved to fix a funding cost in the future.

To borrow £1m at 16% for three months costs an extra £2500 in interest, compared with borrowing at 15%, the agreed rate.

16% cost = £40,000   15% cost = £37,500

(over three months)

difference = £2500 = compensation payment

If rates move in the opposite direction the customer will pay the bank the relevant compensating payment. It should be emphasised that clients do not actually have to borrow the money if they do not wish to, they must make, or receive the compensating payment only. Because only compensating payments are made there is no risk of default to the bank with respect to the underlying sum of money.

There is only the compensating payment at risk should rates move against the customer. For this reason FRAs only represent a small contingent liability and do not affect the customer's banking facility a great deal, 5% of the underlying sum is common.

Settlement/Reference rate

The agreed, predetermined, contract rate will be as stated in the FRA, and will be the forward/forward rate for the contract period. The actual rate being charged on real sums of money in the cash market for the contract period is known as the interest settlement rate. It is stated two days before the contract period begins (i.e. two days before the value day). The settlement rate, sometimes known as the reference rate, is a composite rate published by the British Bankers' Association (BBA) and therefore is known as the BBA interest settlement rate (BBAISR). It is the average rate of a number of BBA Designated Banks at the 11 a.m. LIBOR fix. There are not less than twelve banks on the BBA panel and the settlement rate is taken from an average of any eight. Standard FRA contract periods use this system. Non-standard contract period FRAs use a settlement rate by a method agreed between bank and customer.

Sale and purchase of FRAs

- The **purchase** of an FRA protects against a **rise** in interest rates where a company is to borrow and a bank in the cash market lends.
- The **sale** of an FRA protects against a **fall** in interest rates where a company is to lend (i.e. deposit) and the bank borrow (i.e. take the deposit).

Always look at the position from the company's point of view, not that of the bank/market maker. Remember that the FRA and the necessary cash market arrangements have to be arranged separately to effect a hedge.

Note that it is possible to sell an FRA without previously having bought one! This can be a little difficult to accept at first. The terms buy and sell are merely ways of stating by convention whether borrowing or depositing is required.

Note also, however, that the opposite convention is used for interest rate futures, i.e.

- selling a future protects against a rise in rates;
- buying a future protects against a fall in rates.

An FRA in action

A further numerical example will further illustrate the principle and practice of an FRA, including that concerning the compensation payment/receipt. The example begins here and continues into following sections. Imagine a company needs to borrow £1m in three months' time for a period of three months and wishes to hedge the rate of interest they will have to pay. Using an FRA this will be a 3 v 6, and diagrammatically this is:

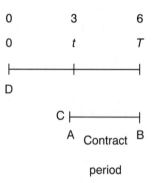

A = value day/spot day

B = maturity day

C = settlement day, two business days before value/spot day

D = deal/transaction day

The company would like to fix the rate of interest for the loan in that it does not wish to pay more than current rates. It believes that interest rates may well have risen by the time it actually borrows the money. Therefore in the example the company will wish to purchase an FRA (go long).

On the deal/transaction day the bank will quote the contract rate. This will be based on a calculation of the forward/forward rate for reasons fully explored later in the chapter (p. 56). In this instance let the contract rate be 10% p.a. If this rate is acceptable to the customer they will go long, purchase the FRA, to protect against a rise in rates.

FRA settlement rates

Two business days before the period of the loan begins, i.e. two days before the value day, the settlement rate is determined. It is this rate with which the contract rate is compared, to ascertain the amount of compensation to be paid and by which party. The way in which the settlement rate is determined is by way of the method given below. This is the FRA market convention (in the UK, FRABBA terms apply) and follows the practice in the Eurocurrency markets. The convention is to make financial transactions relate to the spot date. It takes two working days for money to be transferred, therefore if settlement is to be on the value day, then it must be at the rate two days earlier.

Standard FRA agreements will use as a settlement rate a reference rate (the terms are used interchangeably in FRAs) given by the average of rates from a number of banks on the 'panel'. Clearly rates will relate to different maturities and the one used will be appropriate to the contract period (rate given Telerate pages 3740 and 3750).

Here the FRABBA three-month composite rate will need to be used. We will say the rate is 11% p.a. As a result of this the bank will pay the customer 1%, being the difference between the settlement and contract rate. The 1% will be calculated here on a three-month basis related to the agreed figure of £1m and will be £2426.60 (see p. 54 for calculation).

It should be realised that had rates fallen, payment would have been made by the customer. The point is that by use of the FRA the customer has been able to lock into the contract rate. This is the rate they will effectively pay using the FRA and cash market together, whether rates actually rise or fall.

Remember, with the FRA the actual loan that the company will have to take is quite separate from the FRA obligations and forms no part of it. In this case money will have to be borrowed at the actual rate of 11% with the compensating payment from the FRA effectively reducing the cost to 10%.

FRA compensation formula → APPEDIX

As the settlement payment is made at the beginning of the actual period of the loan rather than at the end of the payment period when interest in the cash market is due, the settlement payment needs to be discounted to represent value at the end of the contract period.

The formula used for settlement of an FRA at maturity is:

when settlement rate (L) is greater than contract rate (R)

$$\frac{(L-R) \times D \times A}{(B \times 100) + (L \times D)}$$

or $\quad \dfrac{L - R \times A \times D/360}{1 + (L \times D/360)}$

When settlement rate is less than contract rate

$$\frac{(R-L) \times D \times A}{(B \times 100) + (L \times D)}$$

or $\quad \dfrac{R - L \times A \times D/360}{1 + (L \times D/360)}$

L = settlement rate expressed as a number, not a percentage
R = contract rate expressed as for L
D = number of days in contract
A = contract amount
B = 360 or 365 as applicable.

Remember, all FRAs are based on a 360 day year, except for sterling where it is 365. There is also a recommended procedure to calculate the compensation amount for FRAs exceeding a year. Note that although the compensation paid is often referred to as interest, in most tax jurisdictions it is not treated as such for tax purposes.

Plugging the figures of the example into the relevant formula gives a settlement payment to the customer by the bank of:

$$\frac{(11 - 10) \times 91 \times 1,000,000}{(365 \times 100) + (11 \times 91)} = \frac{91,000,000}{36,500 + 1001}$$

$$= £2,426.60$$

The first formula given above in each case is the one used in the market as standard and handles the discount value necessity in the compensation payment. All the formula does is apply the interest rate difference to amount and contract period and discount it so that time value of the compensation is the same as that for the cash market interest.

Further FRA market details

The FRA market is most liquid in US dollars, sterling and deutschmarks. Other currency quotes are available, but with wider bid/offer spreads. The market is more liquid in the shorter maturities. The FRABBA currencies are, in addition to the above, Swiss Francs, Japanese Yen, ECU, Australian Dollars and French Francs.

Typical hedged amounts are US$5m to US$100m, with smaller amounts in less liquid markets.

The bank as FRA market maker

Banks can of course use FRAs as an asset-liability management device to reduce their own interest rate risk by entering into FRAs with other banks which are acting as market makers in FRAs.

It therefore follows that a number of banks will themselves be market makers and offer bid/offer prices and make a turn across the spread.

In a two-way quote given by a market maker, the lower rate will be the bid rate, at which the market maker pays fixed interest and receives floating (LIBOR). The higher rate will be the offer rate, at which fixed interest is received. The **market maker** is said to buy at their bid price and sell at their offer price.

Any party to the FRA who sells is said to be short and benefits from a fall in rates as it is they who will be borrowing the underlying, notional sum.

Any party who buys is said to be long and will benefit if rates rise. They will be lending the notional sum. The same terminology is used in the swaps market.

A bank as market maker can cover its own position by any of the following:

- Balancing its book, i.e. taking on sales and purchases for matching amounts and maturities. In this way compensation paid will equal compensation received, with a profit being taken due to the spread across the rates.
- Taking a matched FRA position. The bank will, for instance, purchase from another market maker, to match a customer selling over the same period of time, or vice versa the bank will sell, the customer will purchase.
- Taking out a corresponding forward/forward position.
- Taking out a financial futures contract (Chapter 11).

FRA users

In addition to banks as described above, corporations, non-bank financial institutions and government bodies all use FRAs to hedge. The credit risk to the market maker is quite small in relation to the risk to the principal involved. Even on an untypically long-term FRA, the change in interest rates is not likely to exceed say 5%, therefore compensation payable will be quite small in relation to default of the principal as a whole. If rates move 5% p.a., then compensation will be 5% of the principal, based upon a year. Thus a contingent liability marked against the customer will be quite low, i.e. 5%.

No premium is paid by the customer for an FRA. The only payment is the compensating one should this be necessary. A bank's/market maker's profit is made across the spread.

Should a close-out be necessary this is done by a further contract which contras the original position. FRAs by their very nature must be firm and binding.

It is of course possible for users of FRAs to take a position to speculate upon future interest rate movements. This is simply achieved by not undertaking the cash market activity which would have been taken had a hedge been the motive. Almost invariably this will be counter the written policy of the user organisation.

All participants constantly compare FRA rates with those on other financial instruments seeking arbitrage possibilities. This search activity ensures that spreads are kept narrow.

FRAs and forward contracts – a comparison

FRAs are the interest rate management equivalent to the forward contract and currency risk. Favourable movements in rates cannot be taken advantage of as part of the hedging process. Cost or gain can only be known in relation to spot rate outcome at maturity. Both are firm and binding on the parties and represent a contingent liability, due to the firm and binding obligations.

They are both derivatives of a cash market hedge, forward/forwards with their associated lending or borrowing in the case of FRAs and lending/borrowing of currency in the case of forward contracts. Forward rates are derived from the cash market hedge and so are the contract rates in an FRA. In either case arbitrage ensures that this be so.

Forward/forward – FRA arbitrage

It would be instructive to consider why the rate given by a forward/forward and the contract rate in an FRA must be the same. If they are not then arbitrage can take place. The process is similar to that described with regard to forward rates and currency borrowing/lending. Consider a sum of money of £100,000 and the following central rates:

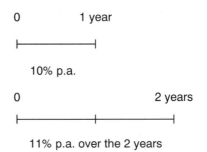

Plugging the rates into the t on T formula gives a forward/forward rate of 12.009% p.a. This will be the FRA rate to be quoted by the market maker/bank.

If the central rate quoted were less than 12.009% then a risk free, arbitrage profit could be made by lending for two years at 11% p.a. giving £123,210 at the maturity of the deposit whilst simultaneously borrowing for two successive years, the first year at 10% and the second year, with an FRA, at a rate below the forward/forward rate as we have suggested to illustrate the point. If the FRA rate were to be say, 11.5% p.a. this would give a total cost of borrowing over the two years of £122,650. As the return on lending this amount was £123,210, an arbitrage profit of £560 could be made.

Were the FRA rate to be above the forward/forward rate then an arbitrage could be effected by borrowing at 11% p.a. over two years and lending at 10% for the first year and at the FRA rate for the second.

Summary

- FRAs are a way of hedging interest rate risk. Gains or losses in the cash market are compensated by payments/receipts from settlement of the FRA position taken.
- Lending/borrowing has to be arranged separately.
- The FRA contract rate is firm and binding and therefore favourable movements in interest rates cannot be enjoyed. However, unfavourable movements are not experienced. What the user gets is certainty.
- If the user does not care for this pay-off profile, other hedges can be used, but it must be appreciated that nothing is for free and that more advantageous outcomes can only be bought at a price.
- As such an FRA does not 'cost', payments by one party are used to compensate the other.

Questions

9.1 You have been quoted the following rates for a 3 v 6 FRA: 5.35–5.60% p.a. You wish to hedge borrowing of £250,000. Will you purchase or sell an FRA? What is the actual compensation paid or received (state which) if cash market rates at three months are 5.40–5.67% p.a.? What is the net sterling cost of borrowing the £250,000?

9.2 Why does an FRA represent a contingent liability?

9.3 Why does the compensation formula for an FRA take into account the time value of money at the end of the actual borrowing period?

10 An introduction to futures

Four chapters are devoted to futures. Chapter 10 outlines basic principles, how futures markets work. Chapter 11 deals specifically with interest rate futures. Chapter 12 covers currency futures. Chapter 13 covers more advanced principles and trading strategies.

It is not the intention of this text to deal with commodity futures markets, but commodities can be used to illustrate basic principles and they are used in this chapter where it is felt it serves a purpose, they are more straightforward than financial futures.

If you have not studied futures before you might at first think they are difficult, many students do, regardless of their course. Part of the problem is that there are a number of things to understand and they cannot all be covered or comprehended at once, so it is difficult to appreciate sometimes the significance of pieces of information and their place in the whole. You may find it worthwhile frequently to go to the summary at the end of this chapter which tries to give a quick overall explanation without a lot of detail. You may even find it worthwhile to give the summary a try first.

Definitions of futures

You may have come across futures before without perhaps realising it. In the film 'Trading Places' the Eddie Murphy character successfully loses a very large sum of money speculating in futures and causes a large margin call upon his two financier benefactors, demonstrating the leverage effect a futures position has.

If you have seen James Dean in 'East of Eden', you might recall that the Father loses a lot of money. In order to make good this loss the James Dean character speculates in soya bean futures. He believes the spot price of beans will rise. You will see later that he must have taken a long position in bean futures to make his profit.

In its simplest form a futures contract is an agreement between two parties to make an exchange of a commodity (the underlying) at a particular named future date at a pre-agreed price.

More developed definitions can be given as follows:

- A future is a contract which provides both a right and an obligation to buy or sell a standard amount of a commodity on a specified future date at a price agreed when the contract is entered into.
- A futures contract is a standardised legally binding agreement to sell or buy a specified asset at a fixed time in the future at an agreed price.
- A futures contract is an agreement for a seller to deliver a specified quantity of a particular grade of a certain commodity to a predetermined location on a certain date at an agreed price. The obligation of the buyer is the opposite, i.e. to take delivery.

With some types of **financial futures contracts** where the underlying asset/commodity is a financial asset the definition becomes:

A futures contract is a binding agreement between two parties to make or take delivery of a commitment at a stated price at a specified future date.

Other kinds of financial futures do relate to delivery of an actual financial asset such as a bond.

A key element of any successful traded futures contract must be the characteristic of standardisation, it is this element which makes the agreement tradeable – i.e. traded for itself. The only negotiable, changeable element, must be the price agreed when entering into the contract.

History of futures

Historically, if there is ever a high degree of price risk in a market over time (or due to distance of delivery) then futures trading is likely to develop. Price risk can be viewed as an important factor which needs to be present for successful futures trading.

Although financial futures are relatively new, commodity futures are very ancient. Financial futures – stock indices, interest rate and currency – came later and the latter two are dealt with specifically in Chapters 11 and 12. New futures contracts are being constantly developed, for example, since December 1992 it has been possible to trade contracts on the Chicago Board of Trade in National Catastrophe Insurance Futures. Each contract reflects the ratio of losses to premiums of insurers in all US states. In this chapter the basic principles which apply to all futures will be described, sometimes using commodity futures as examples.

The honour as to where the first futures market developed is a matter of historical discussion. It is sometimes said that there are examples of futures trading in India back as far as 2000 BC and later in Roman times. However, it was probably not until the 12th century at French and English medieval fairs that anything like modern futures trading took place. In Japan in the 17th century rice was traded for future delivery in the Osaka area and in 1697 there appears to be the first recorded examples of trading in future agreements for rice. It is this trading of the delivery agreement, the future, which leads to the Dojima Rice Market being described as the world's first futures market. Here receipts for the future delivery of rice were traded. It is likely, however, that the fairs letters given as receipts at the French and English medieval fairs were also bought and sold in a similar way. The value of the receipts it was found, changed when the cash value of the commodity for which they were a receipt, changed.

The modern futures markets really developed in the Chicago area of the US in connection with the grain markets. Initially trading was spot and then forward **to arrive**. The latter means that agreements were made to sell or buy grain at a time in the future at a pre-determined price and it was intended that the grain be actually delivered. Due to price uncertainty, especially during the Civil War, it became the practice to sell and re-sell the **agreements**. Agreements were more saleable if they related to standard conditions, it meant that merchants did not have to examine carefully unique contract clauses to see what obligations they were taking on (quality of grain, place of delivery or quantity, for example).

The Chicago Board of Trade (CBOT) opened originally in 1848 and by 1865 had established its *General Rules*. It was these rules which generally facilitated and developed the modern concept of a futures market. It must therefore be the CBOT which can legitimately lay claim to be the first truly exchange traded futures market in the world; it is still the largest.

The New York Cotton Exchange, 1870, began trading in cotton futures and since that date many other exchanges have opened up around the world dealing in a wide variety of futures covering related cash markets.

Future exchanges

Now there are futures markets in most financial centres: Amsterdam, Auckland, Bermuda, Dublin, Frankfurt, Hong Kong, Kuala Lumpur, London, Osaka, Paris, Rio de Janeiro, Sao Paulo, Singapore, Stockholm, Sydney, Tokyo, Toronto, Winnipeg and Zurich – as well as a number of exchanges in the US.

In the US itself exchanges include, in addition to the CBOT, the Chicago Mercantile Exchange (CME). These two exchanges account for ten of the twelve most actively traded futures contracts world-wide. Other exchanges are located in Kansas, Minneapolis and New York.

In the UK futures exchanges are:

- The London International Financial Futures Exchange (LIFFE) which opened in September 1982 in the former Royal Exchange Building, but is now located at Cannon Street Bridge, along with the London Traded Options Market (LTOM). On the former financial futures are traded. LIFFE and LTOM combine to become The London International Financial Futures and Options Exchange. LIFFE is the largest financial futures exchange outside the US, and is therefore regarded as the leading market in Europe for financial futures and options and is the third largest in the world.
- The London Commodity Exchange (LCE), formerly the London Futures and Options Exchange (London FOX) trades futures (and options) on a range of soft commodities.
- The London Metal Exchange (LME), established in 1877, is a major metals market for copper, lead, silver, aluminium, nickel and zinc. It accounts for about half of all commodity futures trading in London.
- The Baltic Futures Exchange (BFE) trades futures in agricultural products and freight. On the trading floor are the following:

- Baltic International Freight Futures (BIFFEX) – the world's first open outcry freight futures exchange;
- London Grain Futures Markets;
- London Meat Futures Exchange;
- London Potato Futures Market;
- Soya Bean Meal Futures Market.
- The International Petroleum Exchange (IPE) opened in 1981 and trades futures (and options) in Brent crude oil, gas oil and unleaded gas, although the latter hardly trades at all.
- The London Securities and Derivatives Exchange (OMLX) trades futures and options on mainly Swedish Financial instruments and stock, often on a clearing basis only, trading being conducted inter-bank.

Financial futures

In May 1972, largely as a result of the breakdown of the Bretton Woods system of fixed exchange rates, the CME formed the International Money Market (IMM) and introduced currency futures for the first time. Since then other exchanges have attempted to develop currency futures, but it is only at the IMM that there has been sustained success. The IMM holds about 90% market share in the US of these contracts.

In October 1975 the CBOT introduced Government National Mortgage Association (GNMA) certificate futures known as 'Ginney Maes' and for the first time it became possible to hedge interest rate exposure using the futures market.

Since that time Ginney Maes futures have disappeared from the market for reasons discussed later in Chapter 20 as an illustration of the necessary features for a successful futures market. As described above, LIFFE opened in 1982 and initially interest rate futures were introduced on three-month sterling time deposits, sterling long gilts and Eurodollar three-month time deposits as well as contracts for four currencies against the US$. Currency futures trading was discontinued in 1990.

Financial futures now represent a very high proportion of futures trading. World-wide, interest rate futures are always the most common contract. In the US they represent about 45% of all contracts (source: Futures Industry Association), currency futures represent about 10% of US futures trades.

The most highly traded individual contract world-wide is the US Treasury Bond (T–Bond) $100,000, traded originally on the CBOT since August 1977, but also now at Singapore and Sydney. It was also traded on LIFFE, but was delisted in 1993. Futures on Japanese Government bonds are also traded in huge volumes and it can be generally seen that long-term bonds are the most active contracts.

Stock index futures (not featured in detail in this text) were introduced in 1982 at the Kansas City Board of Trade as the Value Line Index (VLI).

Forward delivery contracts 'to arrive'

It helps to build up our understanding of what an exchange traded futures contract is by first of all looking at a few basic ideas, by looking at agreements between individuals concerning forward prices and forward delivery.

Buyers of commodities are concerned that prices might rise in the future. Sellers have the opposite concern, that prices might fall. One way of ensuring certain prices in the future is to enter into an agreement, a forward delivery contract, to sell/ buy at an agreed price in the future. Regardless of what happens to the spot market price between the date the agreement is made and the date of exchange, the parties to the agreement, buyer and seller, have removed price risk from their transaction.

Whilst they have removed risk as to price, they have not removed all risk. Their agreement is not free of default risk. If the spot market price were to rise above the agreed price between the date of the agreement and the agreed date of the sale, there would be a temptation for the seller to ignore the agreement and sell at the higher, prevailing spot price. Equally, there would be a temptation for the buyer to renege upon the agreement were the price to fall. There is also the problem that one of the parties will not be able, even if willing, to meet their obligations.

There are also other problems in using this type of forward agreement as a matter of routine in hedging price risk. Seller and buyer have to locate each other, therefore search costs arise. There is also a problem of negotiating not only the price, but the quantity of the commodity, its quality and where it should be delivered, as well as compliance with these terms.

Default risk, search costs and non-standardisation are therefore drawbacks to this type of forward delivery contract, often described as a **to arrive** contract because it is fully intended that the commodity be delivered and taken up at the agreed future date.

Trade in the forward agreement

A further development is for the forward delivery contract itself to be bought and sold and for speculators to enter the scene who do not wish to profit from the sale or purchase of the commodity itself, but from changes in price in the spot market. Thus a futures contract market, not yet exchange traded, developed alongside the actual cash or commodity market. Such a futures market cannot readily develop if there is still lack of standardisation and default risk.

It should be easily apparent to see how the trading of the future contract itself could, given the right circumstances, produce a profit (or loss) for those prepared to trade in the contract, rather than the commodity.

An example:

Suppose a seller of wheat were to sign a forward agreement with a buyer to deliver 5,000 bushels of wheat in three months' time at a price of £5 per bushel. Further imagine that during the period of the agreement that the spot market price were to rise to £6 per bushel. It is apparent that the buyer now has an agreement which itself now has value. He can buy at £5, whereas everyone in the spot market has to buy at £6. If he does not want to take delivery of the wheat, a profit can still be made by selling the agreement itself to someone who does, who can then use the agreement to buy at £5. Ignoring any transactions cost, you should be prepared to buy the agreement for:

(spot price minus forward price) times amount of commodity.
This equals the value of the agreement

$$(£6 - £5) \times 5,000 \text{ bushels} = £5,000$$

Alternatively, had the spot price fallen to $4 per bushel, then the seller would have an agreement worth

$$(£5 - £4) \times 5,000 \text{ bushels} = £5,000$$

They would be able to sell at £5, whereas all other spot sellers would only be able to achieve £4, the prevailing spot.

It can be seen that a gain by one party is made at the expense of the other, this is why futures are described as a **zero sum game**. Note that we have not yet reached exchange traded futures contracts.

Buying long and selling short

The selling and buying of futures contracts is a way of describing commitments, a seller of a future can sell without previously having bought.

In the commodities futures market the following conventions apply:

- Buy a future to agree to take delivery of a commodity. This will protect against a rise in price in the spot market as it produces a gain if spot prices rise, as demonstrated in the example above. Buying a future is said to be going long.
- Sell a future to agree to make delivery of a commodity. This will protect against a fall in price in the spot market as it produces a gain if spot prices fall. Selling a future is said to be going short.

As this text is concerned with financial risk management, it is important to know that matters may at first seem a little confusing for financial futures which relate to interest rates.

Care will be needed when using interest rate futures, as here selling short and buying long have the opposite effects to that achieved in the commodity futures markets and also importantly in the FRA market when related to interest rate changes. This is due to the way in which interest rate futures prices are quoted and the relationship between bond prices and interest rates. The matter is fully described in Chapter 11, it is flagged up here at this introductory stage so that the wrong idea is not created.

Compare the following with the above for commodity futures:

- Selling short an interest rate futures contract protects against a rise in interest rates.
- Purchasing long an interest rate futures contract protects against a fall in interest rates.

In either case the key is to remember the relationship between bond prices and interest rates. As interest rates rise, so bond prices fall. As interest rates fall, so bond prices rise. Thus selling short a future protects against a fall in bond prices and therefore protects against a rise in interest rates.

Purchasing long protects against a rise in bond prices, therefore protects against a fall in interest rates. Thus if you remember that selling and buying futures positions have the same effect for commodity and bond prices the matter is resolved and hopefully no longer confusing.

Even when futures do not relate to bond prices but to deposit/borrowing interest rates, the conventions of buying and selling are retained. A fuller treatment of bond prices/interest rates is given in Chapter 11 (pp. 88–9). In addition compare the FRA conventions:

- Selling short an FRA protects against a fall in interest rates.
- Purchasing long an FRA protects against a rise in interest rates (refer back to p. 51).

Yes, the terminology is inconsistent, you just have to remember this and not get too emotional about it! The way futures are described seems to make the most sense logically. But further note:

- Buying (long) a currency future protects against a rise in currency value.
- Selling (short) a currency future protects against a fall in currency value.

Here the terminology is in fact consistent, although it does not appear to be so. Full details can be found in Chapter 12.

As will be demonstrated at a later stage, any profit in the futures market is used to off-set losses in the cash market or vice versa to achieve an effective hedge.

Futures price and cost of carry

We now look at futures price again. As described earlier, price here does not relate to price paid or received when buying or selling a future, it is merely the price agreed in exchange for a commodity at a future date, therefore futures price. The concept of futures price should become clearer when the concept of **cost of carry** is explained.

If a commodity like wheat is taken, as in earlier examples, a cash market hedge can be constructed to hedge wheat price risk. A future, or a futures contract, is a derivative of this spot market hedge. A seller of wheat will not wish the price to fall in the future when a sale is anticipated. A buyer of wheat will not wish the price to rise. If an agreement is made to deliver a quantity and grade of wheat in three months' time, how might the seller of the wheat arrange affairs so that there is no price risk? If they remain in an open position there is no knowing what the price of wheat will be in three months' time. Therefore a cash market hedge can be constructed as follows.

Wheat will already be held or can be purchased at today's spot. Take today's spot rate which is known and add to this the **cost of carrying** the wheat for three months. These costs will be:

- storage
- insurance
- transport costs involved in making delivery to a named point and
- finance costs of the operation over the three months, i.e. interest forgone on funds used to purchase the commodity and meet other costs.

Therefore:

spot plus cost of carry = agreed price of wheat in three months' time
(i.e. futures price)

Such a strategy will fix the price of wheat for both parties in three months' time. Regardless of what happens to spot during the three months, the agreed price will be received or paid.

That the **entry price** of a futures contract 'should' be the same price is further developed in the next section.

Futures price

A price in the futures agreement or contract has to be agreed. The question arises what must/should this price be?

The price 'should' be today's spot adjusted by the cost of carry for three months. If you agree this price with your counterparty this will become the **entry price**. If the entry price is not 'correct', then an arbitrage can be made using the cash market hedge described above and the simultaneous mispriced futures agreement.

If the entry price of the futures contract (remember this will give the seller of wheat the right to sell the wheat at this agreed, entry price in three months' time) is greater than spot plus cost of carry then an arbitrage profit is possible. Here, in this example, the futures price is 'rich' to the cash price, so on the principle that you sell that which is overpriced (the future) and buy that which is underpriced (commodity at spot), it follows that:

If future (entry) price > spot plus cost of carry then:
(e.g.   £10   >   £8   +   £1.50)

in spot market take a long position, i.e. purchase wheat at spot, carry this for three months

total outlay = spot plus cost of carry
£9.50 = £8 + £1.50

In futures market take a short position, i.e. sell a futures contract.
In three months' time sell the goods you have held over the three months at a total outlay of:

original spot (£8) plus cost of carry (£1.50), for a sum greater than this, (£10) as enabled by the futures contract held, because:

future contract price > spot plus cost of carry (the original
proposition).

£10 > £8 + £1.50

This arbitrage process is called a **cash and carry transaction**. The arbitrage opportunity will be eroded and disappear as such transactions are made. Demand at spot will raise the spot price so that it, when added to the cost of carry, equals the futures price. At the same time there will be a greater demand for short positions in futures and this will drive down the futures price. In both markets the tendency will be to equalise prices. If the futures price equals spot plus full carrying cost, then the futures price will be a **full carry price**.

If the futures price is 'cheap', then buy what is cheap (the future) and sell that which is expensive (commodity at spot). This arbitrage 'should' result in a **full carry futures price**.

Therefore the futures entry price should equal the spot plus cost of carry. The reason why it may not be this idealised price will be discussed later, it is concerned with **basis risk** and the possibility of a **convenience yield** on the actual commodity.

Basis and what makes futures prices change

The principle emerges therefore that spot and future prices differ due to the principle of cost of carry. However, at maturity spot and futures will be identical. If they are not identical it will be possible, a fraction of time before maturity, to take a futures position and an opposite cash market position, arbitrage and profit from the difference. A simple example easily illustrates.

Futures price £10, spot £8. Selling a futures contract (right to deliver at £10) and buying in the spot market at £8 obviously gives a profit of £2 per unit quantity.

If prices are identical at maturity, but differ at the beginning of the period, it follows that even if the spot price were to remain constant (highly unlikely) the futures price would gradually have to change as the contract approached maturity. This is illustrated in Figure 10.1.

This is quite a reasonable statement to make because as time passes and as maturity is approached, the cost of carry necessarily will diminish, at maturity there will be none (unless, for example, the location of the commodity differs from where it must be delivered, in which case delivery carry costs will apply). More realistically the spot price will change over the contract period and the futures price will track it as in Figure 10.2.

It should be readily apparent why the futures price behaves the way it does. At any given time the futures price will be spot plus cost of carry, therefore if spot changes the futures price will change with it, all the while adjusting by the cost of carry which diminishes as maturity approaches.

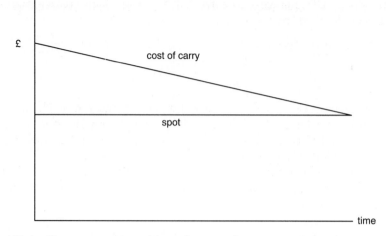

Figure 10.1 *Constant spot price and diminishing cost of carry.*

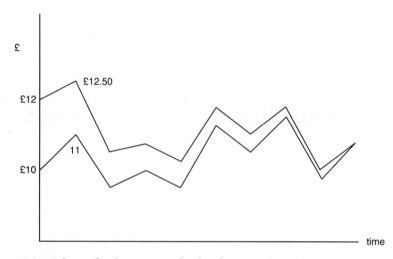

Figure 10.2 *Arbitrage free futures price related to changing spot price.*

If spot is £10 and cost of carry £2, then futures price is £12, If later, spot rises to £11 and cost of carry is now £1.50, the futures price becomes £12.50. Falls in spot will have the opposite effect.

It should now be possible to see how a futures contract can gain and lose value over time as a result of spot and futures price changes.

If you are short a future and the futures price rises, your futures contract will lose value. Take the last set of figures, your futures entry price was £12 and futures price rises to £12.50. You can sell for £12 not £12.50. If you wish to be released from your obligation to sell for £12 you will have to buy it back for £12.50. The individual who holds the right to buy at £12 will only sell it back to you for you to buy at £12.50, after all he could sell it on to someone else today and they would be prepared to buy at £12.50. Thus you have received £12 when you sold originally and have paid back £12.50, a loss of 50p.

The difference between the futures price and the spot price is known as the **basis**.

> basis = spot (cash) price minus futures price

This is the usual way to define basis. However,

> basis = futures price minus spot price

is sometimes used when the future relates to a financial asset.

Note that in many commodity futures contracts basis refers to the difference between spot and futures prices for the nearest contract delivery month, for example, November spot price of wheat compared to December futures price because December is the closest month for which there is a corresponding futures contract.

Futures contracts – standardisation

In addition to the market risk referred to earlier, there is also a problem in making trades in a future due to the difficulty of finding suitable counterparties – sellers finding buyers and buyers finding sellers. Some kind of physical location is needed where they can find each other. A further issue, also previously raised, is the problem of non-standardisation of the specification of the commodity itself. Standard amounts need to be specified and even this is insufficient as the quality is not defined. In a to-arrive situation, if the quality of the commodity is not fully specified, then the danger, and likelihood is that inferior quality will be delivered. If such matters are not fully standardised they have to be separately negotiated which slows the trading process and means that prices have to differ for each futures contract and therefore there is no such thing as market price.

Non-standard amounts, non-standard delivery times and non-standard delivery locations also create further trading difficulties.

In summary, therefore, default risk, search cost and non-standardisation are a bar to the development of a futures market. The solution is found in standardisation of futures contracts and the setting up of an exchange with a clearing house.

The only thing open to negotiation in a futures contract is price and this will be settled on the floor of the exchange. All other matters are standardised:

- The commodity itself is carefully given a technical description which ensures that a reasonably uniform product is delivered if the contract is actually taken to this point. Too restrictive a description would reduce the attractiveness of the future agreement as it would make it too difficult to arrive at. CBOT wheat futures, for example, require wheat to be in the following deliverable grades: no. 1 northern spring wheat, no. 2 soft red, no. 2 hard red winter and no. 2 dark northern spring at par. Each of these grades in turn is given an exact technical description.
- The quantity of the commodity is given a fixed amount for each contract. Very large quantities therefore require a number of contracts. CBOT wheat contracts are in units of 5,000 bushels and are priced and traded in bushels as are all grain contracts. Contracts in other commodities, including financial, are traded and priced per contract.

- Delivery dates are usually standardised to every three months. There are exceptions, CBOT wheat, for example, is July, September, December, March and May.
- Delivery point for the commodity has to be specified. In the case of wheat this will be a list of agreed grain elevators. Where the commodity is actually delivered and differs from the contract specification, in some instances a price adjustment is made. This is only possible if it forms part of the contract terms. Some commodity futures have delivery options. A range of qualities may be delivered, there may be alternative delivery locations or delivery dates. The short position exercises these options (not the long as with a true option, Chapter 14).

Futures contracts are placed into the following categories:

- grains and oil seeds
- livestock and meat
- food and fibre
- metals
- industrial – timber, oil
- financial – interest rate and currency (Chapters 11 and 12) and stock indices.

Clearing house and exchange

The clearing house and exchange are really two separate functions and their use creates an exchange traded future whose properties transform future agreements in the way we have understood them so far.

The exchange, e.g. LIFFE, is the physical location where buyers and sellers meet, thus search time and cost is minimised. The exchange is organised so that trades take place in an open and orderly fashion, although this may not be your first impression when you first see one in action. Information as to price and volume of trading is open to all through a reporting system from the floor of the exchange to displays around the exchange and to information vendors such as Reuters, Telerate, Extel and Datastream. This price and volume transparency, a feature of exchange traded futures (and options), reduces the possibility of insider information and trades.

Individuals on the floor of the exchange have to be members of the exchange, unless they are exchange officials, 'Blue Jackets' at LIFFE. Only traders may execute trades, thus individuals and organisations who wish to buy or sell futures will do so through an appropriate exchange member whose titles vary from exchange to exchange. At LIFFE they are as follows:

- Commission broker – acts as agent for both members and non-member firms.
- Floor broker – acts as agent solely for other members (some of whom may have a presence on the floor).
- Pit broker – acts as agent solely for other members (all of whom have a presence on the floor).
- Broker–trader – primarily a broker, with some authority to trade on their own account.
- Individual trader – primarily trades for their firm on their own account, whilst occasionally executes trades for others.

On the CME and CBOT a floor broker executes customer orders on the floor of the exchange. A floor trader (local) trades on their own account.

On most exchanges each wears a highly coloured jacket which indicates their exchange member firm. This makes identification easier, and helps sort out disputed trades. 'Red Jackets' at LIFFE are 'locals' who trade on their own account. The cost of a full membership seat on different exchanges varies, but in 1994 a seat on the CBOT cost $640,000 up from $375,00 in 1993. At LIFFE the cost was £120,000, enabling trades on all contracts (source: Futures and Options World, Jan 1993:58 and CBOT press release 1 September 1994.) Seats can also be leased.

Most exchanges are organised on an **open outcry** basis, where trading is conducted on the floor of the exchange in pits, a different one for each futures contract. Some trades are possible using computers, e.g. Globex at the CBOT and APT (Automated Pit Trading) at LIFFE, but volume is quite small.

Traders trade in pits and shout their price and quantity bids and offers, augmented by hand signals which will either be taken up or ignored by other traders. Trading is **fill or die**. Bids and offers must be filled immediately, 'whilst the breath is warm', or they die. Futures trading is thus not a held market in the way that most spot markets are. In fact the convention is to use bid and ask, rather than bid and offer. The letter 'O' as an abbreviation on information screens could be confused with the number nought as part of a price.

A trader might come to the pit wishing to buy 20 futures contracts at a given price each. His bid will be, for example, £5 for 20, meaning he is prepared to buy 20 contracts for £5 each. If there are other traders prepared to sell at this price and quantity they will shout their acceptance and the deal is struck. Sometimes large quantities will be split up amongst a number of counterparties. The price agreed becomes the futures price.

Sellers who are offering/asking will shout 20 at £4.95, meaning they are prepared to sell 20 contracts at £4.95 each. The convention is thus:

- bid/buy   price for lots
- ask/sell   lots at price.

Once a trade is made, information is relayed by both traders to their firms' brokers' booths where a dealer's slip is time stamped and completed giving details which must be registered within 30 minutes at LIFFE, otherwise a fine is imposed.

One hour later the seller's and buyer's details are matched. If there is a dispute and it cannot be sorted out mutually between the parties then a Blue Jacket observer in the pit can be consulted or a video of activity in the pit at the time can be played back. In addition all phone lines are audio logged, it may be possible to trace circumstantial evidence via the client's order, if the trade is not own account. Finally a senior pit committee member will make a ruling upon the available evidence.

Further **price and volume transparency** is assured through careful observation of all exchange floor and off floor activity by exchange officials. There is also an element of self-policing in that other traders are likely to report any behaviour of others which may place them at a disadvantage, or even suspicions of such behaviour. This is particularly important at exchanges such as LIFFE where trades for clients and own account trading are permissible with the right kind of exchange seat. Here the danger is that own account trading, getting into the market first before a client, might be of advantage, such 'front running' would be useful if you know that a large client order is in the pipeline which might affect price.

The clearing house has a separate function and in most locations will be a separate company. (CME and NYME clearing houses are divisions of their exchanges.) In London it is the London Clearing House (LCH) since 1991, formerly the International Commodities Clearing House (ICCH) which clears all LIFFE futures trades (and options). Discussion of the role of the clearing house in relation to options occurs in Chapter 14 (pp. 148–9).

All members of the clearing house will be members of the exchange, but not all exchange members will be members of the clearing house. Traders who are not members of the clearing house will have to get their trades cleared by a clearing member. Clearing house membership confers prestige, generates fee income from non-trader members and ensures anonymity for their own trades.

The function of the clearing house is to clear, that is settle transactions made on the exchange on a daily basis and act as a counterparty to all trades. It is in this way that risk of default in the futures market is effectively eliminated and therefore makes trading quicker. Traders do not have to investigate the creditworthiness and reputation for honouring contracts with the original counterparty with whom they originally trade. The counterparty becomes the clearing house in place of the original counterparty with whom the trade was originally agreed.

The clearing house therefore takes the opposite side of all transactions after clearing. It sells to buyers and buys from sellers. This is known as the **principle of interposition** or **substitution**. (Remember, buy/sell denotes the direction of the agreement, rather than its meaning in the spot market. A future can be sold without having previously been bought).

As a result of this clearing activity, the taking of the opposite side of the transaction, a trader can, if he or she wishes, reverse the trade at a later date, via the trading process on the floor of the exchange and eventually, after clearing, have an opposite position at the clearing house. Thus an original short can at a later stage go long. An original long can go short at a later stage. This gives an equal and opposite position at the clearing house after clearing, which cancels out each original position. For this reason a trader does not need to seek out the original trader to reverse the position, any willing trader will do, whose place will of course be taken at the end of the day by the clearing house. The original trader may not wish to trade anyway. Futures markets are highly liquid due to these features.

In fact this process of **off-set** is usually what happens. This **close-out** of a position is the way in which almost all futures positions are settled. Very few commodity futures, 5% or fewer, result in actual delivery of the commodity itself at maturity. Most financial futures are **cash settled**, e.g. LIFFE Short Sterling contract. Some can be settled by physical delivery, e.g. LIFFE UK Long Gilt contract if taken to expiration and delivery. (More detail in Chapter 11.)

Should a trader with a short position actually want to make delivery at the expiry date of the futures contract, they will tell the clearing house and the trader with the oldest long position will be informed by the clearing house that delivery is to take place. For every holder of a short futures position there will be a holder of a long futures position. This should be evidently so, but reference to p. 80 (open interest) will explain. Because the clearing house is still counterparty to both positions settlement is guaranteed. That the clearing house will always be in a position to settle its obligations as counterparty is ensured through a system of **margins** required from traders and holders of futures. These margins are often described as **earnest money** or **good-faith money** in the US, we return to them in the next section.

The exchange combined with the clearing house therefore:

- Brings traders together, this creates:
- Market liquidity, which in turn is further facilitated by:
- The risk transfer mechanism of the clearing house.
- Liquidity is further improved through standardisation of contracts because the only negotiated variable is price.
- Price discovery is easier in an open outcry system where all information is made public.

Margins

A common, misconceived, question is 'How much does it cost to buy a future?' or 'How much will I get if I sell one?' The answer is that it costs nothing and you receive nothing as such. (You will need to pay some commission, but this is a different matter.)

Gains and losses as a result of either going long or short a future are handled by a **margin** system. We should understand that a futures price is not a price paid for the futures position, but it is the price which is paid/received at expiration for the underlying commodity if the futures position is not **off-set, closed-out**.

If you wish to take a position in a futures contract, either long or short, you must deposit an **initial margin**, a sum of money for each contract you wish to enter into. If you are an exchange member initial margin is deposited at the clearing house, you in turn take an initial margin deposit from your client (often larger than that demanded of you).

Depending upon the clearing house, **initial margin** payments can be made in cash or approved securities, e.g. UK gilts, US Treasury bills and bonds, letters of credit from approved banks or shares in the clearing house. Such initial margins usually represent 5%–10% of the underlying value of the commodity which the future controls. For financial futures the margin is usually smaller, e.g. the LIFFE Short Sterling contract (three-month LIBOR sterling interest rate) initial margin was £1200 December 1992, with a contract size of £500,000. For most financial futures the margin is typically less than 3% of the full contract value.

Margins are larger for speculators than for hedgers, the latter having off-setting positions in the cash and futures markets which should cancel each other out in terms of losses and gains (discussed on pp. 77, 78).

Minimum margins are set by each exchange in relation to each contract. The idea is that the initial margin is sufficient to cover at least the maximum allowable price fluctuation per day of a net futures position. Each day the change in value of a futures position is calculated and **marked to market**. If a loss is made by a holder of a futures position, the initial margin should be enough to meet this loss that day.

In reality, when a loss has been incurred, then further **variation margin** is payable. If losses continue to be made each day when marked-to-market, then fresh sums of variation margin have to be paid. Naturally, if a futures position has gained value when marked-to-market variation margin is received. Variation margin received can be withdrawn or held on deposit as desired. Interest is paid on initial margin paid in cash and on variation held on deposit at a margin below LIBOR. It is apparent that variation received originates from holders of futures who have paid, it can thus be described as a zero sum game. All money flows are of course via the clearing house to protect against default risk.

With some contracts a maintenance margin is set. When losses on the futures position fall below this figure, only then does variation become payable to restore the margin to its initial value. Thus any obligations are met as they arise on a daily basis. Should a futures holder not be able to meet their variation margin obligations, then their position is closed out by the member of the exchange they are dealing with. A signed agreement to this effect will be held by the exchange member giving them the authority to do this. Should an exchange member in turn not be in a position to meet their obligations, then they too will be closed out by the clearing house. The payment which has not been met by variation margin payment is of course met from the initial margin.

Daily trading limits are often set for each contract so that price cannot fluctuate by more than a given amount each day above or below the previous **settlement price**. This should limit price panic on an exchange under turbulent conditions and also makes for more orderly clearing in that variation margin payments do not become excessively large on a daily basis. When there is a large increase in price volatility, often larger initial margin deposits are demanded to cover potential larger losses, as occurred February/March 1994 with the LIFFE Bund contract.

The margin system therefore guarantees the credit risk which might otherwise still occur in relation to settlement via the clearing house. It has been described as a margin tree in that each party to the taking of a futures position has margin obligations which must be met. Obligations are passed to and fro along a branch network from seller/buyer to a member of the exchange to the clearing house and in reverse when a contract matures or is closed out, at which time initial margin will be repaid. Variation margin payments or receipts will take care of daily obligations. It is only when variation margin payments due are not made, that there will be recourse to the initial margin, this is its purpose.

As described, the initial margins are quite small in relation to the underlying value of the commodity per contract size. It is for this reason that futures are described as highly leveraged positions. A small margin can control a very high commodity value. A large market position can be taken for a relatively small capital outlay. This high leverage does not create default risk, in fact the system of margins which creates the leverage is designed to minimise the risk. The risk here is of course that of the clearing house. The risk of loss from a futures position taken is still very present if it is taken by the holder for speculative rather than hedging purposes, this is of course a different kind of risk – market risk. The guarantee of the clearing house only extends to exchange members, not the client end user. However, in the UK Securities and Futures Authority (SFA) membership by the exchange member should protect the client.

Thus an exchange traded futures position can be taken for very little outlay, initial margin is not lost, it is returned when a position is closed out. Market risk is always present, however, to participants, they will always have to pay variation margin at daily settlement if required.

Changes in the value of the underlying cause changes in the futures price and cause leveraged, magnified changes to the value of the future. Take a contract size of £500,000, for example the LIFFE Short Sterling contract. If three-month LIBOR changes during the day by 20 basis points (0.20% or 0.0020) then the futures price will change by approximately £250, which is what one party to a contract will have to pay in variation margin. If this is related to the initial margin of about £1200 quoted earlier, this represents a percentage loss of 20% if the position were closed out. Equally the other party will make a large gain of 20%.

In summary, a system of margins ensures that all parties to a future are in a position to fulfil their obligations. Margins ensure that the clearing house can fulfil its obligations as counterparty to all contracts. It is this system of margins which acts as collateral and has ensured to date that clearing house default has occurred only in France and Hong Kong, causing the collapse of the associated market. It is interesting to note that the clearing house at SIMEX was able to honour its obligations at all times following the collapse of Barings Bank. Only a few traders have ever defaulted separate from a clearing house collapse. In addition **guarantee funds** are funds that clearing houses can access if necessary to cover debts owed by clearing house members in default. These funds are provided by remaining clearing house members.

Tick

Tick size is the minimum price change allowed and varies from contract to contract. Tick as a device also speeds up the trading process as it makes price signals made by exchange traders easier. Examples of tick sizes are given below to illustrate:

- LIFFE three-month Eurodeutschmark contract, unit of trading DM 1m. Minimum price movement is 1 basis point, 0.0001 or 0.01%. Contract period is three months, therefore:

    DM 1,000,000 × 0.0001 × 3/12 = DM 25

- LIFFE Short Sterling contract, unit of trading £500,000, contract period three months. Therefore one basis point minimum price change gives:

    £500,000 × 0.0001 × 3/12 = £12.50

Marking to market

There follows a worked example of **daily resettlement** or **marking to market** as it is usually called, showing the entries across the **equity account** the holder of the futures position will have with an exchange member. In turn the exchange member will have an equity account with the clearing house which of course will also be marked to market. Marking to market will take place daily, so that obligations are settled daily as they arise. If obligations are not met, the position is closed out and initial margin used to meet payments, this of course being its purpose as earlier described.

Seller of a commodity futures position

Equity Account £

Day	Settlement price	Initial margin	Variation margin (payments) receipts	Equity	Margin surplus/(call)
1	5.75[a]	2,000	–	2,000	–
2	5.25	2,000	2,500	4,500	2,500
3	5.50	2,000	(1,250)	3,250	1,250
4	5.80	1,750	(1,500)	1,750	(250)
5	5.80 (close-out)	2,000	–	2,000	–

[a] Entry price.
No maintenance margin is assumed for simplicity.
Assume all surplus equity held on deposit (could be withdrawn).

Settlement price is the price used for daily revaluation of open positions which are then marked to market.

Commentary on the equity account entries:

Entry price on day 1 when 1 contract sold, price = £5.75 per bushel of wheat, 1 contract = 5,000 bushels.

Price (i.e. settlement price) on day 2 has moved to £5.25 per bu.

> price change = £0.50 × 5,000 = £2,500
> (i.e. 200 ticks × £12.50 × 1 contract = £2,500)

The seller of the future entering the market on day 1 can (nominally) sell at £5.75, whereas sellers entering the futures market on day 2 can only sell at £5.25, therefore the price movement here represents a gain for the holder.

Price on day 3 = £5.50 per bu.

> price change = £0.25 × 5,000 = £1,250 representing a loss to the holder (opposite to day 2)

Price on day 4 = £5.80 per bu.

> price change = £0.30 × 5,000 = £1500, representing a loss to the holder

At this point they would receive a margin call and have to pay £250 to bring the equity account up to £2,000 immediately for the next day. If the position were closed out immediately at the beginning of day 5 on the instructions of the holder (assume no price movement) the holder of the future would be in the position as shown in the equity account. Initial margin is still intact and is repaid.

If variation margin receipts and payments are examined, it can be seen that total payments of £2,750 have been made and £2500 have been received, a net loss of £250, equalling the margin call of £250.

Marking to market therefore ensures that any obligations which arise due to adverse price movements from the holder's perspective are met as they occur each day. Default risk is therefore minimised and eliminated via initial margin.

The losses were met as they arose on days 3 and 4 and not when the position was closed out. Of course the net loss in this case can be calculated by comparing the opening and closing prices of:

$$£5.75-£5.80 = £0.05 \times \text{no. of bushels in contract, 5,000}$$
$$= £250$$

The fact that variation margin requirements occur over a period of time does affect the calculation of the true cost/gain because cash flows materialise throughout the holding of the futures position and not at the end. Therefore it can be imagined that a net gain taken over time may have needed variation margin payments during the holding of the position. This should not be forgotten.

Hedging and speculating with commodity futures

In this book hedging is taken to mean arranging affairs so that risk is reduced or eliminated. It is worth noting that an alternative meaning is sometimes attached to the term in futures trading – that of trading in order to profit from futures positions, i.e. speculating.

In the previous wheat futures examples, changes in the spot price of the wheat had the following effects upon the value of the future:

- A seller of a future going short saw its value rise when the spot price fell.
- A buyer of a future going long saw its value rise when the spot price rose.

Therefore a short position profits whenever the futures price falls, a long position profits when the futures price rises in the commodities markets. It should become apparent that if you wish to hedge the price of a commodity that opposite positions are taken in the future and spot markets.

Example An individual with a stock of wheat (i.e. long) is fearful that the spot price of wheat will fall. If a short position is taken in the futures market, this position will show a profit if the price of wheat falls. This profit can be taken by closing out the position and used to set against the loss made in the cash market when the wheat is sold at spot. A perfect hedge will be achieved when profit equals loss. The alternative is to take the future to delivery and sell the commodity at expiration for the locked in futures price. Closing out would be more usual.

If spot prices had in fact risen, then a gain would have been made in the cash market, but off-set by the loss in the futures market. In either event a certain net price is achieved by using both markets. It should also be possible to see that if you wish to speculate on price movements over a given period of time, a way of doing so is to take an appropriate position in the futures market in relation to your view as to price movements and take the profit (or loss) on the outcome. There is no need to trade in the actual commodity itself and no cash market position should be taken with the future – to do so would of course hedge the position and make speculative profit unachievable.

A speculator will sell a future when he thinks that the spot price of the underlying commodity will fall and buy a future when he believes the spot price will rise.

Basis risk

As is now explained, the basis may change. Such a change may operate in favour of or against a hedger, depending on the position held. The risk of change in basis is obviously known as **basis risk**. Reasons for changes in basis are discussed more fully in Chapter 13, along with their implications.

A hedger will therefore be subject to basis risk, rather than the outright risk of spot price changes. Basis risk is less than outright risk. Although a change in basis against a hedger will make a hedge incomplete, it can be shown that the outcome is not less than that which otherwise would have been achieved with respect to a hedge, had a different hedge (e.g. a forward contract) been used instead. An illustration of this point is given in Chapter 13.

If at close-out the futures price movement has exactly matched changes in the spot, then losses/gains in the futures market will off-set gains/losses in the spot market. If the use of futures contracts is to be fully understood, then the relationship between spot and futures prices must be fully understood. As the difference between the two is the basis, it follows that basis must be fully understood.

The basis gives the ever-changing relationship between spot and futures prices. There are a number of possible ways to illustrate graphically the relationship between spot and futures prices – the basis. Earlier the point was made that as maturity approaches spot and future prices **converge**, i.e. the basis reduces for the reason that the actual costs involved in cost of carry reduce – cost of carry for one week is necessarily a lesser amount than for one month. Refer to Figure 10.2 which shows the relationship between spot and futures prices over the period of the contract. The futures prices illustrated represent an arbitrage free futures price, representing cost of carry at each stage above the spot. As the spot changes so does the futures price, gradually becoming closer to the spot as maturity approaches due to reduced cost of carry. Basis will therefore be changing and approaches zero as maturity nears. Expressed differently, this means that as maturity nears the futures price and basis converge upon spot.

It follows that if a futures position is closed out before expiration of the contract, that changes in the futures price do not match exactly changes in the spot market. This is known as **delta** and is discussed in later futures and options chapters. If spot price falls over a period of a week, the futures price will fall more rapidly, cost of carry is now one week less.

There are other sources of basis risk connected with price expectations and changes in the cost of carry not related time, e.g. changes in interest rates, insurance or transport costs.

However, futures prices do not always reflect the full cost of carry, for some financials there is a negative carry. Sometimes the futures price will reflect less than the full carry cost, occasionally it will represent more. If the futures price does represent more than cost of carry, commodity traders will quickly take advantage of this by suitable arbitrage, in turn changing spot and futures prices so that basis returns to cost of carry. A reason still has to be found to explain why futures prices may be less than spot plus cost of carry. The reason might be that there is strong demand at spot or that the commodity is in short supply, either of which will push up the price at spot. Buyers may decide they need, for example, wheat at spot now and are willing to pay a higher price to get it now. What has created this demand? Perhaps it is expected that supply of the commodity will be small in relation to demand at a later date and therefore spot prices later in the year are expected to rise. Buyers are willing to buy now to ensure that they are not short of the commodity later, not withstanding cost of carry. In this way they can be assured of continuity of supply and will have partly avoided what they might regard as even higher spot prices later on. In this respect futures prices reflect anticipated **future spot** prices, rather than current spot (plus cost of carry).

The size of the basis is therefore represented by cost of carry plus factors connected with the availability/price of the underlying physical commodity, this latter factor is known as **convenience yield**. The relationship of a futures price lower than current spot (or lower than current spot plus cost of carry) is known as an **inverted market**. Instead of there being a normal carrying cost, there is a negative charge or cost and convenience yield.

When the futures price is above the spot, the futures market is described as **normal**. A plus sign (+) denotes normal, a minus sign (–) denotes inverted.

Basis risk, inverted markets, negative cost of carry and convenience yield are dealt with again in Chapters 11, 12 and 13.

Basis, gains/losses on futures positions

A perfect hedge is where there is no change in basis. As has been observed from observations concerning cost of carry, a change in basis is likely over time. However, to illustrate a perfect hedge imagine the following:

No basis change: buy wheat today at spot £5 per bushel, amount equal to one futures contract quantity = 5,000 bu).
Sell one three-month wheat futures contract at entry price £5.75. (This gives a right to sell wheat in three months' time at £5.75. Basis therefore equals £0.75.)
One month later price of spot wheat has fallen, sell wheat spot at £4.50, therefore cash market loss equals £0.50 per bushel. If basis has not changed to reflect reduced time cost of carry, then at this time futures price will be £5.25 (£4.50 + £0.75).
Futures price has fallen £0.50 (spot plus basis equals futures price).

This fall in the price of the future to the holder of the selling futures position represents a **gain** in the futures market of £0.50, off-setting the loss in the cash market of equal value. The reason for the profit to the futures position is because the seller of the wheat future has a right to sell at £5.75, whereas those taking wheat selling futures positions one month into the contract obtain the right to sell wheat only at £5.25. The original seller of the futures position therefore has an agreement worth £0.50 per bushel more than those taking a selling position one month into the contract. Therefore the seller of the futures position closes out by purchasing a future which cancels out his or her obligation at the clearing house and takes his or her profit on each bushel of wheat as represented by the contract.

A narrowing of the basis would have produced a net gain in that the futures profit would have been greater than the cash market loss. The reverse, a widening of the basis, would produce a net loss. A narrowing of the basis produces a net gain for the following reason:

Basis narrows, therefore futures price is closer to spot, therefore futures price needs to fall more than if basis constant. A price fall of the future produced a gain, therefore a larger fall must give a larger gain. Hedging outcomes can be ascertained by measuring change of basis between taking the futures position and closing it out. If a perfect hedge represents no change in basis, a change in basis results in a hedge which is greater or less than 100% depending upon the direction of change in basis. Worked examples are given in Chapter 11.

Open interest and volume

One of the statistics quoted by exchanges is **open interest**. This is the number of contracts to which longs and shorts are party at any given moment. Every open contract has a seller and a buyer, therefore open interest is the total number of contracts which have not yet been off-set or taken to expiration. Note the following possibilities – if two counterparties enter into a futures contract, each for the first time, then open interest has increased by one contract. If one of the parties then closes out by taking an opposite position and his or her counterparty in the close-out is another individual who is taking up a new position, then open interest remains the same. Alternatively, if the position is closed out by someone also closing out, then open interest falls. Think the possibilities through and you will see that it is so.

Volume is another measure and is a count of the number of contracts traded. It can be appreciated that volume might be high but open interest low if positions are quickly closed out by the majority of counterparties.

Opening and settlement prices

Exchanges also quote opening (open) prices and settlement (sett) prices. Opening price is the first price traded in a future at the beginning of a day's trading. Settlement is the last price traded and is the price used to mark to market. Change in futures price is also quoted for the day. This can cause a little confusion if opening is, for instance, 94.75 and settlement is 94.70 to find that change might be 6 not 5. The reason is that settlement and opening price next day need not necessarily be the same. Newspaper price quotes are discussed for futures on pp. 90, 107 and 118.

Summary

- Futures are agreements to either buy or sell an underlying asset at an agreed price at a stated future date. The problem with agreements between individuals is that search time and costs are incurred in finding partners with the same requirements as yourself; there is lack of standardisation.

- If agreements are standardised so that all elements – quantity, quality, amount, delivery arrangements and time – are kept identical, all that has to be agreed is the price for future delivery. The physical location of an exchange means potential counterparties can find each other easily. Standardisation and an exchange begins to create a liquid market.

- In principle the futures price is related to prevailing spot and cost of carry to expiration of the contract, arbitrages ensure that this is so. If the price of the underlying asset changes, so will the futures price. A rise in spot causes the futures price to rise, subject to cost of carry as time passes.

- If you wish to sell the underlying at a later date you sell, go short a future. You buy a future, go long, if you wish to buy the underlying.

- The short has an agreement whose value increases if the futures price falls. If you can sell, in future time, for £10 compared with £9, £9 being the price new shorts have to accept, then you have an agreement whose value is £1.

- The opposite applies to the long. If they have agreed to buy for £10, instead of the new futures of £9, they are worse off by £1. Therefore, the short loses if the futures price rises and the long gains. The short gains if the futures price falls and the long loses.

- The role of the clearing house is another important part of the story, creating fully exchange traded futures (contracts). There is always risk of default if agreements are solely between individuals. Default risk can be removed by the clearing house becoming counterparty to all trades on the exchange, the principle of interdisposition. Guarantee of performance is due to the margin system and daily marking to market of positions.

- Shorts and longs gain and lose value as futures prices change. Gains by the short are at the expense of the long and vice versa, depending upon the direction of change in the futures price.

- Posting of initial margin before a futures position is taken ensures that any losses can be made good from it, if, on a daily basis, variation margin payments are not made when required. Each day in principle, variation margin is either paid or received. Those who pay, due to adverse price movements, pay indirectly, via the clearing house, to those who are to receive margin due to favourable price movements. It is in this way that the taking of a futures position either 'costs' or 'gains', the initial margin deposit means that at first a futures position can be taken effectively at zero cost, ignoring any commission payable.

- It is not really intended that the majority of futures are taken to expiration and delivery of the underlying. The intention is that positions are closed out, off-set, this is done by reversing the original trade. To close out, a short would go long. A long would close out by going short. Due to the way that the clearing house becomes counterparty to all trades, a close-out can be effected, of course, with a completely different counterparty to the original. Ease of close-out also means that hedges can be lifted at required times which may not necessarily match standard contract expirations. All these features create liquidity in the futures market. In addition close-outs mean that participants in the futures markets are not confined to hedgers, those who wish to have nothing to do with dealing in the cash market can speculate freely in the futures market.

- At close-out longs and shorts will be either net payers or net receivers of variation margin over the time they have held their position. Initial margin will be returned to them intact. Initial margin paid in cash pays interest. If you are a speculator, without positions in the underlying, you will take your profits accordingly. If you are hedging, gains in the futures market will compensate for loss in the cash market, or alternatively, losses in the futures market will cancel out gains in the cash market. In either case a known price will be achieved for the underlying asset which is effectively fixed at the time the hedge is placed.

- A qualification to the last statement can be made in that should the asset underlying the future not be an exact match for the cash market asset, basis risk will be present, i.e. futures price and cash price may not move exactly on a one for one basis in opposite directions, adjusted by change in cost of carry due to time.

Key terms

- basis (p. 69)
- basis risk (p. 78)
- cash and carry arbitrage (p. 67)
- cash settled future (p. 72)
- clearing house (p. 72)
- close-out (p. 72)
- convenience yield (p. 67)
- cost of carry (p. 65)
- delta (p. 78)
- entry price (p. 66)
- equity account (p. 75)
- exchange (p. 70)
- exchange traded (p. 70)
- expiration (p. 73)
- hedges (p. 77)
- initial margin (p. 73)

- long futures (p. 64)
- marking to market (p. 75)
- normal/inverted market (p. 79)
- off-set (p. 72)
- open interest (p. 80)
- opening price (p. 80)
- price transparency (p. 70)
- settlement price (p. 74)
- short futures (p. 64)
- standardisation (p. 69)
- tick (p. 75)
- to arrive (p. 61)
- underlying (p. 59)
- variation margin (p. 74)
- volume transparency (p. 70
- zero sum game (p. 64)

Questions

10.1 You anticipate that spot prices will fall. How do you take a futures position to profit from this?

10.2 Why does initially taking a futures position not actually involve paying any money permanently, apart from variation margin if appropriate?

10.3 You wish to hedge the purchase of an asset at a later date. Describe the futures position you would take to hedge this.

10.4 Futures are described as a zero sum game. Why is this?

10.5 Why is daily marking to market so important a feature of futures markets?

10.6 What are the factors which determine the futures price?

10.7 Why are so few futures actually taken to expiration and delivery?

10.8 If the situation is as described as in Question 10.7, why are delivery arrangements still important nevertheless?

10.9 Why are 1 tick price movements and 1 basis point movements not of equal monetary value in all futures contracts?

10.10 What are the features of an exchange traded future which create price transparency? Why is this desirable?

Further reading

Dubofsky, David (1992) *Options and Financial Futures*, McGraw Hill.

Hull, John (1991) *Introduction to Futures and Options Markets*, Prentice Hall.

Redhead, Keith (1992) *Introduction to the International Money Markets*, Woodhead Faulkner.

11 ▷ Interest rate futures

Material in this chapter assumes knowledge of futures as covered in Chapter 10 and some knowledge of bond markets, although in the latter case a brief reminder is given. Commission and transactions costs are ignored in all worked examples.

Introduction

Futures contracts which enable interest rate risk to be hedged have been available since October 20 1975 when the CBOT introduced futures on **Ginney Maes**. This was shortly followed by the US Treasury bond (T-bond) futures contract on August 22 1977. Since then, world-wide, the US T-bond future has become the most widely used contract of any kind. Interest rate contracts as a whole represent just under half of all futures contracts. The US T-bond contract holds CBOT and world-wide single day trading volume records, on one day, 20 September 1994, 760,885 contracts were traded. Total market volume for the day was 1,540,499. The US T-bond contract represents about half of all CBOT futures trading, during 1993, 79,428,474 such contracts were traded, out of a total of all CBOT contracts, futures and options, of 178,773,105 (source: CBOT).

During 1993 at LIFFE 101,875,805 contracts in total were traded (futures and options). In the year ending August 1994 exchange traded volume was up by 36.42% on the previous year.

The huge growth in the use of futures to hedge interest rates risk stems from the fact that since the early 1970s interest rates have been much more volatile than before. Fixed exchange rate regimes ended in 1973 with the breakdown of the Bretton Woods system, resulting in turn in a greater need for management of floating rates via interest rate changes. In 1979 the US Federal Reserve abandoned interest rate targeting, creating the possibility of greater interest rate volatility. In addition, larger government budget deficits, particularly in the US, resulted in large amounts of funding requiring issue of government debt instruments like T-bonds, T-bills and T-notes and gilts and Treasury bills in the case of the UK. Gradual abolition of exchange controls has meant that large capital flows can occur across national boundaries. All these factors create a need to hedge bond prices. Indeed, some of the over-the-counter hedges offered by some financial institutions, such as FRAs, themselves create a need for the risk taken on by the provider in turn to be hedged via exchange traded instruments like futures.

Prices of long-term instruments like T-bonds and UK gilts are very sensitive to interest rate changes, especially if they have a low coupon, for reasons explained later in the chapter. Thus holders and potential holders of such instruments have a special need to hedge prices and thereby interest rates and this applies equally to bond issuers and potential issuers. Short-term interest rates can also be highly volatile.

Many government instruments have a global market, particularly those of the US, this in turn feeds a global need for hedging the prices of these instruments. Huge trading volumes of government debt instruments and their associated futures contracts necessarily means that cash and futures markets are highly liquid. As a result sales and purchases in either market are not disruptive to the market and its prices.

As will be seen later in this chapter, US T-bond futures can be delivered or received up to two and a half years from the opening of the contract. It is therefore possible to fix prices of T-bonds up to two and a half years ahead. This is of tremendous value to any investor, especially institutional investors.

Many short-term interest rates can be hedged a long way ahead by the use of an appropriate futures contract. Using the CBOT 30-day future, for example, 30-day US dollar rates can be hedged up to 24 months later. Use of the LIFFE Short Sterling contract enables three-month sterling to be hedged up to 10 contract months ahead (10 × 3 months = 30 months).

The importance of the futures market to the US T-bond market is illustrated by an incident, often cited by the CBOT, which occurred in December 1982. At this time the US Treasury postponed an issue of bonds to be auctioned because at the intended time the CBOT was going to be closed for the Christmas holiday. As the bond dealers now had no means of hedging the risk incurred in bidding for bonds, it was felt that to go ahead would have resulted in lower prices being achieved by the US Treasury. As the CBOT remarks 'no hedge – no auction'.

Interest rate contracts

There are a number of interest rate contracts currently traded on exchanges around the world. On LIFFE and the CBOT they include the following (figures quoted by LIFFE and CBOT):

LIFFE	
Short-term	volume by contract Jan–Aug 1994
Three-month Sterling (Short Sterling)*	10,956,967
Three-month Eurodollar (Eurodollar)	85,345
Three-month Eurodeutschmark (Euromark)	21,218,083
Three-month Euro Swiss Franc (Euroswiss)	1,152,644
Three-month ECU (ECU)	413,193
Three-month Eurolire (Lire)	2,406,245

Long-term

Long (UK) Gilt*	14,466,598
German Government Bond (Bund)	26,842,752
German Government Bond, medium term (BOBL)	73,019
Japanese Government Bond (JGB)	433,709
Italian Government Bond (BTP)	8,898,988

CBOT

Short-term

30-day interest rate*	222,769
2-year US T-note	604,979
5-year US T-note	8,280,171

Long term

10-year US T-note	16,505,949
US T-bond*	70,811,581

The asterisked (*) LIFFE and CBOT contracts above will be featured in this chapter to illustrate the principles of hedging interest rate risk by the use of futures and builds upon material in the preceding chapter.

In the case of sterling, three-month rates to 15-year rates can be hedged up to two and a half years ahead. If US dollars are taken it can be seen that rates along the whole of the yield curve, from 30 days to 15 years plus can be hedged in relation to US Treasury securities and for up to two and a half years ahead.

Definition – interest rate futures

LIFFE defines a futures contract as:

> a legally binding agreement on a recognised exchange, e.g. LIFFE, to make or take delivery of a specified instrument, at a fixed date in the future, at a price agreed upon at the time of dealing.

The CBOT definition is:

> an agreement to make delivery (short position) at a later date, or to accept delivery (long position) at a later date, of a fixed amount of a specified grade or quality of a commodity at a specified price.

As discussed in the previous chapter, an important feature of a futures contract is that of standardisation of the contract elements. Using the CBOT US T-bond contract as an example, the underlying cash instrument, the T-bond, is standardised to multiples of $100,000, evaluated to an 8% yield with maturity of not less than 15 years. This differs from the cash market for T-bonds where quantity, coupon rate, maturity and price must all be individually agreed between buyer and seller. In the futures market the only variable is of course price, as determined by open outcry on the exchange floor.

Some interest rate futures contracts are cash settled, for instance LIFFE Three-month Sterling or CBOT 30-day. This is because the contract relates to a deposit, which is non-transferable. Others can be settled by physical delivery, remembering however, that the majority of futures do not reach maturity and are closed out. Nevertheless, the price of the future must relate to the possibility of physical delivery, if this were not so then arbitrage profits would be possible. T-bond and UK gilt futures are deliverable and the delivery process is somewhat intricate with some delivery options affecting price.

Users of interest rate futures

In general terms hedgers and speculators will use futures markets. It should be understood that the term speculator is not used in a pejorative way. A speculator is someone prepared to take on a measurable risk for an appropriate price and potential reward. Those wishing to hedge financial cash market positions will include the following:

- banks
- bond dealers
- building societies
- cash managers
- corporates
- central and local government
- fund managers
- insurance companies
- mortgage lenders
- pension funds
- underwriters.

Bond prices and interest rates

If the use of futures which hedge interest rates are to be understood, then a few basics concerning bond prices will be useful, even if the future is for short-term interest rates.

Fixed income bonds have common characteristics regardless of issuer. A fixed rate of interest, the **coupon** is paid annually or semi-annually related to the nominal value of the bond and is expressed as an annualised percentage.

The holder of a UK gilt, nominal value £50,000 with a coupon of 10.50% paid semi-annually will receive every six months

$$£50,000 \times 10.50\% \times 6/12 = £2,625$$

as a return on his or her investment. The 10.50% here will be the **current yield** on the gilt. However, if sold, the market value of the gilt will only be £50,000 if the prevailing rate of return on debt instruments of equal quality and maturity is 10.50%. As the coupon is fixed, £2,625 will be received by the holder every six months regardless of whether this is a prevailing market rate of return on £50,000.

Therefore if prevailing market rates were higher than 10.50%, say 12%, the price would have to adjust in the market so that a current yield on the outlay would represent 12%. It follows that the market price of the bond must fall in this instance to £43,750. Price must adjust as below:

$$\frac{£2,625 \times 2}{£43,750} = 12\%(.12) \text{ current yield}$$

(×2 because two coupon payments of £2,635 per annum, £43,750 = market price of bond).

If current yields were to fall (say to 8%) then price would rise to £65,625.

$$\frac{£2,625 \times 2}{£65,625} = 8\%(.08)$$

Therefore there is an **inverse relationship** between bond prices and interest rates.

- As interest rates rise bond prices fall.
- As interest rates fall bond prices rise.

The above current yield concept is useful in that it easily illustrates bond price and interest rate relationships, but **yield to maturity** is more commonly used due to its greater accuracy in determining bond prices in reality. However, for our purposes here current yield will suffice as it readily illustrates the price/yield or interest rate relationship.

Buying and selling interest rate futures

- Selling short a future hedges a fall in spot prices of the underlying commodity.
- Buying long a future hedges a rise in spot prices of the underlying commodity.
- As the spot price of the commodity falls, a short futures position gains in value whereas a long futures position loses value.
- The reverse also applies – as the spot price of a commodity rises, a short futures position loses value whereas a long futures position gains value.

Reference to p. 64 will give worked examples.

It has been seen in the previous section that bond prices and interest rates vary inversely. Therefore:

- Selling short an interest rate future hedges a rise in interest rates because it hedges a fall in bond prices.
- Borrowers take short positions, they do not want low bond prices and high interest rates when they sell/issue bonds at some future date.
- Buying long an interest rate future hedges a fall in interest rates because it hedges a rise in bond prices.
- Lenders take long positions. They do not want low interest rates and high bond prices when they purchase bonds at a later date.

Even when contracts like the Three-month Sterling LIFFE and CBOT 30-day interest futures are concerned, where deposits are the underlying cash market instrument rather than bonds, selling short hedges interest rate rises and buying long hedges interest rate falls.

- Depositors (lenders) buy long futures.
- Borrowers sell short futures.

Price quotes – short-term interest rate futures

Futures interest rate contracts are not quoted on a yield per annum basis, 12.50%, but by an index determined by deducting the yield per annum from 100. Therefore a yield of 12.50% gives: 100–12.50 = 87.50, often written as 87-50. This preserves a buy low/sell high principle.

Note that this is the way most things are bought and sold. Do not confuse this with the principle used in earlier chapters for currency transactions in the spot and forward markets where sell low–buy high relate to rates rather than value.

That short-term interest rate futures are quoted this way also has the benefit that when futures prices change, resultant losses or gains to shorts and longs have the same relationships as in other futures contracts whereby if the futures price rises, the short loses and the long gains and vice versa.

Quoted the way they are, if a short sees the futures price rise from 87.50 to 87.75 due to an interest rate change of $\frac{1}{4}$% they will lose from having this futures position. To further illustrate this, look at a close-out example, sell at 87.50, close out by buying back at 87.75 gives a loss of 25 (ticks). Alternatively, if a long buys at 87.50 and sells back at 87.75 this of course creates a gain. Thus the convention is kept that if a futures price rises the short loses, the long gains. If a futures price falls the long loses, the short gains. Returning to fundamentals shows that if you agree to sell something, anything, at 87.50 you have lost out if subsequently you could have sold for 87.75.

With this explanation and remembering the sections on open interest and volume and opening and settlement prices (p. 80), you should be able to understand reports on short-term interest rate futures. An example is reproduced from the *Financial Times* for the LIFFE Short Sterling contract.

Table 11.1 Three-month Sterling Futures (LIFFE) £500,000 points of 100%

	open	sett price	est vol	open interest
Sep	94.17	94.15	5,789	76,586
Dec	93.23	93.16	35,703	150,830
Mar	92.31	92.16	15,946	81,634
Jun	91.72	91.56	7,589	55,534

Basis point and tick

A **basis point** is 1/100 of one percent (0.0001 or 0.01%) and usually represents the smallest movement of short-term futures prices. In all futures contracts price movement is expressed in **ticks**. As the unit of trading for each futures contract differs, it therefore follows that the value of a tick varies from contract to contract.

> Tick = unit of trading × basis point × proportion of year over which contract runs (usually 3 months)

If the LIFFE Three-month Sterling contract is taken as an example:

Unit of trading £500,000 × 0.0001 × $\frac{1}{4}$ = £12.50

This can be compared with the LIFFE Three-month Eurodollar contract where one tick = $25.00

Unit of trading $1,000,000 × 0.0001 × $\frac{1}{4}$

or CBOT 30-day contract where 1 tick = $41.67

($5m × 0.0001 × 30/360)

In the LIFFE Long Gilt future, one unit of trading equals a £50,000 gilt and the minimum price movement is £1/32.

£50,000 × £1/32% = £15.625 (tick)

CBOT US T-bond futures 1 tick = $31.25 (trading unit $100,000 × $1/32%).

Contract highlights of these and other futures are given more fully in later sections. This section explains derivation of the tick.

Futures prices and forward/forward rates

A **theoretical futures price** or **fair value** of a short-term interest rate future such as the LIFFE three-month contracts 'should' reflect the forward/forward rate in the cash market (Chapter 8). If a short sterling contract is used as an example, the futures price should reflect the forward/forward rate in relation to a sterling time deposit which matures on the futures settlement date and a time deposit which matures three months later.

Should this relationship not hold, then an arbitrage will be possible.

Interest rate futures and basis

In Chapter 10 we covered the relationship between cash and futures prices and saw that their movements in general terms parallel one another and converge as maturity of the future approaches. The difference between cash and futures prices was described as the **basis** and it was seen that this was generally more stable than either cash or futures prices. The reason for this was quite straightforward, that even if cash market prices are quite volatile and thereby introduce volatility into the futures price because they parallel one another, with an adjustment for time, the difference between the two market prices remains fairly constant. That prices in either market parallel one another is of course due to the concept of cost of carry and this for short-term interest rate futures is, of course, the forward/forward rate.

Basis can be either **positive** or **negative**. It is positive when the futures price is above the cash price and negative when it is below. Basis for futures which relate to deliverable financial instruments, besides being affected by cost of carry, is also affected by the deliverable supply of the underlying commodity, cost of delivery and interest rate changes. Do not confuse positive and negative basis with positive or negative cost of carry which is discussed later in the chapter (pp. 93–4).

Basis and fair value

Using three-month interest rate futures contracts as an example, the difference between an actual futures price and the price implied by current three-month LIBOR will be **simple basis**. Simple basis, however, has two components: **theoretical basis** and **value basis**. Each component changes in value independently of the other.

Theoretical basis is the difference between the theoretical (fair) futures price and the price implied by the current three-month LIBOR to continue the example.

Value basis is the second component of simple basis and reflects the fact that an actual futures price does not always reflect fair value. Actual price must, however, always approximate to theoretical price or fair value because arbitrage will ensure that this is so. Simple basis is often described as the **basis** (as opposed to basis) when used in connection with interest rate futures.

Cash settlement, EDSP

All short-term interest rate futures are cash settled. This must be so because the underlying notional cash market instrument for delivery into the futures contract is a deposit or cash which is to be borrowed, neither of which can be transferred and therefore there can be no physical delivery.

All cash settled LIFFE contracts use the appropriate cash market offered rates (LIBOR) on the last day of trading to determine the **Exchange Delivery Settlement Price (EDSP)**. Of course, in reality the vast majority of contracts will be closed out by an offsetting position.

The EDSP for LIFFE contracts is based on the appropriate LIBOR rate as given by the British Bankers' Association Interest Settlement Rate (BBAISR) at 11.00 a.m. on the last day of trading. All outstanding futures positions are settled with reference to this rate. For example, if the BBAISR is 5.85% then all positions will be settled at 94.15.

A buyer of five Short Sterling contracts at 96.50 will be settled net at 96.50 minus 94.15 equalling 235 basis points (in reality realised over the life of the futures position by daily marking to market). One basis point this contract equals 1 tick and 1 tick equals £12.50.

$$5 \times 235 \times £12.50 = £14,687.50$$
(no. of contracts × no. of ticks × tick value)

Here there is a net loss on the futures position.
Reason for loss (re-cap):

Buying a future gives a gain if prices rise – you can buy at lower prices than currently available at spot – they have risen. If prices rise, interest rates have fallen.

Therefore, buying a future gives a gain if prices rise/interest rates fall. The opposite is true if prices fall/interest rates rise.

Above, interest rates rose from 3.5% (100 – 96.50) to 5.85% (100 – 94.15). Therefore a net loss is given by the futures position.

Futures prices and the yield curve

(See also the section on positive/negative cost of carry (pp. 104, 105).)

When the yield curve in the cash market is positive, i.e. upward sloping as in Figure 11.1, futures prices will relate to time as in Figure 11.2. The configuration of the yield curve based on futures prices is therefore opposite to that of the cash market yield curve. It follows that a negative cash market yield curve, Figure 11.3, will result in futures prices which behave as in Figure 11.4. Note that the futures prices depicted are snap-shots in time and do not describe their behaviour through time. If Figure 11.2 is taken as an example, it shows that on a given day, with a positive yield curve, futures prices for nearby futures contracts will be higher than prices quoted at the same time for contracts which mature in later time periods. As covered in the previous chapter, cash and futures prices converge towards maturity.

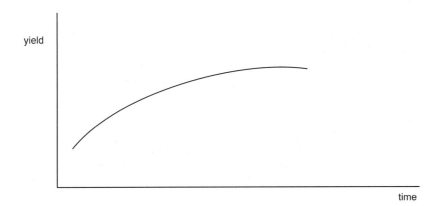

Figure 11.1 *Positive yield curve in cash market.*

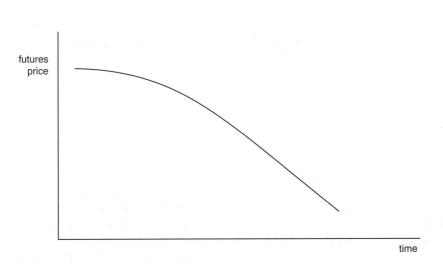

Figure 11.2 *Futures price where yield curve is positive.*

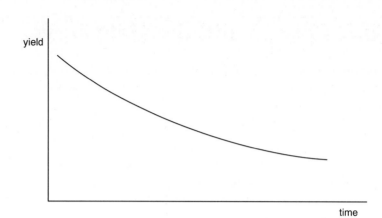

Figure 11.3 *Negative yield curve in cash market.*

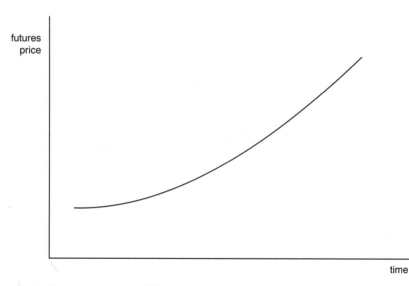

Figure 11.4 *Futures price where yield curve is negative.*

Interest rate risk management and futures

As discussed in Chapter 10, the essential principle of using futures to hedge cash market positions is that losses in the cash market are matched by gains in the futures market, or vice versa. Equal and opposite positions in the cash and futures markets hedge potential loss due to price fluctuations in the cash market.

A large number of hedging strategies are possible depending upon the user's cash market position and what is intended to be achieved. The way in which futures are used will also depend upon types of futures contracts available, current market conditions, the user's circumstances and aims, interest rate expectations and availability and advantages and disadvantages of alternative hedging strategies using other types of hedging techniques.

Investors or portfolio managers can use futures to protect against the consequences of rising interest rates (falling bond prices) by selling futures and protect against the consequences of falling rates by buying futures. Similar strategies can be used by those borrowing funds in the cash market, for instance bond issuers.

Some simple trading strategies to hedge short-term interest rates are now described. As a reminder:

- Hedgers who are long in the cash market (lenders), or who anticipate becoming long at a later date, need to be short in the futures market, i.e. sell.
- Hedgers who are short in the cash market (borrowers), or anticipate being so later, need to take long futures positions, i.e. buy.

The terms **long** and **short hedges** are therefore used and describe the futures contract positions taken to effect the hedge.

- A long hedger wishes to hedge the consequences of a rise in spot prices and therefore the consequences of a fall in interest rates.
- Long hedges lock in a buying price.
- Depositors/lenders use long hedges.

- A short hedger wishes to hedge the consequences of a fall in spot prices and therefore the consequences of a rise in interest rates.
- Short hedges lock in a selling price.
- Borrowers use short hedges.

Hedging short-term interest rates – an introduction

Short-term interest rates tend to fluctuate more than long-term interest rates because they respond much more quickly to changes in money market liquidity. Changes in liquidity in turn are caused by exchange rate changes and changes in economic data and government policy as well as expected changes in all these variables. It will be noted in later sections and further developed in Chapter 13 that long-term security prices tend to fluctuate more than short-term security prices as a response to given yield/interest rate changes.

Various futures contracts are available on exchanges around the world which enable short-term interest rates to be hedged in various currencies. The LIFFE Three-month Sterling and the CBOT 30-day US$ interest rate futures will be used as worked examples.

A short hedge, LIFFE Three-month Sterling

Users of the LIFFE Three-month Sterling futures contract (the Short Sterling) will be lenders/depositors and borrowers in the short-term sterling money markets, issuers and purchasers of short-term securities such as CDs and sterling commercial paper, purchasers of Treasury bills, short-dated gilts and eligible bills, as well as market makers and traders of such instruments. In addition, participants in the sterling swap, FRA, FRN and forward foreign exchange markets may well hedge any net exposure using short-term futures.

Users of these markets will all be exposed to short-term sterling interest rate risk. Each cash market will exhibit slightly different rates of interest and will not be an exact match for the underlying cash market instrument covered by the futures contract, in the case of the Short Sterling this will be three-month sterling LIBOR.

Therefore basis risk will be present when cash and future do not relate exactly. However, as each of the instruments is influenced by the same kind of factors, such basis risk will be minimal and is ignored here. Ways of **weighting** a hedge to take care of differences between the contract underlying instrument and the instrument to be hedged are dealt with later in this section and Chapter 13.

A short hedge involves the selling of a future to protect against rises in interest rates. Borrowers of funds and issuers and sellers of short-term securities will undertake a short hedge.

Table 11.2   LIFFE Three-month Sterling (Short Sterling) interest rate future

Contract highlights	
Trading unit	£500,000
Delivery/expiry months	March, June, September, December
Delivery day/exercise day/expiry day	First business day after the last trading day
Last trading day	11.00 Third Wednesday of delivery month
Quotation	100.00 minus rate of interest
Minimum price	0.01
Movement (Tick size and value)	(£12.50)

Contract standard
Cash settlement based on the Exchange Delivery Settlement Price (EDSP).
EDSP based on the British Bankers' Association Interest Settlement Rate (BBAISR) for three-month sterling deposits at 11.00 a.m. on the last trading day. The settlement price will be 100.00 minus the BBAISR (rounded accordingly).

In addition to the above, it should be noted that futures in this contract are available for 12 delivery months ahead. Thus a contract can be traded for delivery up to 12 × 3 months = 36 months ahead. In reality there is not much liquidity for such **deferred month** contracts so far ahead relative to the liquidity for the current contract and the next two. However, it does illustrate the possibility of hedging interest rate risk concerning the three month position on the yield curve for up to three years ahead. An example of a user of such a far ahead deferred month contract might be a swap market dealer; it would enable him or her to set hedged prices in the swap market. When two additional delivery months were introduced on 17 March 1994, bringing the total from 10 to 12 delivery months, it was found that volume increased for the contract overall and that the two new months appeared to be new business and did not dilute existing liquidity.

A worked example of a short hedge is now given. Imagine the following:

On Wednesday June 16 a corporate treasurer anticipates the need to borrow £5m for three months in three months' time, on September 15. At June 16, three-month LIBOR is 6.00%. The treasurer wishes to hedge against a rise in rates in three months' time, i.e. to lock into a three-month borrowing rate in three months' time.

A hedge is effected by using the short sterling contract as follows:

Cash market	Futures market
June 16	
Do nothing	Sell 10 Sept futures contracts at 93.50
	(implied interest rate 6.50%)
Sept 15	
Borrow £5m at 3m LIBOR at 6.75%	Close out, buy 10 Sept futures at 92.75

Therefore the effective borrowing rate can be calculated as follows:

futures profit = 93.50–92.75 = 0.75%
LIBOR loss = 6.75%–6.00% = 0.75%
6.75%–0.75% = 6.00%

Thus loss in cash market is matched by gain in futures market.

The above example shows the futures position being closed out. An alternative could be to let the short position run to expiration, in which case the result would be the same, except that profit would have been received via the EDSP arrangements.

As an alternative, the net position can be viewed as follows:

Actual borrowing cost in the cash market, September 16:

£5m at 6.75% × 3/12 = £84,375

Gain on futures position June 16–September 15:

10 contracts   × 75 ticks   × £12.50 = £9,375
(£5m divided by £500,000) × (93.50 – 92.75) × tick value

Actual interest minus gain on futures position equals net interest expense:

£84,375–£9,375 = £75,000

Net interest expense related to £5m for 3 months equals:

£75,000/£5m × 12/3 = 0.06 (6%) p.a.

The result is that effectively 6% per annum is paid, even though interest rates did rise over the three-month period. The gain in the futures market matched loss in the cash market.

Positions taken in the cash and futures may not offset each other perfectly. One reason is that sterling LIBOR-linked loan interest is calculated on an actual/365 day basis. Thus a one basis point change in rates charged over, for example, an actual 89 days, would equal an interest cost change on £500,000 of:

0.0001 × £500,000 × 89/365 = £12.19178

whereas in the short sterling contract a one basis point change gives a tick value of £12.50

0.0001 × £500,000 × 3/12

Even this tick value can itself be 'questioned' and is discussed further in Chapter 13.

This introduces the concept of hedge ratios and weighted hedges which are dealt with more specifically later in this chapter and Chapter 13. Briefly here, an exact hedge ratio requires the following calculation (for a short sterling contract to hedge a 3m LIBOR cash market position):

$$\frac{\text{hedged sum}}{\text{contract size}} \times \frac{\text{actual number of days related to the cash market}}{365 \times \text{the number of contracts per year}}$$

$$\times \text{number of contracts per year}$$

Using the 89 days as an example, shows the need for:

$$\frac{\pounds 5m}{\pounds 500,000} \times \frac{89}{365} \times 4 = 9.7534 \text{ contracts}$$

Clearly as only whole contracts can be traded, 10 must be sold, rendering the hedge, in practice, slightly imperfect. Hedges will also be slightly imperfect when, for example, the Short Sterling contract is used to hedge three-month bank CDs. Here cash and futures price movements will not correlate exactly because the futures price is tracking three-month LIBOR, not three-month bank CDs. This is a hedge weighting matter which is partly addressed later in this chapter and more fully in Chapter 13.

A long hedge, CBOT 30-day interest future

Users of the CBOT 30-day interest rate future would be similar individuals and organisations, principally in the US, to the users of the LIFFE Short Sterling contract, except that in this instance the need would be to hedge 30-day US dollar rates. A long hedge would be undertaken by a lender of cash market funds. They wish to hedge the consequences of a fall in rates. A decline in interest rates will be offset by gains in the futures position.

Table 11.3   CBOT 30-day interest rate future

Contract highlights	
Trading unit	$5m
Price basis	100 minus the monthly average overnight fed funds rate (e.g. price of 92.75 for a 7.25 percent rate)
Minimum tick size	$41.67 per basis point (1/100 of one percent of $5m on a 30 day basis)
Trading months	the current calendar month and the next 24 calendar months
Delivery method	cash settlement
Contract standard	the contract will be cash settled against the average daily fed funds rate for the delivery month. The daily fed funds rate is calculated and reported by the Federal Reserve Bank of New York. NB. The actual 30 day rate is not used
Last day of trading	the last business day of the delivery month

To illustrate the use of the 30-day contract in a long hedge, imagine the following scenario:

It is June and a corporate treasurer who has funds to lend during July of $50m is worried that interest rates will fall during June, so that when the funds are actually lent, they will be at a lower rate. July has 31 days, therefore:

$$\frac{\$50m}{\$5m} \times \frac{31}{30} = 10.33 \text{ futures contracts needed}$$

Of course only 10 contracts can be traded.
The hedging strategy requires the purchase of 10 July 30-day futures and to hold the position until expiration or lift the hedge just prior to expiration by close-out.

Imagine the following prices:

	July 1	July 31
30-day futures price	91.85	92.45
implied 30-day rate	8.15%	7.55%
	(100–91.85)	(100–92.45)

Cash market	Futures market
July 1	
deposit $50m at 7.50%	buy 10 futures at 91.85
July 31	
receive back deposit of $50m	sell 10 futures at 92.45
	gain on long position =
plus interest at 7.50% =	10 contracts × 60 ticks × $41.67
$50m plus $322,916.60	
= $50,322,916	= $25,002

interest income + futures gain = net return on funds
$322,916.60   + $25,002   = $347,918.60

Net percentage return on funds therefore equals:

$$\frac{\$347,918.60}{\$50m} \times \frac{360}{31} = 0.0808 \ (8.08\%)$$

This net return of 8.08% achieved via the hedge compares with a cash market return on the funds unhedged of 7.50%, assuming cash market rates did fall to 7.50%.
Note that interest rate at start of hedge was 8.15%, the fact that only 8.08% was achieved is because only 10 contracts could be used, not the actual weighted number required of 10.33.

More advanced interest rate hedges using short-term interest rate futures (e.g. strips, stubs, tails, odd month periods, calendar spreads, inter commodity spreads) are described in Chapter 13.

Cash market price quotes – bonds

We now look at bond market price quotes to help us with bond futures. Cash market bond prices can be described as being at **par**, **discount** or **premium**.

- A bond trading at par trades at its nominal, par value and is a **par bond**.
- A bond trading at a discount trades below its nominal, par value and is a **discount bond**.
- A bond trading at a premium trades above its nominal, par value and is a **premium bond**.

A bond will have par value when its coupon equals current yield/yield to maturity. Such a bond will have a price quote of 100. If interest rates rise, price will fall below 100, to 90 for example. If interest rates fall, price will rise above 100, to 110 for example. Price changes are usually in increments of $\frac{1}{32}$nds. Thus UK gilts at 89-15 ($89^{15}/_{32}$) with a nominal value of £50,000 will be priced at:

$$£50,000 \times 0.8946875 = £44,734.38$$
$$(89^{15}/_{32})$$

US Treasury notes are quoted in one quarter of $\frac{1}{32}$.

$$93\text{-}150 = 93^{15}/_{32} \ (0.9346875)$$
$$93\text{-}151 = 93^{15.25}/_{32} \ (0.934765625)$$

Maturity, coupon and bond price sensitivity

Time to maturity and coupon rates affect bond price sensitivity. A price sensitive bond is one whose price changes as a result of interest rate changes by a greater proportion than the proportionate change in interest rates. In plain language, price changes a lot as a result of a small interest rate change.

Long-term bonds of 15 years maturity will be more price sensitive than short-term notes of five years' maturity with the same coupon. For bonds of equal maturity, the low coupon bond will be more price sensitive than the higher coupon bond. Thus low coupon, long-term bonds are the most price sensitive. The reason is essentially connected with the time value of money.

Bond holders receive a flow of income over time, the coupon payments plus repayment of nominal value at maturity. Long-term bonds distribute their income and repayment over a long period of time. If these income flows are discounted to present value, it can be seen that changes in current market yields affect distant income flows in regard to present value more than closer income flows which necessarily occur for shorter dated bonds. Thus price changes more for long-term bonds for a given change in current yields.

Lower coupon bonds derive a large proportion of their returns in relation to the nominal value at maturity. The opposite is so for higher coupon bonds. Changes in current yields change present values of distant cash flows more so than nearer cash flows. Therefore a high coupon bond, which attains a high proportion of its income flow (which includes repayment of principal) early on will be less affected by current yield changes than a low coupon bond.

In addition to the above, bond price volatility is also related to anticipation of rate changes and supply and demand conditions related to a given bond issue.

More advanced concepts which measure bond price volatility are **duration, basis point value (BPV)** and **convexity** which are dealt with in Chapter 13. Factors which affect bond prices must be understood as changes in cash market bond prices will affect futures prices. Different bonds are deliverable into bond futures contracts and this causes a few complications.

The UK government bond (gilts) market

The UK gilts market is the sixth largest government bond market in the world (4.14% of the total in 1992). In December 1992, 84 different issues were outstanding, representing a nominal value of £140bn, by December 1993 £190bn was outstanding. Most issues (89% 1992, 84.5% 1993) are fixed coupon paid semi-annually after payment of withholding tax. It is the **straight** fixed coupon issues which are the deliverable instruments in the Long Gilt LIFFE futures contract.

Gilt-edged market makers (GEMMs) are the 19 primary and secondary market makers obliged to make continuous two-way prices in a full range of gilts. Total turnover of gilts averaged £4.5bn per day during 1992 of which fixed coupon straights represented £3.4bn. In 1993 average daily trades amounted to £6.3bn.

Gilt prices are quoted per £100 of nominal stock in steps of $\frac{1}{32}$nds. A few shorts (less than seven years to maturity) are quoted in $\frac{1}{64}$ths. A **repo market** was introduced in January 1993. Only GEMMs may borrow gilts.

Interest is accrued on an actual/365 day basis. Stock goes ex-dividend 37 days before the coupon date. Ex-div gilts are not deliverable into the Long Gilt LIFFE future, nor on the business day either side of being ex-div. Three weeks before going ex-div gilts can be traded either ex or cum-div in the cash market.

US Government bond (T-bond) market

US T-bonds are fixed interest bonds with initial maturities greater than 10 years. T-notes have initial maturities of between one and ten years. T-bonds are the deliverable instruments (maturities 15 years plus) into the CBOT T-bond futures contract.

At the end of September 1992 there were $461.8bn of T-bonds outstanding making a total with T-notes and T-bills of about $2 trillion. The primary market is dominated by 36 primary dealers who maintain two way prices. The secondary market is primarily OTC.

Since 1986 T-bonds have been issued with 30 year maturities and since 1984 have been issued straight, i.e. free of call options. Coupon is fixed and paid semi-annually, with interest calculated on an actual/actual day count basis. Bonds are quoted clean of accrued interest and there is no ex-div period. No withholding tax is deducted. Bond prices are quoted in 1/32nds.

Deliverable bonds

All futures contracts are obligations to make or accept delivery of an underlying commodity on specified terms. In the case of futures relating to bonds, the underlying commodity is of course specified bonds. A feature of all bond contracts is that a number of bonds may qualify as deliverable into a futures contract.

If the LIFFE Long Gilt contract is taken as an example, from June 1993 delivery month onwards, gilts deliverable have had the following (abridged) characteristics (deliverable grade):

- maturity between 10 and 15 years;
- no early redemption permitted, redemption payable in a single instalment;
- fixed coupon paid semi-annually in arrears;
- fully paid, not convertible or in bearer form;
- must have been admitted to the Official List of the London Stock Exchange.

A number of gilt issues will meet these criteria at any one time and will have different maturities and coupons and necessarily different prices.

Delivery may be made of any gilts as published by LIFFE and are delivered on or before the tenth business day prior to the First Notice Day. A similar range of underlying instruments applies to other LIFFE and CBOT treasury futures, some of which will appear when specific contracts are examined later in the chapter.

Although futures contracts are delivery obligations, in very few instances does delivery actually take place due to the process of off-set, as we have noted previously. However, delivery in principle must be understood due to its role in the pricing of futures. If futures prices do not reflect the price of the underlying bonds deliverable into a contract then arbitrage profits will be taken, in turn ensuring that futures price does reflect the price of the underlying bond.

CTD bonds

A range of specified bonds is deliverable into bond futures. The option as to which bonds are actually delivered lies with the holder of the short (sell) position. Rationally the seller will deliver the cheapest bond and it follows that the futures price will track this **cheapest to deliver (CTD)** bond.

Bond conversion factor

The futures price will parallel the CTD instrument, however, short futures position holders may still deliver instruments other than the CTD through a **conversion factor** system. This system equates all deliverable bonds to a common value. The CBOT uses 8% as the basis for its conversion factor system in relation to its US T-bond contract and LIFFE uses 9% for the Long Gilt contract. In both cases the factors were selected because they were the prevailing rates at the time the contract was designed. Conversion factor tables are available from each exchange.

In the case of the LIFFE UK Long Gilt futures contract which is based on a 9% coupon, the conversion factor for any 9% instrument will be 1.000. If the instrument eligible for delivery is below 9% coupon, then the conversion factor will be less than 1.000, reflecting the discount. If the delivered instrument has a coupon above 9%, then the conversion factor will be above 1.000 to reflect the premium. Similar conversion factors apply to US T-bonds at 8%.

Cash equivalent price of bonds

If a futures price is multiplied by the conversion factor a **cash equivalent price** or **adjusted futures price** is obtained.

$$\text{Futures price} \times \text{conversion factor} = \text{adjusted futures price or cash equivalent price}$$

Futures equivalent price of bonds

Alternatively to the above, when the cash price of any deliverable bond is divided by the conversion factor, a **futures equivalent price** or **adjusted cash price** is obtained.

$$\frac{\text{cash price}}{\text{conversion factor}} = \text{adjusted cash price or futures equivalent price}$$

Invoice amount/EDSP and bond futures

If a futures contract reaches maturity and bonds have to be delivered, the holder of the long futures position nominated by the exchange to purchase the bonds must pay an invoiced price for the bonds, this will not be the straightforward futures contract settlement price as this will reflect the CTD bond, when in fact a more expensive/cheaper bond may be actually delivered. The calculation of the **invoice amount** will use the conversion factor system and will result in an **Exchange Delivery Settlement Price (EDSP)**, when any accrued interest relating to the bond is added. (EDSP has already been covered in the context of the LIFFE Short Sterling contract earlier (p. 92), here the idea is the same with appropriate changes.)

Invoice amount/EDSP =
futures settlement price × contract size × conversion factor + accrued interest

The LIFFE Long Gilt contract actually uses the following formula:

$$\text{Invoice amount} = (\text{EDSP conversion factor} \times £500) + \text{accrued interest}$$

The £500 is derived by dividing the nominal value of the contract (£50,000) by the quotation (£100).

Bond/futures price relationships – cost of carry

Bonds will have their prices adjusted in the cash market in relation to yield to maturity changes as described on pp. 88–9. The actual market price of a bond can be adjusted to its adjusted cash price/futures equivalent price through the concept of conversion factor. Each bond can have its actual cash market price adjusted this way.

The futures price of a given bond will track its cash-adjusted price which, necessarily due to the conversion factor, will be the same as tracking the actual cash price of the CTD bond. The difference between cash and futures prices, as always, will be the basis. Basis should equal cost of carry, therefore the arbitrage free price of a bond future should reflect the adjusted cash price, net of cost of carry, in which case an investor would be indifferent to cash and futures markets, as cost would be equal. Therefore:

$$\text{Arbitrage free futures bond price} = \text{adjusted bond price less cost of carry}$$

Positive/negative cost of carry and bond futures

Most physical commodities have actual carrying costs – storage, insurance, delivery, financing – this ensures that the futures price is above the cash market price and carrying costs are said to be **negative**, for the reason given shortly.

When the underlying commodity of a futures contract is a financial instrument like a UK gilt or a US T-bond, then cost of carry can be either negative or positive.

If a UK gilt is held it delivers a flow of income. If this flow of income is greater than the financing costs incurred to purchase the gilt, then there is a positive cost of carry, i.e. there is a net gain in holding the gilt. If, however, the financing costs exceed the income then there is a negative carry, i.e. an actual cost of holding the gilt, a net loss.

When there is a negative carry the futures price will be above the cash market price. When there is a positive carry the futures price will be below the cash market price. In each case cash and futures price will converge towards maturity as net carrying cost diminishes over time, as discussed earlier (pp. 67–9).

Therefore, where the yield curve is upward sloping, it should be possible to enjoy a net interest income. This is achieved by borrowing at low short-term rates to finance the holding of the bond over the contract period, whilst at the same time enjoying the high long-term rates payable on the (long-term) bond. Net interest cost will be incurred where the yield curve is downward sloping.

- Where there is positive carry, the futures price should equal the adjusted price of the CTD bond less the positive carry and the futures price will be below the cash market price.
- Where there is negative carry, the futures price should equal the adjusted price of the CTD bond plus the negative carry and the futures price will be above the cash market price.

Positive or negative basis?

- The cash price will be above the futures price (positive basis) whenever spot prices are expected to fall/interest rates rise (positive yield curve).
- The cash price will be below the futures price (negative basis) whenever spot prices are expected to rise/interest rates fall (negative yield curve).

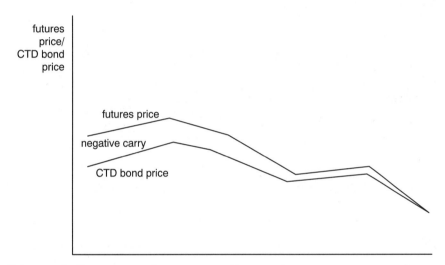

Figure 11.5 *Futures price with negative carry.*

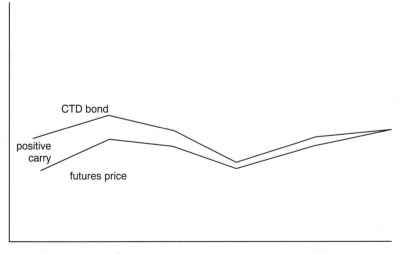

Figure 11.6 *Futures price and positive carry.*

Bond futures prices in reality

In reality the price of a bond future will not always equal the theoretical futures price relationships depicted earlier. The reason for this is the way in which bond futures contracts are designed, in that the short position has choices (options) in relation not only to what to deliver but when to deliver. The 'when to deliver' is 'any delivery day in the business month at seller's choice' for the LIFFE Long Gilt contract and between the last day of futures trading and last delivery day for the CBOT US T-bond contract. These choices are called an **implied put option**. (Terminology as used in options – Chapter 14).

The value of the put option implied by the seller's choices often results in the actual future trading below its theoretical price by a small amount. As a result cash and futures prices will not completely converge on the final day of futures trading.

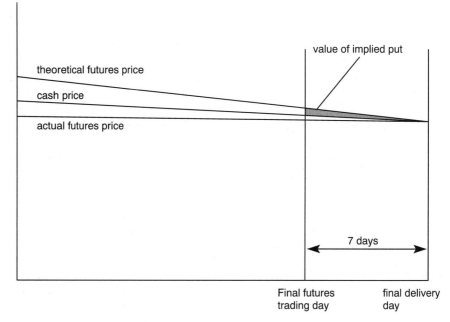

Figure 11.7 *Effect of implied put option on convergence, negative carry example.*

Implied repo rate (IRR) – cost of carry

A theoretical futures price for a commodity reflects cost of carry. For a bond future net cost of carry is the price of financing the purchase of a bond less the coupon return on the bond. This net carrying cost can be either positive or negative as discussed before.

The **implied repo rate (IRR)** refers to the short-term financing rate used to purchase the bond which is implied in the current futures price. In other words, a given futures price implies a short-term financing rate.

Earlier (p. 10) it was seen that:

(1) Arbitrage free futures bond price = adjusted bond cash price – net cost of carry

An arbitrage free futures bond price will be a theoretical futures price if:

(2) Net cost of carry = coupon income − financing rate

The identity (1) above can be rewritten:

(3) Theoretical futures price = adjusted bond cash price − (coupon income − financing rate)

If the actual futures price (as opposed to the theoretical futures price) is put into the identity, then a breakeven financing rate or **implied repo rate (IRR)** can be calculated. Because:

Actual futures price = adjusted bond cash price − (coupon income − IRR)

then:

IRR = actual futures price − adjusted (bond) cash price + coupon income

An IRR can be calculated for every bond or note which is deliverable into a futures contract, using the appropriate adjusted cash prices and coupon rates. The instrument giving the highest IRR will give the highest cash and carry profit and will be the cheapest to deliver. If a holder of a short futures position could finance the purchase of the bond or note below the IRR, a profit could be made by a cash and carry operation, by purchasing the bond in the cash market and selling a futures position against it.

Rich/cheap futures prices

Using the concept of IRR in analysing cash and future price relationships enables market users to determine when actual futures prices are either higher or lower than their theoretical values. Such a determination will necessarily relate to users' own, personal short-term financing costs and the value of the implied put option. If actual is greater than theoretical, futures are described as being **rich**. If actual is less than theoretical, futures are said to be **cheap**.

Contract highlights of the LIFFE Long Gilt future, June 1993 delivery onwards and newspaper quotes

Unit of trading	£50,000 nominal value notional gilt with 9% coupon
Delivery months	March, June, September, December
Delivery day	Any delivery day in business month at seller's choice
Last trading day	11.00 a.m. two business days prior to last business day in delivery month
Quotation	Per £100 nominal
Minimum price movement	£$^1/_{32}$
(Tick size and value)	(£15.625)

Highlights of the Contract standard (specification of gilts deliverable into the contract) were given earlier in the chapter (p. 102).

When looking at quotes for bond futures, an example is given from the *Financial Times* for the LIFFE Long Gilt contract, you must remember that the minimum price movement is £1$\frac{1}{32}$ giving a tick value in our example of £15.625. Thus in the worked example which follows a price change from 91.16 to 87.27 is a 117 tick price change. In price quotes this would be recorded as a 1.17 change.

It is worth seeing why a price move from 91.16 to 87.27 is not a price change of 389 ticks (i.e. 91.16 minus 87.27, treating .16 and .27 as decimals). 91.16 is really $91^{16}/_{32}$ and 87.27 is $87^{27}/_{32}$, thus $91^{16}/_{32}$ minus $87^{27}/_{32}$ equals $117^{1}/_{32}$nds. Note that in the FT example given different figures are used.

Table 11.4 Notional UK Gilt futures (LIFFE) £50,000 32nds of 100%

	open	sett	est. vol	open interest
Sep	99-05	99-03	669	19,104
Dec	98-14	98-11	36,629	99,301
Mar	–	97-23	0	0

A short hedge to protect asset values using LIFFE Long Gilt futures

A short hedge involves the sale of a future to protect the value of a cash market sale of an asset at a later date. The idea is to lock in a selling price of the asset at the later date when the sale is planned.

Assume the following:

A portfolio manager holds £1m nominal value of UK gilts, Treasury Stock 10.00% coupon, redemption year 2003. A rise in interest rates is feared, thus a fall in the price of the gilts in the cash market when it is envisaged that the gilts be sold.

The portfolio manager takes the following action:

On February 15, 20 Long Gilt futures contracts are shorted (sold) in the nearby contract month of June at 91.16.

Cash market position – now	Futures position – now
£1m gilts at 110.00 = £1,100,000 market value	Sell 20 long gilt futures at 91-16 ($91^{16}/_{32}$) (= £915,000)

During the time that the futures and cash market positions have been held interest rates rise to give the following when the futures position is off-set.

Cash market position – later (June 12)	Futures position – later (June 12)
Market value falls to 105.00 = £1,050,000 Loss = £50,000	Buy 20 Long Gilt futures at 87-27 ($87^{27}/_{32}$) (= £878,437.50) Gain = £36,562.50

Alternatively the futures position can be evaluated in terms of tick. Entry price was 91.16 and the position was closed out at 87.27. This is a 117 tick change (remember, price is £$\frac{1}{32}$).

$117 \times £15.625 \times = £36,562.50$
ticks $\times$ tick value $\times$ no. of contracts

Of course in reality each day price changes in the futures market would be marked to market and the net gain of £36,562.50 would be received over the period of time that the futures position was in place in one tick increments through variation margin receipts to the equity account. Due to the timing of these payments the true gain may be slightly different, due to the time value of money and the possibility that variation payments at some stage may have been necessary, even though the eventual outcome was a gain.

It can be seen from the above calculations that all the loss in the cash market is not fully compensated by the gain in the futures market. This is because an **unweighted hedge** has been used.

A weighted long hedge (US T-bond) using conversion factor

A long hedge involves buying a future to hedge the purchase of a commodity (this example US T-bond) at a later date. A long hedge is often called an **anticipatory hedge**. A worked example of a weighted long hedge follows using a conversion factor taken from CBOT publication no. 765.

Imagine US T-bonds are going to be purchased one month later with a coupon of 15% and maturity in 20 years, total nominal value $5m, currently trading at par value. Conversion factor is 1.6927.

Edited US T-bond contract highlights are as below:

Trading unit	One US Treasury bond having a face value of $100,000 or multiple thereof
Deliverable grades	US Treasury bonds that, if callable, are not callable for at least 15 years and, if not callable, have a maturity of at least 15 years. The invoice price equals the futures settlement price times a conversion factor plus accrued interest. The conversion factor bond ($ par value) to yield 8%
Price quote	Points ($1,000) and thirty-seconds of a point; for example, 80-16 equals $80\frac{16}{32}$
Tick size	1/32 of a point ($31.25/contract); par is on the basis of 100 points
Contract months	Mar, Jun, Sep, Dec
Last trading day	Seventh business day preceding the last day of the delivery month
Last delivery day	Last business day of the delivery month

With a conversion factor of 1.6927, the number of contracts therefore needed is:

$5m divided by $100,000 times 1.6927 = 84.64, rounds to 85

Cash market now	Future market now
Plan to buy 50 par value T-bonds totalling $5m later	Buy 85 T-bond contracts at 63–16 (= $5,397,500)

Cash market later	Future market later
Buy 50 T-bond at 110.00 =$5.5m Loss = $500,000	Sell 85 T-bond contracts at 69.26 (= $5,934,062.50) Gain = $536,562.50

Thus the cash market loss is more than off-set by the gain in the futures market by use of a weighted hedge. However, this outcome does point to a danger in that it does not meet the hedging requirement that cash loss/gains are balanced by futures gains/losses. If the net outcome is a gain, in different circumstances a net loss might occur. A net loss would have been incurred had an unweighted hedge of 50 contracts been used instead.

Weighted and unweighted hedges

A hedge needs to be weighted when the cash market instrument and the instrument to which the futures contract refers differ in any way. We have already come across this when dealing with short-term interest rate contracts (p. 98). Weighting is especially important when dealing with any futures contract which allows a basket of bonds to be delivered into the contract, where necessarily each deliverable bond will have different price characteristics.

The LIFFE short-term interest rate future almost exactly matches the cash market instrument to which it applies. This contract relates to three-month sterling LIBOR-based deposits so that a hedge covering £50m requires

$$\frac{£50m}{£500,000} = 100 \text{ contracts}$$

(even this can be qualified slightly as is done so later in the text.)

In the worked example on pp. 108–9, there has been a greater decline in the value of the gilts in the cash market than the decline in the futures price, and therefore gain, in the futures market. This is because an **unweighted hedge** has been used whereby the nominal value of the gilts has been hedged in the futures market. The outcome of the hedge could be improved by altering the number of futures contracts used, i.e. **weight** the hedge.

In the unweighted example (pp. 108–9), the number of the futures contracts used was calculated as:

$$\text{number of futures contracts} = \frac{\text{nominal value of bonds}}{\text{unit of futures trading}}$$

$$= \frac{£1,000,000}{£50,000} = 20$$

Short weighted hedge – price factor

One of the ways in which a hedge can be weighted is in the following manner using the price conversion factor applicable to the bond which is intended to be hedged – in this case UK Treasury Stock 10.00%, 2003, price factor 1.0654428 (price factor given by reference to LIFFE tables).

Weighted hedge:

Number of futures contracts

$$= \frac{\text{nominal value of bonds}}{\text{unit of futures trading}} \times \text{price conversion factor}$$

$$= \frac{£1,000,000}{£50,000} \times 1.0654428 = 21.31$$

As 21.31 futures contracts obviously cannot be held, the number of contracts used is rounded to the nearest whole number, 21 in this case.

Reworking the earlier example (pp. 108–9) as a weighted hedge gives the following, improved result:

Feb 15

Cash market position	Futures position
£1m gilts at 110.00	Sell 21 long gilt futures at 91–16
= £1,100,000 market value	(= £960,750)

June 12

Cash market position	Futures position
Market value falls to	Buy 21 long gilt futures at 87–27
105.00 = £1,050,000	(= £922,359.37)
Loss = £50,000	Gain = £38,390.63

Comparing this result with the unweighted hedge shows that compensation is much closer with the weighted example. When much larger sums of money are involved a much better result in relation to the hedge can be obtained because with large numbers the adjustment in the number of contracts used can be much closer to the ideal. In the above example, 0.30 has to be ignored in relation to 21 contracts. If 0.30 contracts has to be ignored in relation to say 100 contracts, then it can be appreciated that the hedge can be much closer to 100%.

The outcome of a hedge can be measured in percentage terms to give an idea of its 'perfection'. The hedge can be **evaluated** in the following manner:

$$\frac{\text{futures market gain (loss)}}{\text{cash market loss (gain)}} \times 100$$

The unweighted hedge in on pp. 108–9 gives an evaluation of:

$$\frac{£36,562.50}{£50,000} \times 100 = 73.1\%$$

whereas the weighted hedge here can be evaluated at:

$$\frac{£38,390.63}{£50,000} \times 100 = 76.8\%$$

The relationship between the total nominal value of the underlying commodity being hedged and the nominal value of the futures contract held is known as the **hedge ratio** or alternatively as the **cash–futures equivalency ratio or equivalency ratio (ER)**. In the unweighted hedge the ratio was 1.0, in the weighted example it was 1.05, i.e.

$$\frac{£1,050,000}{£1,000,000}$$

Weighted hedges – an alternative

An optimal hedge ratio can also be calculated by the following formula:

$$\frac{\text{standard deviation of change in cash market commodity over period}}{\text{standard deviation of change in futures price over period}} \times \begin{array}{l} \text{coefficient of correlation between change} \\ \text{in price of underlying commodity and change} \\ \text{in futures price over period} \end{array}$$

Clearly in order to obtain the necessary information to input into the formula, historical data has to be used. If both standard deviations are equal, as they will be if the futures price exactly mirrors the spot price, and the spot and futures prices always behave this way, then the coefficient of correlation between the two price changes will also equal 1.0, in which case the optimal hedge ratio will also equal 1.0.

However, if, by way of an example, the futures price 'always' changes twice as much as the spot price, then the optimal hedge ratio would become 0.5. If the 'always' condition does not hold, then the coefficient of correlation between the two prices becomes less than 1, and thereby alters the hedge ratio. These issues are all reflected in the concept of basis risk of course.

Clearly information on price conversion factors is more easily come by than information needed on standard deviations and correlation coefficients. However, price conversion factors only work when the underlying commodity being hedged and the futures contract commodity are identical (in the sense that all UK gilts are identical). Hedging UK gilts deliverable into the LIFFE Long Gilt contract is no problem, neither are gilts not deliverable. But, if the commodity being hedged is only a close approximation to that in the futures contract, here UK corporate sterling bonds, then price conversion may not be sufficiently accurate.

Nevertheless, the necessary rounding in each case to get whole futures contracts may well result in the same hedge ratios being achieved as being the nearest practical quantity. Further consideration of ERs is given in Chapter 13.

Choice of contract – asset and delivery month

If the underlying commodity differs from those available as the underlying commodities in futures contracts, clearly a contract has to be selected whereby the price of the future exhibits price behaviour which closely correlates with price behaviour of the asset being hedged. Here of course, the technique described in the previous section assists the effectiveness of any hedge and minimises the consequences of basis risk.

The choice of the delivery month is also a factor which influences basis risk and therefore the effectiveness of a hedge. It might be intuitively assumed that if the hedge needs to be lifted at the same time as expiration of the contract month, then contracts with that delivery month should be chosen. This is incorrect. Contracts with a later delivery month should be chosen, the reason being that futures prices are often quite erratic during the delivery month, mainly due to the delivery day option. The day when the hedge needs to be lifted for commercial reasons by way of off-set may well be a day when the futures price is less favourable.

An additional reason why a later delivery period should be chosen, especially if a long futures position is being held, is that during the delivery month the long is at risk of having to take delivery of the underlying asset from the few shorts who elect to make delivery. Such an occurrence can be inconvenient and involve additional costs.

Nevertheless, basis risk is greater the longer the time difference between the anticipated lifting of the hedge and the delivery month. A good working rule is therefore to choose a delivery month later, but closest to the anticipated lifting of the hedge.

Basis risk increases when the hedged commodity and the underlying commodity relating to the futures contract differ, as a result spot and futures prices do not exactly parallel one another. In turn this means that losses in one market are not exactly matched by gains in the other market unless adjustments are made to the number of futures contracts entered into.

If the LIFFE Long Gilt contract is taken as an example, in which the underlying commodity is a 9% notional gilt, it can be appreciated that a number of gilts are deliverable into this contract which do not have a 9% coupon. Maturities also differ.

From explanations in earlier sections concerning the effect of maturity and coupon relating to bond price volatility, it can be appreciated that all these issues mean that the price of the hedged commodity and the price of the chosen future will not parallel each other exactly, an element of basis risk will be present.

Summary

- Interest rate futures contracts are the most traded of all futures.
- Short-term interest rate futures are priced 100 minus the implied rate of interest to give a sell high/buy low principle. They are cash settled and if taken to expiration, compensation is paid or received in relation to the EDSP, actual delivery is not appropriate because the underlying relates to a deposit or borrowing which cannot be transferred by its nature.
- Long-term bond futures can be taken to delivery. Here the underlying is a basket of deliverable bonds. The futures price will track the CTD bond and a conversion factor system operates to adjust for prices of the different bonds which are delivered.
- Both short-term and long-term interest rate futures relate to bond prices, rather than interest rates, thus if you wish to hedge rises in interest rates or falls in bond prices, you short a future. If you wish to hedge falls in interest rates or rises in bond prices, you will go long in futures.
- Bond futures follow the convention in the cash bond markets whereby prices move in increments of $\frac{1}{32}$, thus 95.50 cannot be correct, it would mean $95\frac{50}{32}$, i.e. $96\frac{18}{32}$ or 96.18.
- Basis can be either negative or positive. Simple basis, or the basis, has two components, theoretical basis and value basis.
- Cost of carry for bond futures can be either positive or negative. It will be positive if the short-term rate to finance the holding of a bond is exceeded by the flow of coupon income on the bond. An implied repo rate (IRR) can be calculated which shows the short-term financing rate used to purchase the bond which is implied in the actual futures price. The IRR enables a further calculation to be made to determine whether the actual futures price is rich or cheap in relation to an individual's actual financing costs.
- Many hedges need to be weighted in relation to bonds because a number of bonds are deliverable into the basket. One simple way of weighting the hedge is to use the conversion factor. The perfection of a hedge can be evaluated in percentage terms.
- Due to the delivery option of the short in relation to most bond futures which creates price disturbance of the futures price in the month prior to expiration, it is usual practice to hedge using a contract for the following delivery period and close it out when required.
- In all circumstances the usual practice of the futures market is followed whereby close out, off-set is the norm. If you wish to hedge a cash market position you take an opposite position in futures, e.g. if you are long a bond and wish to sell it later, you go short the appropriate number of futures. Cash market losses will be compensated by futures market gains and vice versa.

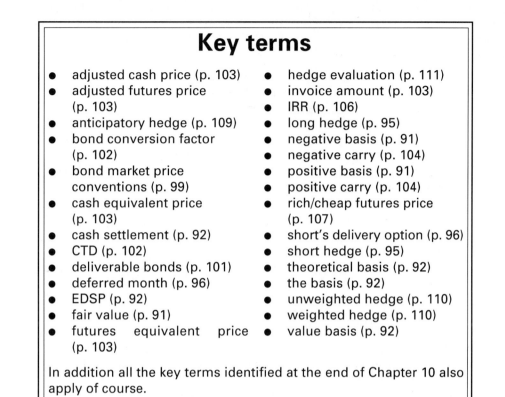

Key terms

- adjusted cash price (p. 103)
- adjusted futures price (p. 103)
- anticipatory hedge (p. 109)
- bond conversion factor (p. 102)
- bond market price conventions (p. 99)
- cash equivalent price (p. 103)
- cash settlement (p. 92)
- CTD (p. 102)
- deliverable bonds (p. 101)
- deferred month (p. 96)
- EDSP (p. 92)
- fair value (p. 91)
- futures equivalent price (p. 103)

- hedge evaluation (p. 111)
- invoice amount (p. 103)
- IRR (p. 106)
- long hedge (p. 95)
- negative basis (p. 91)
- negative carry (p. 104)
- positive basis (p. 91)
- positive carry (p. 104)
- rich/cheap futures price (p. 107)
- short's delivery option (p. 96)
- short hedge (p. 95)
- theoretical basis (p. 92)
- the basis (p. 92)
- unweighted hedge (p. 110)
- weighted hedge (p. 110)
- value basis (p. 92)

In addition all the key terms identified at the end of Chapter 10 also apply of course.

Questions

11.1 You are long one LIFFE Long Gilt future. Your entry price is 102.15, settlement price is 103.28. What is your variation margin payment or receipt?

11.2 What does CTD mean? What is its significance?

11.3 What does EDSP mean? How is it used?

11.4 When a futures contract is traded on the floor of an exchange it may be that: open interest increases, decreases or stays the same? Explain.

11.5 What is meant by a hedge ratio?

11.6 Consider a short hedger's position when basis weakens unexpectedly. Does the hedger's position improve or deteriorate?

11.7 A speculator in LIFFE Long Gilt futures conducts the following trades:

April 1	sells 15 June contracts
April 3	purchase 20 June contracts
April 5	sell 5 June contracts

If the following opening and settlement prices apply, mark the positions to market each day and calculate the net loss/gain over the period. Assume entry prices are at the opening price and close-outs are at settlement price.

	open	sett
April 1	92.37	92.35
2	92.35	92.58
3	92.58	92.44
4	92.44	92.17
5	92.17	92.02

11.8 If you are a corporate wishing to issue £ bonds at a later date what position would you take in the futures market? What kind of risk would you be subject to?

11.9 You hold a long position in a LIFFE Short Sterling contract. Interest rates rise, would you gain or lose from your futures position?

11.10 What does it mean if cost of carry for a Long Gilt future is negative? What is the relationship of the futures price to the price of gilts in the cash market if cost of carry is positive?

11.11 What is meant by IRR? How can it be used?

11.12 What is meant by the short's delivery option in relation to the LIFFE Long Gilt future? What implications does it have when placing hedges?

11.13 a) Explain the features of hedging translation exposure by means of the balance sheet [3]

b) What are the arguments against such a strategy? [8]

c) What is meant by a 'long hedge' and a 'short hedge' of interest rate exposures in financial futures? (A description of financial futures themselves is not required.) [9]

(CIOB Multinational Corporate Banking, Finance and Investment, October 1992.)

Further reading

Edwards, F. R. and Ma, C. W. (1992) *Futures and Options*, McGraw Hill.

Fabozzi, F. (1992) *Bond Markets*, 2nd edn, Prentice Hall.

Hull, John (1993) *Options, Futures and Other Derivative Securities*, 2nd edn, Prentice Hall.

Currency futures

Introduction

This chapter deals with the hedging of currency risk by the use of currency futures. It assumes a knowledge and understanding of basic futures market concepts as covered in Chapter 10, as well as material in Chapters 2–5.

Currency futures were first introduced in May 1972 when the Chicago Mercantile Exchange (CME) formed the International Money Market (IMM). It is only on this exchange that currency futures have enjoyed any real and lasting success. The IMM holds about 90% market share in the US of currency futures. The only other major exchange which trades currency contracts successfully is the Singapore Mercantile Exchange (SIMEX) which is a partner of the IMM. Together they jointly clear currency futures. Trading in Singapore occurs mainly when the IMM is closed at night. A Mutual Offset System (MOS) operates by which IMM firms can have trades executed on SIMEX and transferred back to the IMM as a new or liquidating trade. SIMEX firms have the same facility in relation to the IMM. This applies to currency futures in sterling, yen and deutschmarks only. Trading on LIFFE in currency futures was discontinued in all traded currencies during 1990 due to lack of demand. The Mid America Commodity Exchange (MidAm), affiliated to the CBOT, also trades currency futures.

IMM, SIMEX and MidAm trade the futures contracts against the US dollar as in Table 12.1.

A feature of the MidAm contracts is that the trading units are smaller than those on the IMM, giving rise to lower margin requirements and the ability to remain in a futures position more easily during times of adverse price movements – variation margin payments being smaller per contract. Fine tuning of the hedge is also more easily achieved in that the number of contracts closer to the ideal can be used.

Table 12.1 IMM, SIMEX and MidAm currency futures contracts against the US dollar

	MidAm unit of trading	tick	IMM/SIMEX unit of trading	tick
Pound Sterling	£12,50	$6.25	£62,500	$12.50
Canadian Dollar	CD50,000	$5.00	CD100,000	$10.00
Deutschmark	DM62,500	$6.25	DM125,000	$12.50
Japanese Yen	Y6,250,000	$6.25	Y12,500,000	$12.50
Swiss Franc	SF62,500	$6.25	SF125,000	$12.50
Australian Dollar	—	—	AD100,00	$10.00

In addition the IMM also trades a 'cross rate' future Deutschmark/Japanese Yen.

Currency futures – a definition

A currency future is a binding obligation to buy or sell a particular currency against another (usually the US$) at a designated rate of exchange on a specified later date. Like all futures contracts the only variable is the price, in this case the exchange rate.

Price quotes – currency futures

The quoted price is the US dollar price of one unit of the other currency e.g. £1 = $2 or DM1 = $0.65. All currency futures use this notation when written against the US$, regardless of the practice in the spot market. However, the DM/JY future quotes JY/DM, i.e. DM1 = JY. This is the opposite price notation. The DM/JY future has a trading unit of DM 125,000. Read this in conjunction with paragraph 2, p. 119

A typical newspaper quote would be as in Table 12.2 taken from the *Financial Times*, 23 June 1994 for 22 June.

Table 12.2 Sterling futures (IMM) £62,500 per £

	Open	Sett	Change	High	Low	Est. vol	Open int
Sep	1.5402	1.5304	–0.0126	1.5426	1.5260	10,411	39,621
Dec	1.5400	1.5286	–0.0124	1.5400	1.5240	268	513
Mar	—	1.5276	–0.0120	—	1.5230	1	17

Buying long and selling short

Buying long a currency future means you agree to buy the trading unit amount of the non-US$ currency for a stated amount of dollars (i.e. at an agreed exchange rate). For example, going long a sterling future at £1 = $2 means you agree to buy £62,500 for $125,000 at an agreed later date (IMM contract).

Going long – buy 'currency', sell US dollars.

Selling short a currency future means you agree to sell the trading unit of the non-US currency for a stated amount of dollars. For example, going short a Japanese Yen future at JPY100 = $0.9065 means you agree to sell JPY12,500,000 at a later date for $137,892.99.

Going short – sell 'currency', buy US dollars.

Note: when non-dollar 'cross rate' futures are used, e.g. DM/JY, the long will buy DMs and pay JY. The short delivers DMs and receives JY. Refer back to the section on price quotes (p. 118) to check you follow the difference in price notation for this contract.

If the exchange rate rises, the value of sterling rises relative to the US dollar. The long will always gain if the value of the underlying commodity rises, they will be able to buy at the lower, locked-in price. 'Currency' can be bought for fewer US dollars at a 'low' futures rate relative to spot.

If the exchange rate falls the value of sterling falls relative to the US$. A long is locked into the higher futures price relative to spot and will therefore lose.

- The short will profit if the exchange rate falls and will lose if it rises.
- The long will profit if the exchange rate rises and will lose if the exchange rate falls.

A short will always lose if the value in the spot market rises, they will be locked into selling at a 'low' price when higher prices are obtainable in the cash market. If the exchange rate rises then the value of sterling rises relative to the US dollar; however, the short will not be able to sell sterling at a higher spot rate and thus obtains fewer dollars than in the cash market and therefore loses from the short futures position. A small numerical example should illustrate giving the opposite case.

A short seller of one sterling IMM futures contract with a futures price of £1 = $2 is obligated to sell £62,500 for $125,000 at expiration. If the spot rate were to fall to £1 = $1.75 (i.e. the value of sterling falls relative to the dollar) then the short will still be able to sell at £1 = $2 and sell the £62,500 for $125,000. The dollar sum realised could then be sold at spot for £1 = 1.75 (ignoring any spread) for £71,428.57, giving a gain of £8,928.57.

As has now been seen many times, in reality the position will be closed out and variation margin receipts taken to set against the cash market position. Different permutations of long and short outcomes can be tried to verify the summary above.

From these conclusions it can be seen that a UK importer will take a short position, such a position gains when the exchange rate falls and a UK importer wants to hedge such falls. An importer would prefer the exchange rate to be high, more US dollars would be exchanged for every unit of sterling.

A UK exporter does not wish to see the exchange rate rise, a long position gains from a rise and will therefore be used.

Important – positions taken by exporters and importers are from a UK perspective or non-US perspective. US importers will take long positions, US exporters will take short positions.

US exporters will be in receipt of sterling (or to them other non-dollar currencies). They will wish to sell sterling for dollars and hedge this need via a short position where the obligation is to sell the sterling for dollars.

US importers will wish to buy sterling in exchange for dollars. A long position will put a hedge in place where the obligation is to buy sterling for dollars.

Remember:

- UK importers will use a short hedge.
- UK exporters will use a long hedge.

Cost of carry – currency futures

As with other futures contracts, currency futures prices relate to a cost of carry model. As a currency future approaches maturity the futures price and spot price converge as the cost of carry reduces and becomes zero at maturity.

A theoretical currency futures price will be the price at which a profitable cash and carry arbitrage does not exist, specifically it will be where a covered interest rate arbitrage is not profitable.

> A theoretical currency futures price is a function of the prevailing spot rate of exchange and relative interest rates between the two currencies concerned, for instance the relationship between US dollar and sterling interest rates.

The futures price minus the spot price is called the **swap** when a currency future is involved. Naturally the swap will tend towards zero as the contract approaches its delivery date.

Consider the following currency cash and carry covered interest arbitrage operation:

Today (time t) borrow US dollars for three months (time t, T).

Exchange the US dollars into sterling at spot.

Carry (deposit) the sterling sum for three months until time T.

At three months (time T) sell the sterling sum accrued with interest for US dollars at a rate locked into by a short futures position taken at time t.

(Remember, a short sells the non-US currency, buys US dollars.)

If the sum of money realised at time T in sterling gives a smaller or greater sum when exchanged for US dollars than is required to repay the US dollar borrowing, then the future has been 'incorrectly' priced and there is an arbitrage opportunity.

There now follows a worked numerical example of the cash and carry described.

IMM futures contract trading unit £62,500 used.

Today's spot (time t) £1 = $1.55.

Three-month sterling interest rate (time t, T) = 6.00% p.a.

Three-month US dollar interest rate (time t, T) = 4.00% p.a.

The sum necessary to realise £62,500 at time T at 6.00% p.a. is

$$\frac{£62,500}{1 + (0.06 \times 90/360)} = £61,576.35$$

The US dollar sum which has to be borrowed is therefore £61,576.35 × $1.55 = $95,443.34.

At time t $95,443.34 is borrowed for three months (time t, T) at 4.00%.

The sum owing at time T will be: $95,443.34 × (1 + 0.04 × 90/360) = $96,397.77.

At time t, a short futures position obligating the sale of £62,500 at time T for a given number of US dollars is also taken.

At time T £62,500 is sold for US dollars as per the futures contract.

If the future has been 'correctly' priced the US dollar sum realised should be $96,397.77, i.e. that necessary to repay the borrowing. The futures price therefore should be: $96,397.97/£62,500, i.e. £1 = $1.5424.

If the future is incorrectly priced at, for example, £1 = $1.50 (as opposed to £1 = $1.5424), then the US$ cost of £62,500 at time T would be $93,750.

This sum is insufficient to meet the US dollar liability of $96,397.97. As a result of this mispricing, an arbitrage could be undertaken to realise an arbitrage profit. It would work as follows:

At time t borrow £61,576.35 for three months (t, T) at 6.00% p.a.

At time T repayment including interest will be £62,500.

At time t take a long futures position to buy £62,500 (sell US dollars) at time T at £1 = $1.50.

At time t take the borrowed £61,576.35 and exchange at spot £1 = $1.55 for $95,443.34.

At time t deposit $95,443.34 for three months (time t, T) at 4.00% p.a.

At time T this will be $95,443.34 × (1 + 0.04 × 90/360) = $954.43, giving $96,397.77.

At time T exchange $96,397.77 for sterling at the futures rate of £1 = $1.50. This will realise $96,397.77/$1.50 = £64,265.18.

At time T the borrowed sterling (£62,500) has to be repaid.

As £64,265.18 is now available to do this an arbitrage profit has been made of £1765.18.

If the future were incorrectly priced above its theoretical price, then again an arbitrage could be undertaken to realise a profit.

Suppose the future is priced at £1 = $1.60 (as opposed to £1 = $1.5424).

At time t borrow US dollars for three months (t, T) at 4.00% p.a.

The sum should be sufficient to realise £62,500 at time T at 6.00% p.a.

The necessary sterling sum is:

$$\frac{£62,500}{1 + 0.06 \times 90/360} = £61,576.35$$

The US dollar sum which should be borrowed is: £61,576.35 × $1.55 = $95,443.94.

The US dollar sum owed at time T will be: $95,443.94 × (1 + 0.04 × 90/360) = $96,397.77.

At time t a short futures position is taken to sell £62,500 at time T at £1 = $1.60.

At time T £62,500 is sold for US dollars at £1 = $1.60 giving $100,000, $3602.23 more than needed to repay the $96,397.77 borrowed, representing the arbitrage profit.

All the above worked examples ignore transactions costs and interest rate and exchange rate spreads.

Currency futures and interest rate parity

The interest rate parity (IRP) theory states that a currency futures price, i.e. exchange rate, must differ from the prevailing spot rate by an amount which reflects the interest rate differential between the two currencies concerned, this being the swap. In the worked examples above the currencies would be US dollars and sterling.

In most instances market imperfections or restrictions ensure that IRP conditions do not totally explain currency futures prices.

Using the notation of t and T and in addition:

F_{tT} = futures price covering period between t and T
S_t = spot at time t
R^{US} = US dollar annual rate of interest (base currency)
R^{FC} = currency, i.e. non-US dollar rate of interest (underlying currency)
FC = 'foreign', i.e. non-US dollar currency (underlying)
$ = US dollars

then:

$$F_{tT}(\$/FC) = S_t(\$/FC) \times \frac{(1 + R^{US} \times T - t/360)}{(1 + R^{FC} \times T - t/360)}$$

Plugging in the numbers used in the illustration in the previous section gives:

$$\text{futures price} = \$1.55 \times \frac{1+(0.04 \times 90/360)}{1+(0.06 \times 90/360)}$$

$$= 1.55 \times \frac{1.01}{1.015}$$

$$= 1.524$$

Clearly this illustrates that via the formula we get the same result we obtained when we went through the process step by step in the previous section.

Caution: it is wise to be clear that we talk about the futures price and then quote a rate. When we talk about the futures price being too high/too low relative to its theoretical price, be sure that you understand we are referring to the rate being too high/too low.

It will be useful to remember that in our formula, for certain currencies (e.g. sterling), the interest rate basis is actual/365 and for others actual/360 (e.g. US dollars) rather than the 90/360 we have used. This has also been ignored in the step by step examples. Suitable adjustments should therefore be made in practice.

An alternative to the formula used is:

$$F_{tT}(\$/FC) = S_t(\$/FC) \times [1+(R^{US} - R^{FC}) \times (T - t/360)]$$

This will be less accurate when for one of the currencies a 360-day year is not applicable.

Both formulae show that a theoretical futures price is a function of the current spot and relative interest rates of the currencies concerned.

Calculating the swap

We have already seen that the currency futures price minus the prevailing spot is called the swap. If you wish to calculate the swap, as opposed to the futures price directly, the following formula can be used for currencies against the dollar:

swap =
spot rate × (dollar interest rate – currency interest rate) × days to delivery/360

For sterling against the dollar 365 days would be used.

Implied repo rate – currency futures

Another way to decide whether an arbitrage is possible for an individual is via the concept of implied repo rate (IRR) (pp. 106, 107). If an IRR is calculated and it is higher than your own cost of borrowing, then a covered interest rate arbitrage is possible.

Using the same rates as before:

spot = £1 = $1.55
futures price = £1 = $1.5424
US$ three-month interest rate = 4.00% p.a.
Sterling three-month interest rate = 6.00% p.a.

$$IRR = \frac{360(F_{tT}) - 360(S_t) + F_{tT}(T-t)(R^{FC})}{(T-t)(S_t)}$$

$$= \frac{(360 \times 1.5424) - (360 \times 1.55) + (1.5424 \times 90 \times 0.06)}{90 \times 1.55}$$

$$= \frac{555.264 - 558 + 8.32896}{139.5}$$

$$= 0.400929 = 4.00929\% \text{ p.a.}$$

If it is possible to borrow US dollars at an annual rate of less than 4.00929% p.a., ignoring transactions costs, an arbitrage opportunity exists.

Our answer here illustrates that the future is correctly priced in that 1.5424 is indeed correct. Different futures prices would give a different IRR. Using the figures we have we would expect the IRR to be 4.00% p.a., it is only compounding errors in the calculation on p. 121 which ensure small differences in the expected answer.

The IRR can also be worked from the point of view of a given US$ rate and then see if sterling can be borrowed at below the IRR cost. To calculate the sterling IRR the formula can be rewritten:

$$IRR = \frac{360(S_t) - 360(F_{tT}) + F_{tT}(T-t)(R^{US})}{(T-t)(S_t)}$$

Inserting the relevant figures this gives an IRR for sterling of 5.94167% p.a.

A short hedge

UK importers will go short in the currency futures market to hedge exchange risk. UK importers will need to pay away non-sterling at a later date, therefore they need to sell sterling and buy foreign currency.

Most currency futures are written against the US dollar, i.e. the US dollar is the base currency, therefore going short, selling a future, creates an obligation to sell a non-dollar currency (for a UK importer it will be sterling) in exchange for US dollars.

Two futures contracts can be used to hedge sterling against currencies other than the US dollar by creating a synthetic currency future.

Example Suppose a UK importer has to make a payment of $1m in three months' time (September) and wishes to hedge against the consequences of a change in value of the US$ against sterling using the IMM contract.

Taking the rates used earlier (p. 121) spot today, £1 = $1.55.

Futures price £1 = $1.5424 for a three-month contract.

On the final day of the contract an off-setting position will be taken and dollars purchased in the spot market. Any gains/losses in the spot market will be hedged by losses/gains in the futures market.

Each contract is for £62,500.

$$£62,500 \times \$1.5424 = \$96,400$$

$1,000,000/$96,400 = 10.37 contracts, 10 contracts will therefore be shorted.

Cash market	Futures market
June	
Spot = $1.55 $1m = £645,161.29	Sell 10 September sterling futures at $1.5424 × £62,500 × 10 = $964,000
September	
Spot = $1.52 Purchase $1m = £657,894.73	Buy 10 Sept sterling futures at $1.52 = $950,000
Spot market loss	**Futures market gain**
£12,733.44	$14,000 at $1.52 = £9,210.52

Hedge evaluation:

£9,210.52/£12,733.44 = 72.3%

It is instructive to compare this outcome with the use of a forward contract, which can be used for the exact amount of $1m of course.

Example   Using the interest rates of $ = 4.00% and £ = 6.00% as before, the three-month forward rate will be as follows (refer to pp. 33–5):
Borrow sterling at 6.00% p.a. for $T - t$, spot = $1.55.
Hold US dollars realised on deposit at 4.00% p.a. for $T - t$ to realise $1m.

$1,000,000/(1 + 0.04 ×90/360) = $990,099
$990,099/$1.55 = £638,773.54
£638,773.54 at 6.00% p.a. for $T - t$ =
£638,773.54 ×(1 + 0.06 × 90/360) = £648,355.14
$990,099/£648,355.14 = £1 = $1.5271

£1 = $1.5271 is the effective forward rate.
$1m at $1.5271, sterling cost = £654,835.96.

Compare this with a futures hedge:

spot cost	£657,894.73
less futures gain	£9,210.52
	£648,684.21

Transactions costs need to be added to this figure for a fair comparison (no such commissions using a forward contract – it's all captured in the rate).

10 contracts, commission = £22 per round turn per contract
(Source: Lind–Waldock & Company.)

£22 × 10 = £220, add to cost, total = £648,904.21, representing a saving compared with a forward contract of £5,931.75.

A long hedge

UK exporters will need to sell currency, the proceeds of their sale, at a later date in exchange for sterling. They will therefore buy sterling, requiring a long hedge. A US dollar/sterling IMM futures contract will be used to illustrate.

May 21 spot is £1 = $1.5410–1.5420.
At close of business on the IMM the settlement rate for the September sterling future is $1.5318. It is anticipated that $2m will be received by the exporter July 1, when an off-setting position will be taken.
Contracts needed:

£62,500 × $1.5318 = $95,737.50
$2,000,000/$95,737.50 = 20.89

i.e. 21 contracts needed.

Cash market	Futures market
May 21	
Spot $1.5420 $2m = £1,297,016.80	Buy 21 September sterling futures at $1.5318 £62,500 × 21 = £1,312,500 = $2,010,487.50
July 1	
Sell $2m, buy sterling at spot £1 = $1.5045 Realises £1,329,345.20	Sell 21 September sterling futures at $1 = $1.5056 = £62,500 × 21 = $1,976,100
Net cash market gain	**Futures market loss**
= £32,328.44	at $1.5056 = £22,839.73

Hedge evaluation:

£22,839.73 ÷ £32,328.40 = 70.6%

Compare this with using, for instance, a 1/2-month forward contract.
Forward rate = $1.5420–0.72 c pm = $1.5348.
$2m at $1.5348 = £1,303,101.38.
Futures hedge

spot cost	£1,329,345.20
futures loss	22,839.73
net proceeds	£1,306,505.57

Even when taking transactions cost (estimated £462) into account, the futures hedge is clearly much better in this instance.

Summary

- Volumes in currency futures are not so large as those for interest rates. Currency futures are traded principally at IMM/CME.
- Most currency futures trade an underlying currency against the US dollar, but cross currency contracts like the DEM/JPY are becoming more popular. US dollar contracts are priced as one unit of the underlying against a given number of units of the US dollar, e.g. £1 = $2, regardless of the spot market convention. Cross rate futures quote the opposite way, the DM/JY future quotes JY/DM, where deutschmarks are the underlying.
- Going long you buy the underlying, sell US dollars.
- Going short you sell the underlying, buy US dollars.
- Longs profit when the exchange rate rises, lose when it falls.
- Shorts profit when the exchange rate falls, lose when it rises.
- A UK importer will take a short futures position.
- A UK exporter will take a long futures position.
- The IRR theory states that a currency futures price is a function of the prevailing spot and the interest rate differential of the currencies concerned. Futures price minus the spot is called the swap instead of basis.

Key terms

- implied repo rate (p. 123)
- interest rate parity (p. 122)
- mutual offset system (MOS) (p. 117)
- the swap (p. 120)

Questions

12.1   What is MOS in relation to the IMM and SIMEX?

12.2   What is said to be the advantage MidAm contracts have over those at IMM and SIMEX?

12.3   When the contract relates to US dollars and another currency, which is the underlying?

12.4   What are the price quote conventions for US dollars futures and cross currency futures?

12.5   If the exchange rate falls from £1 = $1.80 to £1 = $1.70 will a short profit or lose?

12.6   Will a UK exporter with US dollar receivables go long or short to hedge?

12.7   What is meant by the swap in the futures market?

12.8   What does the IRR theory state?

12.9   If your own cost of borrowing is higher than the IRR, what can you do to realise an arbitrage profit?

12.10 If Yen interest rates exceed US Dollar interest rates which statement(s) about currency futures is true and why?

    (a)   Yen futures trade at successively higher levels in successively distant months.

    (b)   Yen futures trade at successively lower levels in successively distant months.

    (c)   The discount of futures to spot decreases as maturity approaches.

    (d)   Yen are overpriced relative to US Dollars.

        (Securities Institute, Financial Futures and Options, July 1993.)

Further reading

Sutton, William (1990) *The Currency Options Handbook*, 2nd edn, Woodhead Faulkner.

13 Advanced futures concepts

Introduction

In the previous chapters we have seen in outline the use of futures to hedge interest and currency risk, building upon basic principles and material covered in Chapter 10. In this chapter we shall be looking at more advanced matters which cover situations which cannot be fully and effectively hedged without additional techniques. In particular we shall look at ways of weighting hedges that were not covered in Chapter 11 and at ways of hedging a cash market position when there is no exact matching futures contract. Income enhancement techniques which involve 'trading' futures will also be covered, but it should be noted that these involve taking a view of cash market prices at a later date. Hedging of course is a technique for managing the consequences of such unpredictable price movements. Trading and hedging can thus be viewed as opposites. Trading creates magnified overall gains or losses, the aim of hedging is to produce overall neutral positions – neither gains nor losses.

Equivalency/hedge ratio, further considerations

The issue of hedge weighting has already been addressed (pp. 97–8). Further consideration is now given to this matter. If cash market and futures market price changes exactly mirror each other, giving a hedge ratio of 100%, a perfect hedge could be achieved using futures. In practice prices do not mirror each other exactly and that they do not is of course known as basis risk. Somehow basis risk has to be managed and is achieved by the use of a **cash–futures equivalency ratio**, also known as a hedge ratio.

This **equivalency ratio (ER)** gives the number of futures contracts required to off-set price changes in the cash market. Adjustments to the number of futures contracts required is very important to perfect a hedge where the underlying instrument deliverable into the futures contract is only similar, and not an exact match, to the cash market instrument held.

Even, for example, when the LIFFE Long Gilt contract is considered, there will not be an exact price change match between the cash and futures markets, even when the gilt held has a 9% coupon with maturity between 10 and 15 years, i.e. is deliverable into the contract. The reason is that the futures price tracks the cheapest to deliver and the gilt held may not be the CTD, even if it is, there may still not be a 100% correlation between cash and futures price changes due to changes in yield.

If there is a 100% perfect hedge, whereby changes in the cash market are perfectly off-set in the futures market then it follows:

change in cash price = change in futures price

In practice there will be some variance between changes and the object is to minimise this. The fact that cash and futures price sensitivities do not correlate 100% means that an equivalency ratio (ER) has to be used to minimise the effects of the variance upon the hedge.

Thus in reality:

change in cash price = change in futures price × ER

ERs work as follows: if the cash instrument has a price volatility, twice that of the future for example, then the ER becomes 2:

20% change in cash price = 10% change in futures price × 2

It should be self-evident that if cash market prices change by twice as much as the futures price, then it will require two futures contracts for every cash market unit for a 100% effective hedge. Losses/gains on one futures contract will only be half those experienced in the cash market, therefore two futures contracts will be needed to match cash losses/gains.

For example:

You are hedging the purchase at a later date of a cash market instrument, current spot = £50,000.

Spot price rises 10% over the period of the hedge to £55,000, giving a cash market loss of £5,000.

If one futures contract were used to hedge this position whose price sensitivity were half that of the cash instrument, then the futures position would only gain £2,500 in value over the period of the hedge. Thus two contracts would be needed to provide £5,000 compensation for the cash market loss.

ERs are sensitive to time and price levels. As time changes and a futures contract approaches maturity, then futures and cash prices converge. The variance between cash and futures prices also changes as the cash price level changes. This means that the ER must be adjusted as time and price change.

There are various ways in which an ER can be determined and they are covered in the following sections (one method, conversion factors for bond futures, has already been used (pp. 109, 110)).

As a result of basis risk, to perfect a hedge, the number of futures contracts has to be chosen carefully and in many instances the actual futures contract has to be carefully chosen when there is no exact match between the futures underlying instrument and the cash market. For example, bank CDs held or to be issued in the cash market cannot be directly hedged by a bank CD futures contract, there isn't one, although such contracts have existed in the past. A futures contract must therefore be selected whose price behaviour closely correlates with the price behaviour of the CDs. If a suitable futures contract is not found with this characteristic, then basis risk is greater. Other derivatives traded over the counter, whilst they may not exhibit such basis risk, do in fact come with a high premium cost to cover the issuer for taking and managing the risk.

Conversion factor weighting

Examples of using CF weighting to hedge UK gilts were given earlier (pp. 109, 110). Such a method does not lead to a futures position which exactly matches changes in the cash market. The futures price will track the CTD and the CF is adjusting for the volatility of the actual instrument held, as a result there will be basis risk.

Other, more accurate, ways of matching futures and cash price sensitivity can be used. They are:

- basis point value (BPV)
- duration
- convexity
- standard deviations related to coefficients of price correlation (p. 112).

Bonds and duration

Duration is often described as a way of comparing apples with oranges. Duration enables a comparison to be made between different bonds in relation to price sensitivity to interest rate changes. It is a technique which with a single number captures the price sensitivity of a fixed coupon bond following interest rate changes. A high number, a high duration, means high price sensitivity and vice versa. Formally duration measures the proportionate change in price of a bond following a small proportionate change in yield.

A bond with a duration of, for instance, 6.25 means that, for a one basis point change in yield of the bond, its price will change 0.0625%. Thus if the nominal value of a bond were £105, then a one basis point change in yield would alter the price by:

$$£105 \times 0.0625\% = £0.065$$

The duration of a bond is calculated by way of a formula whose derivation is not discussed here. Duration can be ascertained as part of the futures price quotation process from traders or can be found by the use of suitable programmed calculators or software packages. However for those who wish to see, the formula is:

Macaulay duration

$$\frac{\displaystyle\sum_{t=1}^{D=M} \frac{tC_t}{(1+r)^t}}{\displaystyle\sum_{t=1}^{m} \frac{C_t}{(1+r)^t}}$$

t = time until receipt of each cash flow
C = cash flow
$\dfrac{C_t}{(1+r)}$ = present value of cash flow

Duration price sensitivity is affected by the following factors (remember – the higher the duration, the higher the price sensitivity):

1. Maturity – as maturity increases, duration increases;
2. Coupon – the lower the coupon, the higher the duration;
3. Coupon frequency – the more often a coupon payment is made per year, the lower is the duration;
4. Yield – as yield increases duration decreases.

Clearly items 1–4 could pull duration in opposing directions, the calculation gives a net outcome, enabling dissimilar bonds to be compared with respect to price sensitivity.

The concept of duration can be easily understood by reference to Figures 13.1 and 13.2.

The shaded areas represent the present values of the coupon payments and the principal at maturity. Duration is at the point of balance where

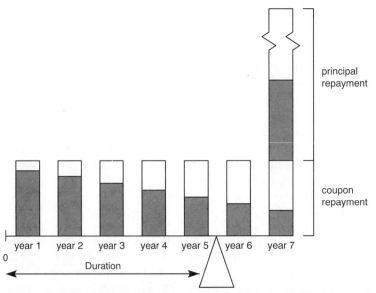

Source: CBOT, Understanding Duration and Convexity Handbook of Fixed Income Securities, quoting Handbook of Fixed Income Securities, Fabozzi & Pollack.

Figure 13.1 *Cash flows and present values of a 7-year bond.*

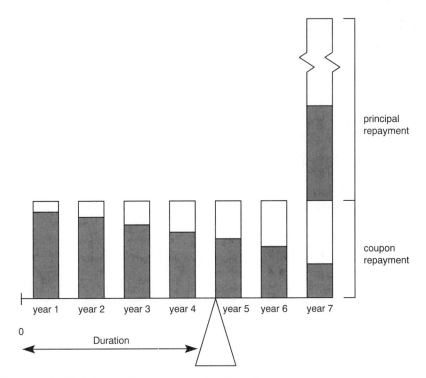

Figure 13.2 *Cash flows and present values of a 14-year bond.*

net present value to the left of the duration point equals net present value to the right of the duration point (imagine a see-saw in balance). It is the weighted value of all the cash flows appropriate to a bond.

Duration can be used to weight hedges because it is a measure of interest rate/bond price sensitivity. It is also a concept which can be used as a way of enhancing portfolio value by the use of futures to alter duration effectively of a portfolio, without direct use of the cash market.

Bonds and BPV

Basis point value (BPV) is the price change of a bond following a one basis point (0.01%) change in the yield of that bond. As an example, if the yield on a bond changes from 10.00% to 10.01%, i.e. a one basis point change, and the price of the bond were then to change £50, £50 would be that bond's BPV at that particular yield level and maturity. BPV changes as yield and time to maturity change. This can be seen from the formulas below – duration and yield being the variables.

BPV is calculated using the following formula (based on Macaulay duration and yield to maturity):

$$\text{BPV} = \frac{\text{Duration}}{(1 + \text{yield}/2)} \times \text{bond value} \times 0.001$$

A BPV for a portfolio of bonds can also be determined by taking the sum of the weighted BPV for each bond in the portfolio.

Weighting the hedge with BPV

To determine the ER/hedge ratio using BPV the following calculation must be undertaken:

$$ER = \frac{BPV \text{ of cash instrument}}{BPV \text{ of futures contract}}$$

That this is so can be seen from the identities described earlier (pp. 129–31).

change in cash price = change in futures price × ER

ER therefore must equal:

$$\frac{\text{change in cash price}}{\text{change in futures price}}$$

The value of the cash position and the futures position will change according to their BPVs, therefore BPV can be substituted for price changes giving the original identity of

$$ER = \frac{BPV \text{ of cash instrument}}{BPV \text{ of futures contract}}$$

The question naturally arises: how do you determine the BPV of a futures contract? You calculate the BPV of the cheapest to deliver (CTD) instrument and then adjust by its conversion factor:

BPV of futures contract = BPV of CTD/CF

The BPV of the cash portfolio must be used with the BPV of one futures contract. The formula therefore becomes:

$$ER = \frac{BPV \text{ of cash portfolio}}{BPV \text{ of futures contract}}$$

To determine the ER necessary to hedge a bond portfolio, look at the following example:

UK gilt portfolio 10 × £50,000, BPV per gilt £50

CTD gilt BPV £45, CF 1.25

BPV of gilt portfolio = £50 × 10 = £500

BPV of futures contract = £45 /1.25 = £36

ER = £500/£36 = 13.89

i.e. 14 contracts should be used to hedge the portfolio.

Another formulation often used would rearrange the same figures as:

$$\frac{£500,000}{£50,000} \times \frac{£50}{£45} \times 1.25 = 13.89$$

$$\frac{\text{i.e. value of portfolio}}{\text{nominal value of future}} \times \frac{BPV \text{ per gilt}}{BPV \text{ future}} \times CF$$

Note that an unweighted hedge would require 10 contracts to be used.

Further note that using BPV and duration allows an ER to be determined with any accuracy only when small changes in yield are used. Inaccuracy will creep in when larger changes are experienced. This is due to **convexity** which is dealt with below.

ER and duration

The concept of duration can be used to determine the ER/hedge ratio necessary to hedge a cash market position or anticipated position.

Changes in bond futures prices approximate to:

$$\frac{\text{change in price of CTD bond in cash market}}{\text{conversion factor (CF) of CTD bond}}$$

Therefore if a bond which is not the cheapest to deliver is being hedged, then adjustments must be made. The hedge ratio becomes:

$$\frac{\text{change in price of actual cash market bond to be hedged}}{\text{change in price of CTD bond}} \times CF$$

If a hedge ratio is to be determined using duration to hedge the actual cash market bond, it follows that:

- The CTD bond must be identified
- You must determine, for a given change in yield, how much the price of the CTD bond and the actual bond will change.

In order to determine the latter, the duration of each bond must be known. When this has been determined, then the relevant figures can be inserted into the following formula. Items above the line refer to the actual bond being hedged, those below to the CTD bond.

$$ER = \frac{\text{bond duration} \times \text{bond price} \times (1 + \text{yield to maturity}) \times \text{change in yield}}{\text{bond duration} \times \text{bond price} \times (1 + \text{yield to maturity}) \times \text{change in yield}} \times CF$$

If it is assumed that the change in yields on both bonds is the same then they can be deleted from the formula as they will cancel each other out. It should be realised that this is achieving, by a different route, a weighting as given by the BPV method. Remember BPV is calculated as:

$$BPV = \frac{\text{duration}}{(1 + \text{yield} / 2)} \times \text{bond value} \times 0.0001$$

Convexity and ERs

Duration and convexity can be used to determine the expected change in the price of a bond due to a change in yield. Duration gives a percentage change in price, BPV gives a monetary value change for every basis point change, i.e. basis point value.

The approximate change in price following a yield change is:

(modified) duration × yield change (in percentage points)

The change in price in percentage points is only approximate due to the principle of convexity. The above formula using duration works well enough for small changes in yield only. When yield changes are large, price changes are too small when interest rates increase and too large when they fall, if price changes are calculated using the above formula.

We will not be calculating convexity here, in any case it can be calculated in various ways – take convexity as given. However, it may be useful to look briefly at outcomes and consequences for ERs. Figure 13.3 shows a price/yield relationship of a given bond, it can be seen to be convex.

Duration only captures price changes as if they were a straight line at a tangent to it. For every small yield change, price errors can be seen to be very small, but when there is a large yield change, a large error creeps in, as illustrated in Figures 13.3 and 13.4.

Relatively small yield changes from y_1 to y_2, little difference between movement along the convex curve and movement along the straight line which represents changes in price as suggested by measures of duration.

A large change in yield from y_2 to y_3 shows an error in price change. To incorporate percentage price changes due to convexity into the ER, use the following formula:

$$\tfrac{1}{2} \times \text{convexity} \times (\text{percentage point yield change})^2$$

Yield change from 8% to 10% is written as 0.02 in the formula.

The answer given by this formula is added to the percentage change in price as given by duration to give a true percentage change in price (following a given percentage change in yield).

A complete formula to determine an ER using convexity would be as follows:

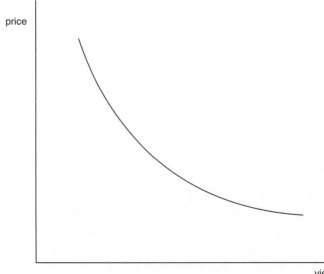

Figure 13.3 *Price/yield relationship of a given bond – convex.*

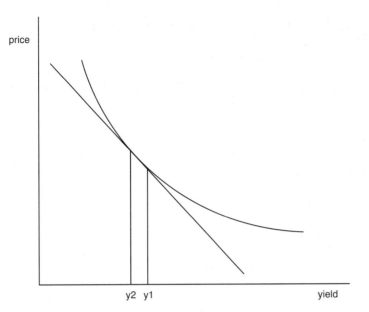

Figure 13.4 *Duration – smalll yield change, small price error.*

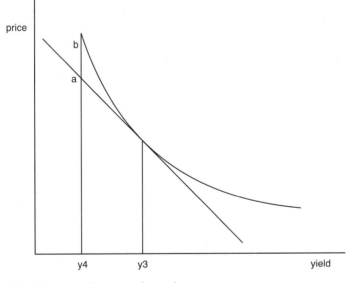

Figure 13.5 *Duration – large price change, large price error.*

$$ER = \frac{CF \times \text{bond duration} \times \text{bond price} \times (1 + \text{yield to maturity}) \times [^{1}/_{2} \times \text{convexity} \times (\text{percentage point yield change})^{2}]}{\text{bond duration} \times \text{bond price} \times (1 + \text{yield to maturity}) \times [^{1}/_{2} \times \text{convexity} \times (\text{percentage point yield change})^{2}]}$$

CF of course is the conversion factor of the relevant bond.

Note that a convex price/yield relationship exists for non-callable bonds, i.e. those with a fixed maturity.

Contract strips

Interest rate exposure may well run over a period of time equal to a number of contract periods. Such risk may be hedged by using a **contract strip**. By way of illustration, see the following example:

On March 17 there is an identified need to borrow £1m in three months' time for a period of six months. At March 17 three-month LIBOR is 6% p.a.

```
├──────────────┼──────────────┼──────────────┤
March 17      June 16        Sept 15       Dec 22

               ├──────────────────────────────┤
               need to hedge borrowing
               of £1m this time period
```

Use the LIFFE Short Sterling contract (nominal £500,000) to hedge. Contract matures third Wednesday of each delivery month – March, June, September and December.

Sell two June short sterling contracts at the beginning of the contract period March 17, expiration June 16 – price 94.56.

Sell two September short sterling contracts March 17, expiration September 15 – price 94.75.

Target borrowing rate as given by futures prices on March 17 =

$$(1 + 5.44/4) \times (1 + 5.25/4)$$
$$2.36 \times 2.3125 = 5.4575\% \text{ p.a.}$$

On June 16, three-month LIBOR is 5.875% p.a. and six-month LIBOR is 6.00% p.a.

If the June contract is taken to expiration it will be settled at an EDSP of 94.125.

The September contract on June 16 is closed out (bought) at 94.11.

On June 16 £1m is actually borrowed in the cash market at six-month LIBOR 6.00% p.a.

Outcome:

March 17   sell 2 June futures at 94.56
                   sell 2 Sept futures at 94.75

June 16   settle 2 June futures at EDSP 94.125
                   buy 2 Sept futures at 94.11

Profit June 94.56 – 94.125 = 0.435%.

Profit September 94.75 – 94.11 = 0.64%.

Total profit on futures position = 1.075%.

Per annum futures profit therefore is 1.075% /2 = 0.5375%.

Cash market cost of 6 month LIBOR is 6.00% p.a.

    6.00–0.5375 = 5.4625% p.a.

The effective borrowing rate is therefore 5.4625% p.a. This has hedged the cash market where the rate is 6.00% p.a.

Rolling/stack hedge

In the previous section we have seen that a strip involves using a number of contracts with differing expiry dates to hedge an extended period of time. An extended period of time, covering a number of contract periods can also be hedged using a **rolling hedge**, sometimes known as a **stack** or **stacking hedge**.

A rolling hedge uses a number of contracts with the same expiry date. As the contracts near expiry the holder of the futures position rolls out of the contracts by closing them out and enters into new contracts with later delivery dates. One of the advantages of a rolling hedge is that liquidity will almost certainly be greater in the nearby delivery contracts than in the distant contracts which will be used in a strip. In addition, contracts in nearby delivery periods are more likely to be more accurately priced; they will be closer to their theoretical/fair price position.

A rolling hedge will definitely have to be used to hedge a period of time which is later than any available contract period. A rolling hedge involves more transactions cost than a strip because there is a continuous need to close out and enter into new contracts.

Diagrammatically the steps used in a rolling hedge are:

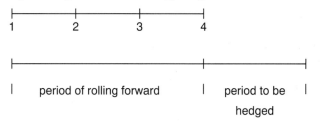

1. enter into original contracts

2. close out position and enter into new contracts

3. repeat of 2

4. close out position

Hedging odd time periods – stubs and tails

The strip and rolling hedges illustrated in the previous sections used whole futures contract periods. It will often be the case, however, that a hedge requires the use of part of a contract period.

Stubs and **tails** describe part of a futures contract period. Most futures contracts cover a period of time of three months, if these contracts are used for less than three months, the hedger will be hedging either a stub or a tail period.

Some examples will illustrate the point, using the LIFFE Short Sterling contract.

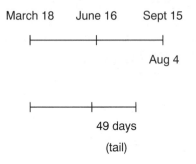

A hedge covering the period March 18 to August 4, dates inclusive, has a complete contract period at its beginning from March 18 to June 16. It then has a tail period of a further 49 days in the next contract month, initially this is a deferred month, becoming the current month on June 17. Two contract periods are therefore necessary, the first could be taken to expiration and settled via the EDSP, the second could be off-set on August 4.

A further example:

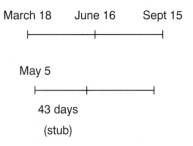

A hedge covering the period May 5 to September 15, dates inclusive, has a period of time in the current month of 43 days plus a complete contract period. The 43 days at the beginning of the hedge would be called a stub period. Stubs and tails refer to the part of the hedge period therefore and not contract periods.

A hedge has to be carefully weighted especially when a tail is involved. As a rule of thumb, a hedge involving a tail needs to weight the tail as a fraction of the contract period, whereas a stub is best treated as if it were a whole contract period with regard to weighting.

A cross hedge

There will be many instances where you wish to hedge a cash market position and there is not an exactly matching futures contract. As a result it is certain that cash market prices will behave differently to the futures price for any chosen contract. Necessarily, the futures price will be tracking changes in the cash market instrument to which it actually relates.

There are no futures contracts in, for example, commercial paper (CP), corporate bonds or bank certificates of deposit (CDs), although the latter did have a futures contract for a short while. The problem with these instruments is that they will be sold by issuers with widely differing credit ratings, as well as maturities and coupons. As a result it is difficult to envisage a futures market for a large number of instruments without a degree of homogeneity as experienced with regard to US T-bonds or UK gilts. US T-bond and UK gilt futures are complicated enough in relation to their delivery arrangements and conversion factors where there is near homogeneity.

The lack of an exact match between cash and future does not mean that a hedge cannot be put in place. A **cross hedge** can be employed, but it will result in a less than perfect hedge performance.

If CP and CDs need to be hedged, the closest futures contracts will be, if in sterling, the LIFFE Short Sterling contract, or if in US dollars, the LIFFE Eurodollar contract or the IMM three-month US T-bill contract. In order to choose which futures contract is the most applicable, a study should be made of changes in price of CP and CDs and the instrument underlying the available futures. It is likely that there will be a fairly close correlation between price movements in CP, CDs and three month sterling deposit rates, or, if US dollars are considered, between CP, CDs and Eurodollar three month rates and US T-bill rates. It is likely that if maturities are three months for CP and CDs then there will be a closer correlation in price changes than if maturities were one month. In any event it must be appreciated that the relationship being identified and used is an historical one, a relationship which need not necessarily hold true over the period of time an actual hedge is in place.

As an example we will hedge the issue of one month commercial paper denominated in US dollars (USCP) using the LIFFE three month Eurodollar contract.

Assume that the hedge is to cover the issue of USCP $25m at some time in the future. The issuer wishes to protect against a rise in interest rates as this will mean that the sum realised at the sale of the CP when issued will be less than anticipated. The issuer will therefore need to short a suitable number of Eurodollar contracts. In order to weight the hedge a number of factors need to be taken into account.

CP is one month maturity	Eurodollar underlying deposit is for three months
Credit risk on CP is that of corporate issuer	Underlying deposit rate based upon 3m Eurodollar BBAISR, no specific credit rating

As a result of these factors, CP rates and Eurodollar rates and thereby the futures price will behave differently. In turn this will be reflected in differences in the dollar value of a basis point change in the CP and the dollar value of a basis point change in the futures price. These values will reflect the way in which the two different interest rates are expected to move in relation to each other.

The dollar value of a basis point movement in the futures price will be $25, i.e. 1 tick.

$$\$1,000,000 \times 0.0001 \times 90/360 = \$25$$

The dollar value of a basis point movement in USCP of the same unit value ($1,000,000) will be

$$\$1,000,000 \times 0.0001 \times 30/360 = \$8.33$$

The next step is to determine the historical price behaviour of the two prices in relation to each other. An analysis would reveal that they move in a way closely related to each other, the exact historical relationship could in fact be determined.

Assume here that CP rates move by 75% of the movement in 3m Eurodollar LIBOR rates. This means that for every 10 basis point movement in the LIBOR rate, CP moves 7.5 basis points.

In order to weight the hedge to determine the number of contracts needed, the following calculation should be made:

$$\frac{\text{Amount to hedge}}{\text{Unit of trading}} \qquad \frac{\$25,000,000}{\$1,000,000} = 25$$

$$\text{basis point value ratio} \qquad \frac{\$8.33}{\$25} = 0.33$$

$$\text{correlation ratio} \qquad \frac{7.5}{10} = 0.75$$

number of contracts needed:
$$25 \times 0.33 \times 0.75 = 6.19 \text{ i.e. } 6$$

Six contracts will hedge the anticipated position 'well' if the relationship between CP and Eurodollar LIBOR holds in the way suggested by the analysis.

Futures and portfolio management

The focus of this book is risk management, the use of cash markets and their derivatives to hedge against different kinds of financial risk. Futures, however, can be used to manage investment portfolio objectives, they can be used to manage risk and return on investment portfolios. Futures can be used, for example, to alter the risk and return characteristics of an individual bond or portfolio of bonds.

The use of futures in portfolio management involves taking a view on movements in interest rates, this is something quite different to the attitude taken in hedging decisions where it is taken that you do not know either the direction or magnitude of change and therefore wish to hedge the consequences of such unknown movements.

A further chapter could easily be devoted to **futures trading strategies** where the objective is to take a futures position or positions in an attempt to make a profit. Naturally it will also be possible to make a loss should the expectation you have about rate movements actually not happen. Futures trading could in these cases be taken as examples of speculation. Here we view the use of futures in portfolio management as being somewhat between hedging and speculating and that is the reason why this section has been included. Further justification for inclusion is that a technique is used to decrease duration and this can be viewed as a hedge against rises in interest rates and as a way of protecting portfolio asset values.

Let us look at an example of the use of futures to alter portfolio duration.

If you expect a fall in interest rates you will also expect a rise in bond prices. Bond prices will rise by a larger proportion, the higher the duration of the bond or bonds in a portfolio.

To take advantage of this expectation in relation to your bond portfolio, you could sell some of your low duration bonds. When and if interest rates do fall, you will experience greater appreciation in the capital value of high duration bonds than in those of low duration. Thus this rearrangement of the portfolio is designed to maximise its return. This strategy is seen in the bond markets as a standard response to anticipated interest rate falls. The opposite strategy of selling high duration bonds and replacing with low duration bonds in anticipation of interest rate rises is also equally recognised as sound and in no way being unduly speculative.

Transactions costs will be incurred and a degree of portfolio 'disruption' will be experienced if bonds are actually sold. Arguably there is a better way to adjust portfolio duration with lower costs and nil portfolio disruption. Duration can be effectively adjusted by appropriate use of futures, leaving the actual cash market holding of bonds intact, this has an additional advantage if parts of the entire portfolio are the responsibility of different, individual, managers who have the responsibility to be optimally invested in their sector. Disruption of the portfolio could cause sub-managers' performance on an individual basis to decline. The use of futures by the manager with overall responsibility for the entire portfolio can be undertaken without affecting individual managers' reported performance. It is possible that the futures decisions may not even be known to the sub-managers.

In addition to futures being used by portfolio managers to alter duration of a portfolio, futures can also be used for asset allocation and the creation of synthetic instruments.

Changing portfolio duration using futures

- Selling futures decreases duration and decreases interest rate sensitivity of a bond portfolio.
- Buying futures increases duration and increases interest rate sensitivity of a bond portfolio.

The value of a bond futures contract changes when interest rates change. If interest rates change by one basis point, it is possible to calculate the resulting change in price of the future, tracking as it does the CTD bond. As seen earlier (p. 134) the result of a change in a futures price following a one basis point change in interest rates is known as the basis point value (BPV) of the futures contract.

If the BPV of a futures contract is calculated, related to the BPV of the cash market holding of the bonds and the BPV of the bond holding desired (target BPV), then the number of futures contracts necessary to alter duration can be calculated:

$$\text{number of futures contracts} = \frac{\text{BPV target} - \text{BPV portfolio}}{\text{BPV futures}}$$

BPV target – BPV portfolio gives the change required in the portfolio. Dividing by the BPV of the futures contract gives the number of contracts necessary to create this change in value.

A worked example, selling futures to increase duration and price sensitivity of a portfolio:

portfolio duration	5.2
target duration	10.0
portfolio yield to maturity	6.85%
portfolio value	£50m
BPV future	£72.55

$$\text{BPV of portfolio} = \frac{5.2}{1+0.0685/2} \times £50m \times 0.0001 = £25{,}135$$

$$\text{BPV target} = \frac{10.00}{1+0.0685/2} \times £50m \times 0.0001 = £48{,}344$$

number of contracts needed to achieve a duration of 10

$$= \frac{£48{,}344 - £25{,}135}{£72.55} = 319.90, \text{ i.e/ } 320 \text{ contracts}$$

Summary

- The principle by which futures can be used to hedge positions is that gains/ losses in the cash market are off-set by losses/gains in the futures market. The 'compensation' in the futures market does not, however, always lead to a hedge ratio of 100%. Adjustments must be made to the number of futures contracts necessary to approximate to a 100% compensation by the use of a cash–futures equivalency ratio, or simply equivalency ratio (ER). Adjustment is especially important when the instrument which is the underlying in the futures contract and the actual cash market instrument being hedged are not the same, this will be so even when, for example, UK gilts are hedged which are not deliverable into the basket.
- As a basic principle, if the cash market instrument changes price by twice the amount the futures price changes, then two futures contracts will be required for each cash market unit.
- ER can be determined by using basis point value (BPV), duration or convexity. Each method is a way of measuring price sensitivity of a fixed coupon bond to interest rate changes. Standard deviation related to coefficients of price correlation (p. 112) can also be used.
- Contract strips enable a hedge to be effected when the hedge period runs over a number of contract periods, as an alternative a rolling or stack hedge can be used.
- Hedging odd time periods, covering part of a contract period, can be implemented by using stubs and tails.
- Cross hedges can be used where the underlying and the cash market instrument are not a close match.

- Futures trading strategies can also be used in portfolio management, whereby the duration of a portfolio can be adjusted without disruption to the portfolio itself. Selling futures decreases portfolio duration, buying futures increases duration.

Key terms

- basis point value (BPV) (p. 133)
- contract strips (p. 138)
- convexity (p. 135)
- cross hedge (p. 140)
- duration(P. 131)
- equivalency ration (ER) (p. 129)

- portfolio disruption (p. 143)
- rolling/stack hedge (p. 139)
- stubs (p. 140)
- tails (p. 140)
- trading strategies (p. 142)

Questions

13.1 Explain the term equivalency ratio (ER). What does it show?

13.2 For a hedge ratio to be 100%, what are the necessary conditions?

13.3 Outline the meaning of BPV, duration and convexity.

13.4 High duration means high or low price sensitivity?

13.5 How much will the price of a bond whose price is currently £110.15 change if it has a duration of 7.15 and there is a two basis point change in its yield?

13.6 What are the factors which affect the duration of a bond?

13.7 Why are duration and convexity only accurate measures of price sensitivity if small changes in yield are experienced?

13.8 What is the advantage of a rolling hedge over a contract strip?

13.9 What is the difference between a stub and a tail?

13.10 What is a cross hedge?

13.11 How can you increase the interest rate sensitivity of a bond portfolio without disrupting the portfolio using futures?

Further reading

Dubofsky, David (1992) *Options and Financial Futures*, McGraw Hill.

Fabozzi, Frank (1993) *Bond Markets*, 2nd edn, Prentice Hall.

Labusowski, J. and Nyhoff, J. (1988) *Trading Options & Futures*, Wiley.

14 ► An introduction to traded options

Four chapters are devoted to traded options: Chapter 14 outlines basic option principles; Chapter 15 deals with currency options; Chapter 16 covers interest rate options, including options on bond futures and Chapter 17 covers option pricing.

Definition of options

The word option suggests a choice and this is exactly what is involved with an **option**, it conveys a choice, either this or that. More formally:

> An option conveys the right but not the obligation to buy or sell a particular commodity at a specified price on or before a specified date.

The definition used by LIFFE is as follows:

> [An option is] a contractual agreement that gives the option buyer the right, but not the obligation, to purchase (in the case of a call option) or to sell (in the case of a put option) a specified instrument at a specified price at any time of the option buyer's choosing by or before a fixed date in the future. Upon exercise of the right by the option holder, an option seller is obliged to deliver the specified instrument at the specified price.

The right to choose, therefore the option, is sold by the **seller (writer)** of the option to the **purchaser (holder)** in return for a **payment (premium)**. The right conveyed by the option only lasts a certain period of time and then the right expires – at its **maturity** or **expiration**.

The seller of an option has no choice. He must meet his obligation to buy/sell if the right of the purchaser to do so is **exercised** at the agreed **exercise/strike rate**. His reward is of course the premium he receives. Therefore at best the seller can receive the premium and no more. At worse he may lose a large sum if he has to buy/sell at a price which differs greatly from the prevailing spot price in the cash market. For the writer therefore, there is substantial **downside risk**.

It is the purchaser therefore who has choice, he does not have to exercise the right to buy/sell at the strike rate agreed if it is better from his perspective to buy/sell at spot, he can instead **walk away** from the option. In this respect options differ from futures where holders of positions do have the obligation to buy/sell the underlying asset. At worst the purchaser will lose the premium, but can gain substantially if the option is worth exercising. **Upside potential** is therefore great for the option purchaser.

That purchasers and sellers have different rights and obligations means that options can be described as **unilateral contracts**. The purchaser acquires rights to the underlying asset and the seller is obligated to satisfy those rights.

OTC/traded options

Credit risk on an option is asymmetrical. To the writer there is no credit risk. He is paid the premium up front and therefore cannot go unpaid for taking on risk related to price change of the underlying asset.

For the purchaser credit risk is quite different. He will pay the premium up front to the writer and is carrying the risk that the writer will not honour his obligation if required to do so.

With traded options credit risk for either party (the writer will not be paid instantly) is effectively removed by the use of a clearing house which will act as counterparty to trades and be able to guarantee performance and settlement.

The system will work in a similar fashion to that used in the futures market. The clearing house takes the opposite side to every position taken by purchasers and sellers.

Trading on the exchange can only be conducted by exchange members who have bought a seat on the exchange. As with futures trading there are different classes of members. Ultimately all trades must go via a clearing member.

Although the guarantee from the clearing house only extends to a clearing member and not to a non-clearing member or option writer or purchaser, the Securities and Futures Authority (SFA) regulations in the UK ensure clearing traders' clients are effectively safeguarded.

In London it is the London Clearing House (LCH) since 1991, formerly the International Commodities Clearing House (ICCH) which clears all LIFFE trades, as with futures.

As an example of the way the system safeguards market participants, LCH quotes the example of the failure of Drexel Burnham Lambert in February 1990 'a major player on all the exchanges, where client positions were transferred and house positions closed out, with no market disruption nor loss to LCH'. A far more well known example is of course the collapse of Barings Bank in February 1995 due to its trading activities principally at SIMEX in Singapore. An outline of the events leading up to and following the collapse is given in Chapter 21, along with a preliminary analysis. The six major banks which own LCH currently provide backing for LCH's counterparty risk to the extent of £150m.

Traded option buyers pay the premium to the clearing house via a trader. Option writers guarantee their ability to meet their obligations via a margin system operated by the trader who trades for them. In turn clearing members are subject to a margin system. As trades occur members of the exchange have their accounts debited and credited to reflect gains and losses, and these in turn are passed to clients' accounts.

Purchasers are not subject to a margin system, once the premium is paid no further losses can be incurred by them. However, all options traded at LIFFE are **traded futures style** whereby a margining system applies to the purchaser as well as the writer. There are a number of advantages to this and they are further discussed in Chapter 16.

On all other exchanges buyers need not put up margin. As a result once the premium has been paid there will no margin calls when temporary adverse price movements occur. Option buyers not subject to a margin system thus have 'staying power' to maintain a position which is not the case, in contrast, for a holder of a futures position.

A key feature of traded options is their standard terms. Each contract sets standard strike prices, unit quantities, option periods and a careful specification of the underlying asset and its delivery arrangements, even if in almost all cases such arrangements are not actually used due to close-out of positions similar to that which happens in futures markets.

Like futures, traded options are usually bought and sold on an open outcry basis and in a similar way they are not a **held** market. Bid/ask prices can be agreed with other traders in the trading pit – so long as the breath is warm. It is a **fill or die system**. Ask is the price at which a trader is prepared to sell, bid at which a trader is prepared to buy – either on their own account, or for a client. Price in relation to an option is of course the premium and should not be confused with the strike price or rate which is the price at which the underlying can be exchanged at the option of the buyer.

OTC options are written and bought in very large volumes, but here credit risk exists for the purchaser who pays the premium up front.

Puts and calls

Puts and calls are separate option contracts, not a counterpart to each other. If a purchaser buys the right but not the obligation to sell the underlying asset to the writer the option is known as a **put option**, or simply as a *put*.

If a purchaser buys the right but not the obligation to buy the underlying asset from the writer the option will be a **call option**.

To get the matter clear, look at buying and selling the **underlying asset** from the option purchaser's point of view.

Therefore:

- buyers call
- sellers put.

Because there are sellers of options and purchasers of options it is therefore possible to distinguish:

- buyers of calls (long calls)
- sellers of calls (short calls)
- buyers of puts (long puts)
- sellers of puts (short puts).

Sellers have **short** option positions.
Buyers have **long** option positions.

In practice, due to the way traded options are dealt with by a clearing house, buyers and sellers do not have the permanent relationship and obligation or rights between each other as suggested so far. Their initial relationship does not bind them together for the life of the option. Their obligations, rights and relationship become between the clearing house, traders and themselves. Of course many traders will buy and sell options on their own account.

- Sellers of options can be referred to as **writers** or **grantors**.
- Buyers are sometimes referred to as **takers** of options and are also of course the **holders** of options.

Strike/exercise price

The price at which calls and puts are to be exercised or walked away from is the **strike** or **exercise price**. This price is usually near to the prevailing spot price of the underlying asset when the option is first entered into. One of the benefits of exchange traded options is that option terms are standardised and this as seen applies to strike prices. Strike prices are set by the exchange so that options for a given maturity can be traded above, below and at the spot of the underlying asset. For example, a spot price of a commodity when an option is first traded may be £1.54. Strike prices may therefore be set at £1.55, £1.60 and £1.50. If the spot moves outside these bands then the strike price of subsequent trades will change to new positions. After each day's trading new strike prices will therefore be created by the exchange if prices in the underlying asset have moved outside the previous strike rates.

The term **series** is also used for strike price, e.g. 'a £1.55 series put'.

Note, in contrast, an **option series** (calls and puts) is all options of a given class with same expiration and strike price. An **option class** is all options of the same type, e.g. all currency option calls for dollars/sterling regardless of expiration and strike price.

American, European and Asian options

Options are either **American-** or **European-style**, with some **Asian** options now becoming available. Asian options are available only OTC at the moment, but there are plans to introduce them in traded form at the CBOE in 1994.

American options convey the right but not the obligation to the purchaser to buy/sell the underlying asset at any time between purchase of the option and its maturity. Maturity is alternatively described as **expiration date** or simply **expiration**, or the **exercise date** or **strike date**.

European options convey the right but not the obligation to the purchaser to buy/sell the underlying asset at expiration only.

The **exercise day** for an American option, the day on which the right to buy/sell may be exercised, is any day before expiration. For a European option the exercise day will be at expiration.

Asian options convey the right but not the obligation to the purchaser to buy/sell the underlying asset at a strike price which is the average of its spot price over a given period of time. They are available on currencies, oil and some metals.

Note, the terms Asian, American and European options do not mean that they relate to their geographical location – most options traded on European exchanges are American. The words American and European describe when rights can be exercised. Asian refers to the determination of strike price.

History of options

Options may have existed as far back as 400 BC in ancient Greece and Rome. There are records of options on agricultural commodities, especially wheat, during the middle ages in England. In the early 17th century options were written on tulip bulbs in Amsterdam. In 1636 the options market collapsed when the cash market price of tulip bulbs fell rapidly. Sellers of options refused to purchase bulbs at the high prices they were obligated to pay under the option agreement they had entered into. This illustrates well the principle that enforcement of performance is necessary if an options market is to develop. When there is an OTC market there is always the danger that an option writer will default if they have to buy or sell at prices which are at a disadvantage to them.

An OTC options market in the US was fairly active in agricultural commodities and common stock (shares) from the 1860s. During the early 1900s the Put and Call Brokers and Dealers Association was set up. A mechanism was created to enable sellers and buyers to get in touch with each other (broker function). If a suitable seller could not be found, acting as a dealer a member firm would sell an option at a price. This was an OTC market with no face to face dealing, no market dealing to determine premium and no secondary market. There was no way of guaranteeing that obligations would be honoured by option writers. These deficiencies ensured that options did not develop in use.

Much later, the CBOT wanted to begin to trade futures on shares but were refused by the Securities and Exchange Commission (SEC). In response the CBOT developed stock options and opened the Chicago Board Options Exchange (CBOE) on 26 April 1973 and for the first time the problems with OTC options were removed by the use of standard bands for strike prices, standard maturities, standard specification for the underlying asset and standard delivery arrangements. Counterparty default risk was removed by the use of a clearing house and a margin system for sellers. In addition a location was provided where buyers and sellers could meet. In general an open outcry system would give price transparency and fair premium prices.

At first call options only were traded. Put options were introduced 3 June 1977. Options on futures were initially banned by the US Congress in 1978, but were reintroduced 1 October 1982.

Underlying assets

There are a number of 'commodities' used as the underlying asset for options. They are:

- physical commodities, agricultural products like wheat, plus oil, timber, metals etc.;

- currencies;
- stock (equities);
- future contracts (these are often used as a substitute for the cash market asset due to their greater liquidity, e.g. options on bond futures);
- indexes.

The most numerically common options are on stock, i.e. shares in companies such as IBM, Allied Lyons, Asda.

Option exchanges

Most exchanges identified on p. 61 as Futures Exchanges also trade options on the same underlying assets as in the futures market. Exchanges exist in most financial centres.

In the UK

In London, LIFFE incorporates options trading on underlying financial assets on a different part of the trading floor as the London Traded Options Market (LTOM). In fact LTOM was formed in 1978, before LIFFE as a trading exchange which began in 1982. LIFFE and LTOM merged in March 1992 to become the London International Financial Futures and Options Exchange – still referred to as LIFFE.

Options traded at LIFFE are:

- Options on short-term interest rate futures:
  - Three-month Sterling
  - Three-month Eurodollar
  - Three-month Euromark
  - Three-month Euroswiss

- Options on long-term bond futures:
  - Long Gilt German Government Bond (Bund)
  - Italian Government Bond

- Index option:
  - FT-SE 100

- Equity options

Other options exchanges in London are:

- London Commodity Exchange (was London Fox until 1 July 1993) – here underlying assets include coffee, cocoa, white sugar, the Baltic Freight Index (BIFFEX) and wheat.
- The London Securities and Derivatives Exchange (OMLX) – this was OM London until 1 April 1993. Underlying assets traded are mainly Swedish stock options.

Other major options exchanges are:

In the US

- Chicago Board Options Exchange (CBOE) – here all types of options are traded: stock, stock indices, T-bonds, T-notes and currencies as well as many commodities.
- Many US exchanges trade stock (share) options.
- There is a large currency options market at the Philadelphia Stock Exchange.
- The International Money Market (IMM) division of the CME trades a range of financial options.

Outside the US

There are options exchanges in:

- Amsterdam
- the European Options Exchange (EOE)
- France (MONEP)
- Germany (DTB)
- Singapore
- Switzerland (SOFFEX)
- Sydney
- Tokyo.

Contract specifications

As with all traded derivatives, standardisation is important. Option contracts carefully specify the contract elements, leaving only in this case the option premium to be determined on the market. As an example the following highlights apply to the LIFFE option on Long Gilt Futures:

Unit of trading	1 long gilt futures contract
Delivery months	March, June, September, December
Quotation	Multiples of 1/64
Minimum price movement	£1/64
(Tick size and value)	(£7.8125)
Exercise price intervals	£1
Introduction of new exercise prices	Thirteen exercise prices will be listed for each new series. Additional exercise prices will be introduced on the business day after the Long Gilt futures contract settlement price is within £16/32 of the sixth highest or lowest existing exercise price.

Intrinsic value

An option is said to have **intrinsic value** when the strike price is better than the spot price from the purchaser's perspective. Clearly the strike/spot relationship will have a different outcome depending upon whether the position held is a call or a put.

If the strike price is £5 and the spot is £4, then the purchaser (the long) of a put has intrinsic value. They can sell the underlying commodity notionally to the seller of the option for £5, whereas ordinary spot sellers will have to sell at £4. The purchaser's intrinsic value is £1 for every unit they have the right to sell under the option contract.

Therefore, when purchasing a put:

intrinsic value = strike price − spot price

If the purchaser has a call option there is no intrinsic value using the above strike and spot rates. They will be better off **walking away** from the option, there being no obligation to buy at £5 when the underlying commodity can be bought spot for £4.

Therefore, when purchasing a call:

intrinsic value = spot price − strike price

It will pay to exercise a call if, for instance, strike is £10 and spot is £12, giving intrinsic value of £2.

In contrast the option writer's position is as follows: if the purchaser has no intrinsic value, the option will not be exercised and the premium received will represent profit.

If the purchaser has intrinsic value then the option will be exercised, the higher the intrinsic value to the purchaser, the greater the overall loss the writer will experience. Using the above figures for the put, having to buy at strike £5 and then sell at spot £4 the writer will make a £1 loss for every unit allowed to be delivered by the long. Of course the writer can set the premium received against any loss, however, in many circumstances the difference between strike and spot will be sufficiently large to wipe out the premium received.

Premium, intrinsic and time value

The premium paid to purchase an option must relate in some way to whether or not the strike gives intrinsic value. If strike is £5 and spot is £4 and the purchaser buys a put, allowing a sale at £5 instead of at £4 then the value of the option, the premium, must be at least the intrinsic value. If the premium were less than intrinsic value it would pay to purchase the option and exercise it at a profit.

Again using strike £5 and spot £4, if the right to sell the underlying commodity by the purchaser, a put, relates to 50,000 units the intrinsic value becomes (at least)

(£5 − £4) × 50,000 = £50,000
(strike − spot) × traded number of units

If the purchaser buys a call at £5 when the spot is £4 there is no intrinsic value for the purchaser. An option with no intrinsic value does not mean that the premium will be zero. As long as time remains to expiration there will be **time value**.

Option premiums consist of two elements, intrinsic value and time value. Sometimes intrinsic value will be zero, but the longer an option has to run until expiration, the greater is the time value and the higher its premium will be. Time value is a reflection of the opportunity of the spot price of the underlying asset to change so that there is intrinsic value for the purchaser. At expiration an option will have no time value, thus time value falls as expiration approaches. For this reason an option is often described as a wasting asset for the purchaser. Time value is thus the potential of the option to gain intrinsic value during its remaining time to expiration. A key feature is the **volatility** of the underlying. Clearly the more volatile the underlying, the greater is the possibility that an option will gain, or lose, intrinsic value. As discussed in detail in Chapter 17, volatility is an important variable in the determination of option premiums.

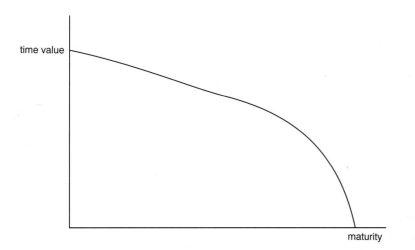

Figure 14.1   *The relationship between time value and maturity.*

In-, out-, at-the-money

- An option with intrinsic value is said to be **in-the-money**. If it has a high intrinsic value it will be **deep-in-the-money**.
- An option with no intrinsic value is **out-of-the-money** and **deep-out-of-the-money** if there is a large difference between strike and spot prices.
- If the spot and strike prices are identical then the option is **at-the-money (ATM)**.

In-, out- and at-the-money can be summarised as follows:

Prices	calls	puts
spot > strike	in-the-money	out-of-the-money
spot = strike	at-the-money	at-the-money
spot < strike	out-of-the-money	in-the-money

Option purchasers will only exercise their rights and not walk away when they can make a gross profit, thus in-the-money options will be exercised. If the position is closed out before expiration there will also be some time value. A net profit can easily be determined by deducting the premium paid from the close-out proceeds (i.e. premium received).

Out-of-the-money positions will not be exercised, the net loss to the purchaser will be the premium paid.

At-the-money positions may or may not be exercised, there will be no benefit either way.

The above analysis ignores transaction costs. For an option that is just in-the-money, it may be cheaper for the purchaser to walk away, especially if time value is very low.

An option deep-out-of-the-money has only a small potential to become in-the-money and have intrinsic value, its time value will thus be low. However, the longer the time to expiration, the greater its time value, other things being equal. A deep-in-the-money option will also have little time value, especially if there is a long time to expiration, here there is potential to lose intrinsic value.

Time value will be a high proportion of the premium when an option is at-the-money. In fact time value will be 100% of the premium because there is no intrinsic value.

For a purchaser the value of an option clearly cannot be less than zero – no intrinsic or time value, no further expense just walk away. Options can be referred to as a limited liability instrument for this reason.

> Premium, the price paid to buy the right but not the obligation to buy/sell is thus:
>
> time value + intrinsic value

Call options with low strikes relative to spot are more expensive because they give the holder the right to buy the underlying asset at a low price. In terms of in-, out- and at-the-money, premiums must be higher for options at- and in-the-money because of intrinsic value for in-the-money, and the chance of becoming in-the-money for an option at the money. See Figures 14.2 and 14.3 to illustrate.

If option pricing, i.e. premium determination is to be fully understood, then the potential of time to alter a premium's value must be understood. Intrinsic value is quite straightforward as described, it relates spot to strike price. Further discussion of option pricing occurs in Chapter 17.

Pay-off diagrams

If reference is made to the section on puts and calls (pp. 149, 150) it can be seen that there can be long and short positions on calls and puts. In each a

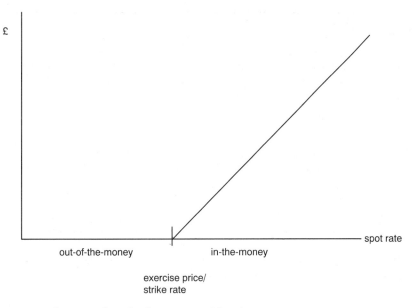

out-of-the-money   in-the-money

£   spot rate

exercise price/
strike rate

Figure 14.2   *Intrinsic value related to in-, out- and at-the-money.*

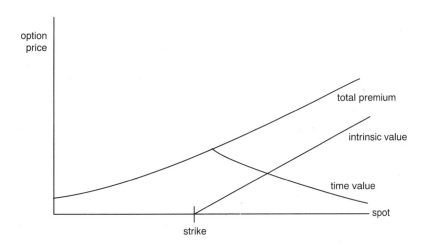

option
price

total premium

intrinsic value

time value

spot

strike

Figure 14.3   *Option price (time and intrinsic value) related to underlying spot.*

pay-off diagram can be produced to illustrate graphically how the value of each position changes as the strike/spot price relationship changes.

Note that the explanation which follows relates to profit and loss on **naked options**. A naked option is where the option position stands alone, it is not used in conjunction with a cash market position in the underlying asset, or another option position. In addition the pay-off profiles assume the option is held to expiration and not exercised early or closed out. In this way the gains/losses on the option alone can be identified.

Pay-off for a naked long call

A long call, the purchase of a call, is an option to buy an asset at the strike price. It is a strategy to take advantage of any increase in the price of the underlying asset.

Suppose the following applies:

	£
Current spot price of underlying asset	100
Strike price	100
Premium paid by purchaser of the call	5
Expiration	1 month

- If the spot price at expiration is below the strike of £100 the option will not be exercised, it is better to buy at spot. The purchaser will lose the premium paid of £5 and no more.
- If the spot at expiration is equal to the strike of £100 there is still no reason to exercise the option, the premium, however, will be lost.
- If the spot at expiration is greater than the strike, then it will pay the purchaser to exercise the option, i.e. buy at £100 and sell the asset at spot for a larger sum.

It is worth noting that if the spot at expiration is less than £105 there will still be a net loss to the purchaser. Imagine spot at expiration to be £104. The purchaser will exercise the right to buy at strike £100 and sell at spot £104, a gain of £4. However, as the premium was £5, a net loss of £1 will be experienced. It is important to see that it is still rational to exercise at anything above strike as the gain can be set against the cost of the premium. Once the spot rises above the strike plus premium, a net profit can be earned by a long call.

Breakeven point with all naked calls, short and long, is:

strike + premium

The above analysis can be illustrated with a pay-off diagram as in Figure 14.4.

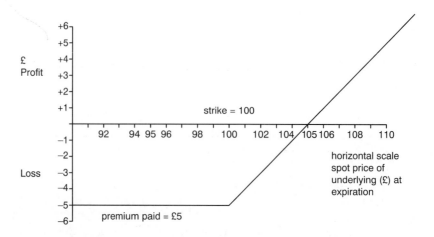

Figure 14.4 *Profit/loss diagram when purchasing a call.*

Examples of outcomes for the long call

Spot	Exercise	(Loss)/profit (£)
98	no	(5)
101	yes	(4)
103	yes	(2)
105	yes	breakeven
108	yes	3

Pay-off for a naked short call

A short call, the writing of a call, is the obligation to sell an asset at the strike price if the long call chooses to exercise. Here the strategy is designed to profit from falls in the price of the underlying asset.

Let the following apply (as the long call example)

	£
Current spot price of the underlying asset	100
Strike price	100
Premium received from purchaser	5
Expiration	1 month

The pay-off to the short call is the mirror image of that of the long call. Profit for the long is loss for the short and vice versa. For example, the maximum loss for the long was the premium of £5.

The maximum gain for the short is the £5 premium. Naturally the option will be exercised or not as the case may be, under the same spot/strike relationships as with the long call above.

Breakeven point will be:

strike + premium   (£100 + £5 = £105)

The situation can be illustrated by Figure 14.5.

Examples of outcomes for the short call

(Compare with outcomes for long call – a mirror image.)

Spot	Exercise (by long call)	(Loss) profit (£)
98	no	5
101	yes	4
103	yes	2
105	yes	breakeven
108	yes	(3)

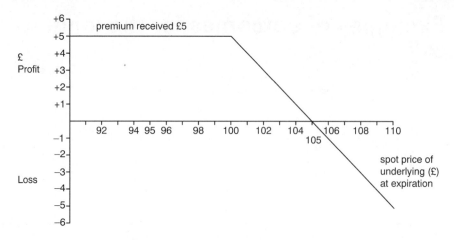

Figure 14.5 *Profit/loss diagram when selling a call (short call).*

The potential loss is therefore unlimited, as spot rises losses occur. The main reason for writing naked calls is that if stable spot prices are anticipated, then premium income can be earned by keeping the time value of the option without any off-setting expense, because the option will not be exercised.

Pay-off for a naked long put

A long put, the purchase of a put, is an option to sell an asset at the strike price. It is a strategy designed to take advantage of a fall in the spot price of the underlying asset. As with any long position the loss is limited to the premium paid with an upside potential profit, as the spot price falls in this case. In theory maximum profit will be attained here should the spot fall to zero.

Breakeven point for all naked puts is:

strike – premium

As before let the following apply:

	£
Current spot price of the underlying asset	100
Strike price	100
Premium paid to purchase the put	5
Expiration	1 month

Figure 14.6 illustrates the pay-off situation:

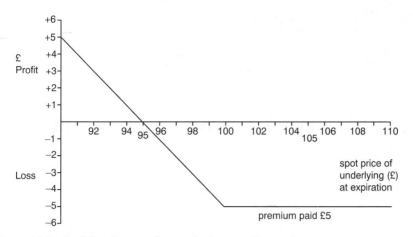

Figure 14.6 *Profit/loss diagram when purchasing a put (long put).*

Examples of outcomes for the naked long put

Spot	Exercise	(Loss) profit (£)
102	no	(5)
99	yes	(4)
95	yes	breakeven
94	yes	1

Pay-off for a naked short put

A short put, the writer of a put, has the obligation to buy an asset at the strike price if the long put chooses to exercise. The short put gains as the price of the underlying asset rises, i.e. as the price of the underlying rises, the less likely it is that the long will sell at the strike, spot will be better. Thus the short put keeps the premium.

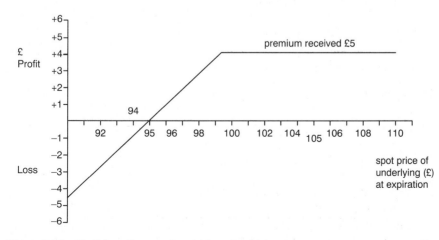

Figure 14.7 *Profit/loss diagram when writing a put (short put).*

The short will also gain if the spot price stays fairly constant, in that the premium will have been earned.

The profit and loss profile for a short put mirrors that of the long put. Loss is limited by the extent to which spot price falls. Using the same data set as before, Figure 14.7 illustrates the pay-off situation:

Examples of outcomes for the naked short put

Spot	Exercise (by the long put)	(Loss) profit (£)
102	no	5
99	yes	4
97	yes	2
95	yes	breakeven
94	yes	(1)

Summary of naked short and long calls and puts

- Naked long calls and short puts, i.e. purchasing calls and selling/writing puts, give rise to gains from the option position if price of the underlying asset rises and losses if the underlying asset price falls.
- Naked short calls and long puts, i.e. selling/writing calls and purchasing puts, give rise to gains from the option position if price of the underlying asset falls and losses if the underlying asset price rises.

In considering the view taken of anticipated spot prices, if you are:

- very bullish   buy a call
- quite bullish   write a put
- quite bearish   write a call
- very bearish   buy a put

The more bullish or bearish you are, the more attractive it will be to purchase out-of-the-money calls or puts. Premiums will be lower, giving greater leverage, with no extra downside risk than exists for an at- or in-the-money option.

The breakeven point for purchasing calls is:

strike price + premium paid

The breakeven point for purchasing puts is:

strike price – premium paid

This can be checked with reference to the relevant pay-off diagrams.

Hedge strategies

As the focus of this text is management of different types of financial price risk in relation to various cash markets, i.e. underlying assets, we now need to consider the position of hedging strategies using options, rather than taking a position in options for speculative purposes as with a naked position. Naked options have been discussed so that pay-offs from options can be seen in isolation and once understood can then be used in conjunction with a cash market position to demonstrate hedge strategies.

What is needed is a **covered option** position to cover asset price risk. This involves taking an option position appropriate to the cash market position, or anticipated position, so that changes in the value of one position will partially or wholly off-set changes in the value of the other.

Changes in the price of the underlying and changes in premiums are not always one to one. In relation to intrinsic value, for in-the-money options, change will be one to one, but due to time value being the other option premium component, the total premium price change may be less than one to one. A consequence of this is that when hedging it may be necessary to adjust the weighting of the hedge during its life. Thus a **dynamic hedge** may be necessary. This issue is further discussed in Chapter 17 in relation to options. Hedge weighting in relation to futures was covered in Chapter 11 as well as in Chapter 13.

Straightforward hedging strategies are dealt with first, they are:

- the **covered call writing strategy**, sometimes referred to as a **buy/write strategy** or a **short call hedge**;
- the **covered long put**, sometimes referred to as the **protective put buying strategy**;
- the **covered long call**.

Later sections deal with more complicated hedges which are cheaper, but hedge smaller asset price changes.

Covered call writing

If an underlying asset is held and a call option is written on it, this will be a covered call. There will be a long asset position and a short option position. It is a short hedge.

The profit/loss pay-off on the long asset position only as the spot price changes can be seen in Figure 14.8.

Referring to Figure 14.8, if the underlying asset is held and has been purchased at £100 and it remains at a spot of £100, then no gain or loss is made. If spot falls to £98, then a loss of £2 is made. Thus price changes and profit/loss can be represented by a 45° line.

If the price of the asset were to fall, creating a loss, this would be off-set, compensated by the premium received by writing the call. The premium received might:

- match the fall in the price of the asset;

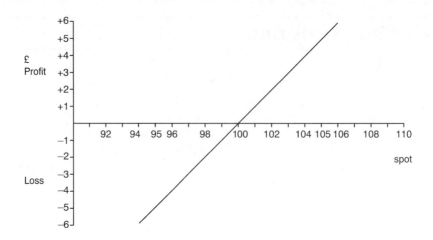

Figure 14.8 *Pay-off diagram long an underlying asset.*

- partially off-set the fall in price of the asset;
- not fully compensate for the fall in the asset price, i.e. create an overall net loss; such loss, however, not so large as that from an open position, due to receipt of the premium.

Suppose the following:

	£
Asset held, spot price	100
Call option sold for premium	5
Strike price	100

Three outcomes are possible:

- If the price of the asset were to fall by £5, the long position represents a loss of £5. Will the option be exercised by the call purchaser? – No, the strike price is £100, it is better to buy at spot £95. As a result the call option writer will have the premium of £5, and no further expense. The net result is the loss on the long position of £5 is off-set by the gain from the short position, the premium of £5.
- If the price of the underlying asset falls, say £3 to £97, the long position causes a loss of £3. Will the option be exercised? – No, it is better for the option purchaser to buy at spot than at strike. The call writer thus has a premium gain of £5, set against the loss of £3 on the asset. Thus there is a **net gain** of £2.
- If the price of the underlying asset falls say £10 to £90, the long position represents a loss of £10. Again, as above, the option will not be exercised. The call writer will still have the premium gain of £5 to off-set the loss on the long position, but this time there will be an overall **net loss** of £5.

Thus so long as the price of the asset does not decline by more than the premium, the covered call writer will not experience a net loss.

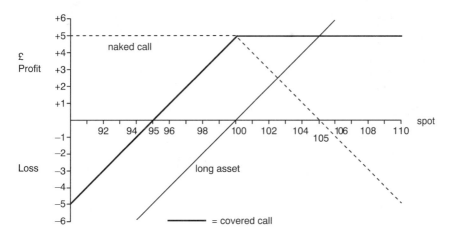

Figure 14.9 *Profit/loss diagram for a covered call.*

However, what if the price of the underlying asset were to rise? What if it were to rise to £110? The option purchaser would exercise the option, it would be better to buy at the strike of £100 than the spot of £110.

Here the covered call writer has foregone the profit which would have arisen from the long position alone, but in return has the premium income instead. Thus the chance of upside potential has been sacrificed for the guaranteed premium income.

In general, selling calls necessarily provides income and the possibility of cushioning the effect of a fall in the price of holding the underlying asset. Downside risk is therefore reduced at the expense of **capping** potential profit. Potential net profit can never be greater than the premium income, possible gains in the cash market have to be foregone, thus effectively a **ceiling price** for the underlying is achieved.

These outcomes can be illustrated graphically as in Figure 14.9.

The pay-off for the covered call is derived by taking the two separate positions – the long asset position (Figure 14.8) and the option position of a (naked) short call (Figure 14.5) and adding them vertically. Some examples:

Asset price	Asset gain/(loss)	Naked call gain/(loss)	Net gain/(loss), i.e. covered call net gain/(loss)
100	–	5	5
102	2	3	5
104	4	1	5
98	(2)	5	3
96	(4)	5	1
93	(6)	5	(1)

As an alternative, the pay-off table could be constructed first and then the final column of figures, i.e. that for the covered call, could be plotted alone.

Note that the pay-off for a covered call is the same as that for a naked short put (Figure 14.7).

Protective put buying – to hedge large asset price falls

A covered short call does not protect the value of the underlying asset – its price might fall by an amount greater than the premium received, so that a net loss occurs.

A protective put does protect the value of an underlying asset which is held. If a put option is purchased in conjunction with a long asset position, then the purchaser of the option can always sell the asset for at least the strike price in return for the premium paid. Therefore in effective net terms the value of the asset can never fall below the **floor price** of the strike price less the premium paid.

It can also be seen that should the spot price of the asset rise, the asset can be sold at this increased price by walking away from the option, at the expense only of the premium paid. Therefore as long as the asset increases in price by an amount which exceeds the premium paid, in net effective terms, gains in the spot market can be enjoyed with the downside risk minimised. Upside potential is only mitigated by premium paid.

Suppose the same information as on p. 164.

	£
Asset held, spot price	100
Put option purchased for	5
Strike price	100

- If the spot price of the asset rises to £106 the option will not be exercised, the asset will be sold at £106, a profit of £6, reduced by the premium paid of £5, giving an overall net gain of £1. Upside potential has been enjoyed.
- If the spot price of the asset falls to £99, the option will be exercised at the strike of £100, thus the value of the asset has been protected, but at the expense of the premium paid. The downside risk is at maximum as below:
- If the spot falls to £94, the option will be exercised at strike £100, its value is protected at the expense of the premium paid of £5. No matter how far spot falls, the value of the asset in net terms will be £100 less £5 premium, i.e. £95. Thus value is protected in net terms to a minimum (floor price) of £95.

The various outcomes are illustrated in Figure 14.10.

Covered long call – to hedge a rise in price

A covered long call enables the purchase of the underlying asset at a later date at no more than the strike price (i.e. when the hedge is placed you are short of the underlying asset). Should spot prices fall, the option can be allowed to expire and the call purchaser can walk away and purchase at spot.

Thus a covered long call fixes a ceiling price for a purchaser, yet enables falling asset prices to be taken advantage of.

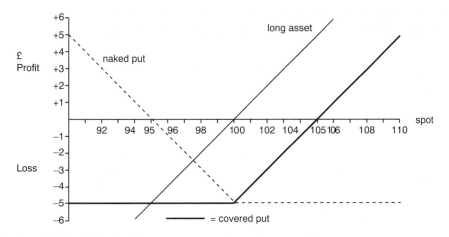

Figure 14.10 *Profit/loss diagram for a protective put (covered put).*

Suppose the following:

	£
Current spot price of asset	100
Strike price	100
Premium	5
Expiration	1 month

At a cost of the £5 premium the purchaser of a call option will be able to buy the underlying asset at a maximum price of £100, the strike rate. If the spot rises above £100 the option will be exercised. If the spot declines the option will be allowed to expire and the asset will be purchased at spot. The greater the fall in the asset price, the greater will be the profit to the covered long call. The facility to achieve these outcomes is, of course, purchased at the expense of the premium paid. Therefore more accurately the maximum (ceiling) price will be the strike plus premium, £100 plus £5, £105.

Possible outcomes:

- If spot rises to £106 the option will be exercised and the asset bought for the strike of £100. Premium was £5, giving a ceiling price of £105.
- If spot stays at £100 either exercise or not (ignoring transactions cost). Cost to buy asset is therefore £100 plus premium of £5; this gives ceiling price of £105.
- If spot falls to £94, walk away from the option, buy asset at spot, participate in profit gain at the expense of a £5 premium, therefore obtaining a net gain of £1.

The maximum loss on the covered position is the premium paid. Profits are gained as the spot falls. Net profit occurs when spot falls below £95. All these outcomes can be seen by examination of Figures 14.11 and 14.12.

Note that if a call were purchased with a strike below current spot, i.e. in-the-money, this locks in a lower maximum price. However this benefit does not come for free. An in-the-money option will have intrinsic value and thus the premium will be higher. In addition if spot declines the profit will be less than had the option been at-the-money. Thus a low price ceiling is guaranteed at greater expense and lower profit potential.

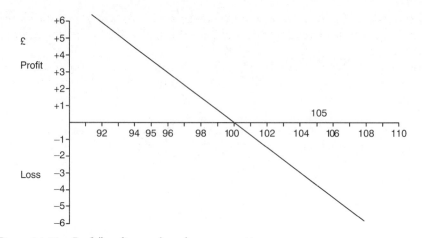

Figure 14.11 *Profit/loss diagram for a short asset position.*

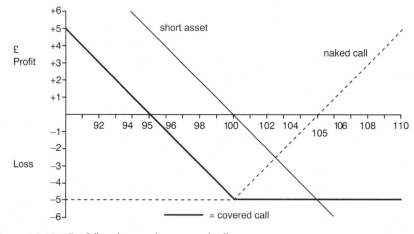

Figure 14.12 *Profit/loss diagram for a covered call.*

In contrast an out-of-the-money option will have no intrinsic value, only time value, therefore the premium will be low. This low cost hedge, however, gives a higher ceiling price, but does give higher profit potential as spot falls.

Put–call parity relationship

The price (i.e. premium) for a call and a put on the same underlying asset, with same expiration and at-the-money strike price, will have to be the same, arbitrage ensures that this is so. This is the **put–call parity relationship**.

Consider the following when the premium is not the same:

- Buy the underlying asset at spot £100 (long the asset).
- Sell a call option at a premium of £5 (short call).
- Buy a put option at a premium of £4 (long put).

Mispriced in this way the combined three positions will always produce an arbitrage profit of £1, regardless of how the spot price of the underlying asset changes.

The premium received for writing the call will be £5, the premium paid for buying the put will be £4. If the spot rises above the strike, the buyer of the call will exercise and the writer of the call will deliver the asset at the strike. However, at the same time the buyer of a put will also exercise and sell at the strike. The delivery and purchase of the asset are carried out by the same person at the same strike price, therefore the only thing to consider is the net profit of £1 (the difference between £5 premium received and £1 premium paid).

A numerical example may make matters a little easier to follow.

Consider strike £100:
Spot price rises to £105 (having been bought at £100).
The sequence is therefore:
Call writer receives (+)£5 premium, put buyer pays premium (–)£4.
Call writer sells asset at strike of £100 (because call buyer exercises), therefore receives (+)£100.
Put buyer buys asset at strike of £100, therefore pays (–)£100.
(Remember – call writer and put buyer are the same.)
Looking only at the figures this is:

$$+5 - 4 + 100 - 100 = 1$$

The arbitrage profit of £1 will be made at any asset price as can be seen by substituting any figure for the +£100 and –£100.
Note that if the strike is below spot £1 arbitrage profit will still be earned, this time the sequence is:
Call writer receives (+)£5 premium, put buyer pays premium (–)£4.
Call buyer does not exercise, therefore no further money flow to or from call writer.
Put buyer does not exercise, therefore no further money flow.
Figures only therefore become:

$$+£5 - £4 = £1$$

If the time value of money is ignored, as in the above examples (no cost of carry for the asset), then it follows that for no arbitrage profit to be possible:

long the asset + short call + long put = 0

If this is not the case then market participants will adjust their activities so that prices changes to eliminate the arbitrage profit. The spot price of the asset and the premiums for puts and calls will adjust so that the three positions do sum to zero.
Look at the following information:

current spot	£ 10
strike	£ 12
premium to purchase long put	£ 2.50

The long put is in-the-money by £2, therefore intrinsic value being £2 it follows that time value must be 50p. It also follows that the premium for a long call will be 50p, it is out-of-the-money, but it will still have the same time value due to put–call parity. Look at newspaper quotes and you will be able to see that this relationship holds. There is further coverage and examples in Chapters 15 and 16.

Closing out/off-setting

We have seen that options convey rights but not obligations. If there is intrinsic value it will be profitable for a purchaser to exercise the right to buy/sell. In reality, as with futures contracts, very few options are taken to maturity/expiration by the purchaser buying/selling the underlying asset from/to the writer at the strike price. In practice most options are closed out by taking an off-setting position. This is also referred to as **squaring out**.

A purchaser can, having purchased, sell the option to off-set. Having bought a call, a call is sold. Having bought a put, a put is sold. Naturally, due to trading being arranged on an organised exchange, it does not follow that the call or put has to be sold back to the original writer. It is the clearing house which becomes the counterparty to each option position and thus an off-set cancels out any obligations or rights.

In a similar fashion, a writer of an option can off-set their position by buying the same option. If a call has been sold a call is purchased. If a put has been sold a put is purchased. The exchange clearing house will of course also be the counterparty.

Profit at off-set will be achieved by the difference in the premium paid and then received back by an original purchaser and the difference between premium received and premium paid for an original writer. Premiums paid/received will of course relate to time and any intrinsic value.

For the purchaser of an option the maximum outlay is of course the premium paid. For a writer, maximum gain will be premium received in return for carrying the risk of having to buy/sell the underlying asset. If the spot falls and a writer has sold a put so that intrinsic value is gained by the holder, then the writer can of course close out their position at any time in order to limit further loss, at the expense of premium payment.

Many writers will limit potential loss by writing options against an opposite futures, cash or option position. Any loss on the options position is then set against, wholly or in part, by gain in the other position.

Exercising an option

When the holder of an option actually wishes to exercise the option rather than close out they must do so through an exchange member or via a broker who in turn must use an exchange member. As far as the exchange clearing house is concerned it is the exchange member who has the position with it.

The exchange member must place an exercise order with the clearing house; on receipt of this the clearing house will select at random another member who has an outstanding opposite position in the same option series. If the holder has a call the selected writer must sell the underlying asset at the strike price. If the holder has a put the writer must buy at the strike price. Writers in the above circumstances are described as being **assigned**. It follows that writers of American options might be assigned at any time the position is held and they must remember this. However, for the long it is optimal to close out and receive remaining time value. Most clearing houses have rules which automatically exercise in-the-money options with a value greater than a minimum amount, designed to cover transaction costs.

An option does not have to be exercised of course, it can be sold for value to close out, or be allowed to expire if it has no value.

Choice of strike and expiration

From what has been seen of intrinsic and time value, it follows that the premium will be higher for those options at- and in-the-money, because of their intrinsic value and greater probability of being profitable to the purchaser. Other things being equal, premiums will be higher for options with a long time to expiration, due to time value. Extra time is usually bought at proportionately smaller extra cost – two months to expiration does not usually cost twice that for one month. Reasons for this are covered in Chapter 17.

Taking different strike prices, with appropriate premiums, produces pay-offs for a naked long call, as illustrated in Figure 14.13.

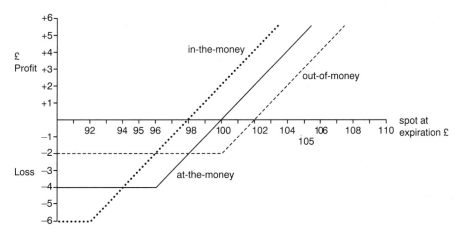

Figure 14.13 *Pay-offs for naked long calls at various strikes.*

Spreads, straddles and strangles

If covered positions are taken it follows that, in the case of long covered calls, different ceiling prices can be fixed with different profit participation according to the strike used.

Purchasing calls to hedge spot market positions may be regarded as expensive price insurance due to the cost of the premium. Less expensive hedging strategies involve the use of **spreads**, **straddles** and **strangles**.

As in the treatment earlier of various options positions, the option positions alone are discussed first, followed by a few examples of their use in hedging strategies.

Spreads

Spreads involve taking simultaneously two option positions on the same underlying asset, so that the combined positions allow speculation on relative price changes.

Spreads involve simultaneous purchase and sale of different options on the same underlying asset. The pay-off from these two positions change as the price spread of the two premiums widens or narrows as the underlying spot changes. The two options in a spread are described as **legs**.

A **vertical spread** is where the legs of the spread have different strikes but the same expiration, it can also be called a **money** or **price spread**.
A **horizontal spread** is where the legs have different expirations but the same strike, it can also be called a **calendar** or **time spread**.
A **diagonal spread** is where the legs have different strikes and expirations.

In each case the option legs will relate to the same underlying asset.

Vertical call spreads

Bullish and bearish vertical spreads can be created with puts and calls with the same strike but different expirations on the same underlying asset.

Vertical Bullish spreads create profit when spot asset prices rise.
Vertical Bearish spreads create profit when spot asset prices fall.

A bull vertical call spread

Buy a call with a low strike and, simultaneously, sell a call with a high strike (same expirations). This is a **long bull call spread**.
Suppose:

	£
Current spot of the underlying asset	100
Premium paid for low strike call	4
Low strike	96
Premium received for writing high strike call	2
High strike	102

(Refer to Figure 14.13 if you are unable to remember why premiums should differ.)

Figure 14.4 shows that if spot is at or below £96, the maximum loss will occur and it will be £2. This maximum loss is referred to as a **net debit**.
Maximum loss will be:

premium paid – premium received

i.e. £4–£2 = £2 (net debit)

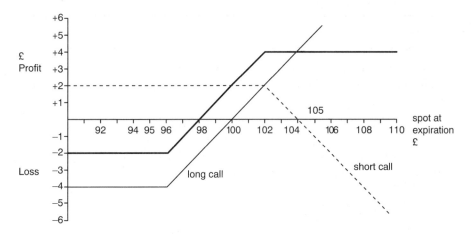

Figure 14.14 *Pay-off diagram for a bull vertical call spread.*

If spot is £102 or above, then maximum profit will occur and will be £4.

When spot is above £102, both options will be in-the-money. The long position will gain value, whereas the short position will be losing value because it will be required to buy at high spot prices, thus high strike gains minus low strike losses will give a gain from the two option positions, adjusted by the net premium paid:

maximum profit = high strike – low strike – net premium
£102 – £96 – £2 = £4

If spot lies between the two strikes (therefore £96 in-the-money and £102 out-of-the-money) there may or may not be a net profit, this will depend upon the breakeven point which is:

low strike + net premium paid
£96 + £2 = £98

When spot is £96 or less, both options will be out-of-the-money and thus the net debit will be the total cost incurred.

The bull vertical call spread is cheaper than a straightforward call purchase (compare the net cost of £2 with the premium to purchase the call of £4). See Figure 14.14 for a pay-off diagram for a bull vertical call spread.

A bull vertical put spread

Buy a put with low strike and, simultaneously, sell a put with a high strike (same expirations).

Suppose the following:

	£
Current spot of underlying asset	100
Premium paid to purchase low strike put	2
Low strike	98
Premium received to write high strike put	3
High strike	103

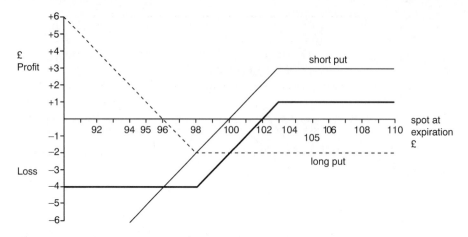

Figure 14.15 *Pay-off diagram for a bull vertical put spread.*

Because the premium paid is less than the premium received (see Figure 14.13 for reasons) the net premium will be positive, i.e. there is a **net credit**.

If the underlying spot is above the high strike, both options will be out-of-the-money and will not be exercised. The maximum gain, the net credit, will be:

premium received – premium paid

£3   – £2   = £1

If the spot is below the low strike, both options will be in-the-money and will be exercised.

- The put writer will be obligated to buy at £103.
- The purchaser of the put will sell at £98.
- Simultaneous option positions generate net premium income of £1.

Therefore the money flows are:

–£103 + £98 + £1 = –£4

Rewritten, this becomes:

maximum loss = £103 – £98 – £1 = £4
Breakeven = high strike – net premium
= £103 – £1 = £102

See Figure 14.15 for a pay-off diagram for a bull vertical put spread.

A bear vertical call spread

Buy a call with a high strike and, simultaneously, sell a call with a low strike (same expirations).

Suppose:

	£
Spot of underlying asset	100
Premium paid to purchase a high strike call	2
Premium received for writing a low strike call	4
High strike	103
Low strike	97

If spot falls below £97, e.g. to £96, both options expire out-of-the-money. Here the position will be as follows:

- Receive £4 for writing the low strike call.
- Pay £2 for purchasing high strike call.

Therefore net gain = £4 – £2 = £2 (i.e. net credit). This will be the maximum profit on the two option positions.

If the spot becomes above £103, say £105, the purchaser of the high strike call will have intrinsic value, the option will be exercised at £103. The simultaneous writer of the low strike call will find that the option will also be exercised, it too is in-the-money. The writer will have to sell at the strike of £97.

Money flows will therefore be:

Pay (–)£103, pay premium (–)£2, sell (+)£97, receive premium(+)£4.

For any spot above £103, the cash flows will be identical, i.e. a net loss of £4 Rewritten, maximum loss will therefore be:

high strike – low strike – net premium

£103 – £97 – £2 = £4

Breakeven will occur when spot is somewhere between both strikes, in this case £99. Breakeven can be calculated as:

high strike – net premium

£103 – £4 = £99

See Figure 14.16 for a pay-off diagram for bear vertical call spread.

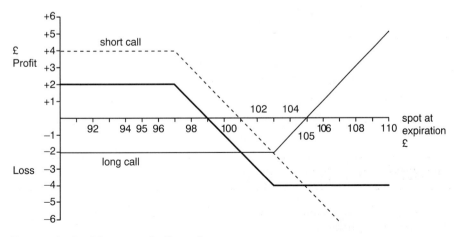

Figure 14.16 *A bear vertical call spread.*

When the underlying is above 102 there is full profit participation. Below 98 losses begin to occur. Between 98 and 102 changes in the value of the underlying are neutralised.

A bear vertical put spread

Buy a put with a high strike and, simultaneously, sell a put with a low strike (same expirations). This is a **long bear put spread**.

Suppose the following:

	£
Spot of the underlying asset is	100
Premium paid to buy a put with high strike	4
Premium received to sell a put with low strike	2
High strike	102
Low strike	98

net premium received = +£2 – £4 = –£2, i.e. net debit

If spot is below the low strike of £98, say £97, then:

- The put writer will find that the option will be exercised, it is in-the-money. The put writer will have to buy the asset at strike £98.
- The simultaneous purchaser of the put will also exercise and receive £102 by selling the asset.

Money flows will therefore be:
Buy asset at (–)£98, receive premium income (+)£2, sell asset (+)£102, pay premium (–)£4 = £2.

As long as the spot is at or below the low strike of £98, a £2 gain will be made, this will be the maximum gain. It can be expressed as:

high strike – low strike – net premium

If spot is above the high strike of £102, say £103, then:

- The put writer will find that the option will not be exercised, it is out-of-the-money, he will retain the premium of £2.
- The purchaser of the put will not exercise, the only expense will be the premium paid of £4.

Money flows will therefore be:
Receive premium income (+)£2, pay premium (–)£4 = (–)£2.
The net loss, the net debit of £2 is the maximum loss which can be made. This can be rewritten as:

maximum loss = premium paid–premium received
= £4 – £2 = £2
breakeven = high strike–net premium
= £102 – £2 = £100

The difference between bear vertical call and bear vertical put strategies is that a call spread will be profitable even if spot prices do not fall.

See Figure 14.17 for a pay-off diagram for a bear vertical put spread.

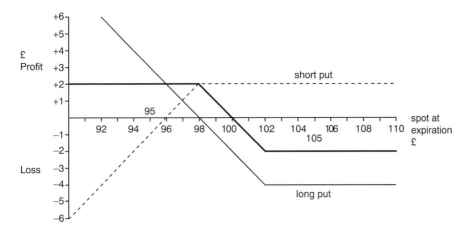

Figure 14.17 *A bear vertical put spread.*

Horizontal spreads

A horizontal spread is where the legs of the spread have two different strikes, but the same expiration.

Bullish and bearish horizontal spreads can be created.

Bullish horizontal spread

Sell a call with a given strike and short time to expiration and, simultaneously, buy a call with the same strike and a longer time to expiration (typically the strike would be above the current spot).

A bearish horizontal spread

Purchase a call with a given strike and short expiration and, simultaneously, sell a call with the same strike and a longer expiration. This is sometimes called a **reverse calendar spread** (typically the strike would be below the current spot).

Both types of horizontal spread could be used when it is believed the underlying spot will be stable. Time value of the shorter option will decline at a faster rate than the time value of the longer option period. This loss on the shorter period will be smaller than the loss on the longer period.

A **neutral calendar spread** has a strike near to the current spot.

With a reverse calendar spread a small profit occurs when spot is much higher than strike or much lower than strike of the shorter maturity option.

Straddles

Straddles are an example of an option **combination**, this is where both puts and calls are used simultaneously. A straddle is purchased by buying a call

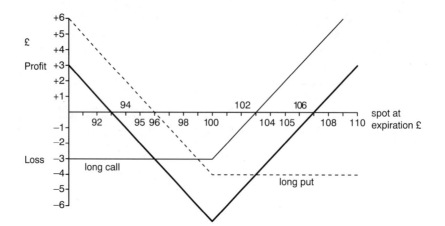

Figure 14.18 *Profit/loss diagram for a bottom straddle.*

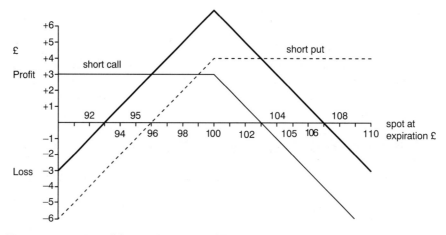

Figure 14.19 *Pay-off diagram for a top straddle.*

and a put on the same underlying asset with same strike and expiration. It is sometimes called a **bottom straddle** due to the shape of its pay-off.

Profit is gained when the price of the underlying asset changes in either direction, i.e. when there is price volatility. A loss occurs when spot stays near to strike, as seen in Figure 14.18.

A straddle is written by selling a put and a call with the same strike and expiration. It is sometimes called a **top straddle**. Profit is gained when the spot of the underlying asset is stable (Figure 14.19). However, if spot moves by a large amount, either up or down, then losses become large and are theoretically unlimited.

Strangles

Strangles are an option combination. A strangle is purchased by buying a put and a call at different exercise prices, but with the same expiration. It is sometimes called a **bottom vertical combination**. The call strike is higher than the put strike. The premium paid for the call is lower than that paid

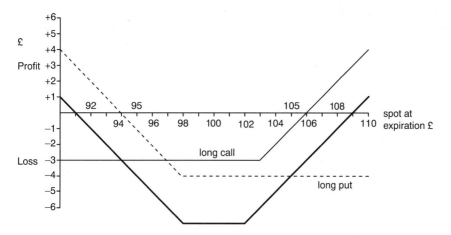

Figure 14.20 *Pay-off diagram for a bottom straddle.*

for the put. Profit is gained by price volatility in either direction of the underlying asset (Figure 14.20).

A strangle is written by selling a call and a put with different exercise prices, but the same expirations. It is sometimes called a **top vertical combination**. Its pay-off profile is a mirror image of that for a bottom strangle. Strangles are similar to straddles. With straddles spot price has to move further to gain profit.

Further points

When using options to hedge or to take speculative positions there are a number of factors which will alter the actual pay-offs in practice. A few are given below.

- Positions do not need to be held until expiration. European option positions can always be closed out. American options can be closed out or exercised before expiration.
- Trades cannot be made free of transactions cost, brokerage commission has to be paid.
- Margin requirements and their costs for option writers have been ignored.
- Bid/ask spreads exist, therefore when closing out this represents a trading cost.
- A writer of an American option may find themselves having to fulfil their obligations before expiration if the option is exercised by the purchaser.

Hedging using more complex trading strategies

Once the pay-offs from complex trading strategies are understood, it is then possible to use them in appropriate hedging strategies to hedge actual or anticipated cash market positions, as has already been seen with more simple strategies.

Hedging small price rises using a long bull call spread

A long call hedging strategy to hedge an anticipated purchase of the underlying asset (Figure 14.12) might be thought by some hedgers to be too expensive due to the premium which has to be paid for the call. A less expensive form of price insurance will be to use a vertical long bull call spread, where the net premium will be lower (refer to Figures 14.21 and 14.14). However, as explained below, the spread only provides limited price protection – you get what you pay for!

If spot falls between £96 and £102 there is a net gain of £2. Once price falls below £96 there is full profit participation. At prices above £104 net losses start to occur.

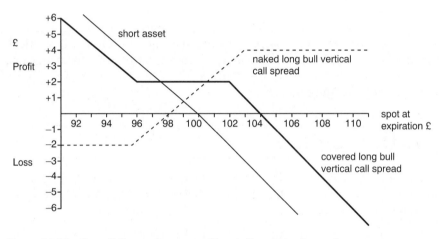

Figure 14.21 *Pay-off diagram for a covered long bull vertical call spread.*

Hedging small price falls using a long bear put spread

Using a long bear put spread is a less costly way of hedging price falls, at the expense of limited protection. The hedge will be used when the underlying asset is already held and its sale is anticipated at a later date. If spot prices increase they can be fully enjoyed only at the expense of the net premium paid, but should spot prices fall, only limited losses will be protected (reference to Figure 14.17 may be useful). The covered long bear put spread is illustrated in Figure 14.22.

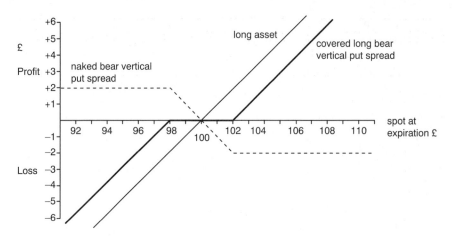

Figure 14.22 *Pay-off diagram for a covered long bear vertical put spread.*

Open interest and volume

In a similar way to the practice in the futures market, open interest and volume statistics are quoted in the options market.

Volume is the number of contracts traded and separate figures are quoted for calls and puts.

Open interest is the number of contracts which have not yet been taken to expiration or off-set. Here too, figures are given separately for calls and puts (see also p. 80 for open interest and volume in the futures market).

Newspaper price quote examples are given in Chapters 15 and 16 for interest rate and currency options and are discussed there.

Summary

- An option is a choice which can be purchased by the long and is sold by the short.
- A call option buyer purchases the right but not the obligation to purchase an underlying asset at a strike/exercise price on or before expiration (American) or at expiration (European).
- A put option buyer has the right to sell.
- The counterparty to the (long) buyer is the (short) seller/writer of the option. Thus the counterparty to a long call is a short call. A short call

has the obligation to sell, a short put has the obligation to buy if the option is exercised by the long.

- A premium is paid by the long to the short and this is the option price, not the strike. With some traded options (all at LIFFE) a futures style margin system operates. On other exchanges only the short is subject to margins.

- All traded options are traded on an organised exchange and trades are cleared through a clearing house, this avoids default risk, reduces search cost and creates liquidity.

- The premium consists of two elements, intrinsic and time value. Options with intrinsic value are said to be in-the-money. For a call to be in the money it will be possible for the long to buy at the strike better than at the prevailing spot. In-the-money puts enable the long to sell at a strike which is higher than the spot. Time value relates to time to expiration and the possibility that the option will gain intrinsic value, related to the volatility of the underlying.

- For the long it is all upside potential, there is no downside risk, at worse the premium will be foregone. For the short there is only downside risk, no upside potential. With American options there is always the possibility that the long will exercise and be assigned to them by the exchange. However, it is optimal for the long to close out and receive time value.

- In common with futures, few options are actually taken to expiration or exercised, but are closed out by taking an opposite position. As an example, a long call would close out by writing a short call for the same strike and expiration and thus cancel obligations. Any gains or losses would be taken by the difference between the premium paid as the long and received by the short. If traded futures style then gains and losses would be taken daily when marked to market.

- Naked options can be taken for speculative purposes or used to cover cash market positions by way of a hedge. It is possible to take multi-option positions to alter pay-offs and profit opportunities and these include spreads, straddles and strangles. Option pay-off diagrams can be drawn for different option positions at expiration. Common hedging strategies include protective puts which create a floor price and covered calls which create a ceiling price.

Key terms

- American (p. 150)
- Asian (p. 150)
- assigned (p. 170)
- asymmetrical contract (p. 148)
- ATM (p. 155)
- breakeven points (p. 158)
- call (p. 149)
- ceiling price (p. 165)
- clearing house (p. 148)
- close-out (p. 170)
- deep-in/deep-out-of-the-money (p. 155)
- downside risk (p. 147)
- European (p. 150)
- exchange (p. 148)
- exercise (p. 147)
- exercise day (p. 150)
- exercise rate (p. 147)
- expiration (p. 147)
- fill or die (p. 149)
- floor price (p. 166)
- futures style margining (p. 149)
- grantor (p. 150)
- holder (p. 147)
- in-, out-, at-the-money (p. 155)
- intrinsic value (p. 154)
- long (p. 149)
- naked/covered option positions (p. 157)
- net credit (p. 174)
- net debit (p. 176)
- off-set (p. 170)
- open interest (p. 181)
- open outcry (p. 149)
- option class (p. 150)
- option combinations (p. 177)
- option legs (p. 172)
- option series (p. 150)
- pay-off diagrams (p. 156)
- premium (p. 147)
- purchaser (p. 147)
- put (p. 149)
- put–call parity (p. 168)
- right but not the obligation (p. 148)
- short (p. 149)
- spreads (p. 171)
- square out (p. 170)
- standardisation (p. 153)
- staying power (p. 149)
- straddles (p. 177)
- strangles (p. 178)
- strike (p. 150)
- strike rate (p. 147)
- takers (p. 150)
- time value (p. 154)
- underlying (p. 149)
- unilateral contract (p. 148)
- upside potential (p. 148)
- volatility (p. 155)
- volume (p. 181)
- walk away (p. 148)
- writer (p. 147)

Questions

14.1 Why are options described as unilateral contracts?

14.2 Give alternative terms for the long and the short.

14.3 Distinguish between the premium and the strike. Which is the option price?

14.4 Which party to an option has upside potential? Which has downside risk?

14.5 Distinguish the default risk for the short and the long. How does a margin system overcome this?

14.6 What is meant by open interest?

14.7 Does a long call have the right but not the obligation to buy or sell the underlying?

14.8 What is the obligation of a short put, to buy or sell the underlying if the option is exercised?

14.9　Who will be the counterparty to a long call?

14.10　What is an option series? An option class?

14.11　Distinguish between American- and European-style options.

14.12　Spot is £12, strike £10, which will be in-the-money, a call or a put?

14.13　What are the two elements of an option price?

14.14　What is meant by deep-out-of-the-money?

14.15　What is meant by ATM?

14.16　Sketch a pay-off diagram 'shape' for:

 a) a naked long put;

 b) a naked short call;

 c) a covered long put.

14.17　What is the breakeven point for a naked long put?

14.18　What option position would you take to create a floor price?

14.19　What might happen to a short put in an American-style option?

14.20　Consider the following information

spot	£15
strike	£12
premium for a long call	£4

What will be the minimum premium demanded by a short put?

14.21　Which multiple option position could you take to profit from anticipated low volatility of the underlying?

14.22　Which multiple option position could you take to hedge anticipated small price rises in the underlying?

Further reading

Dubofsky, David (1992) *Options and Financial Futures*, McGraw Hill.

Hull, J. (1991) *Introduction to Futures & Options Markets*, Prentice Hall.

Redhead, Keith (1990) *Introduction to Financial Futures and Options*, Woodhead Faulkner.

Redhead, Keith (1992) *Introduction to International Money Markets*, Woodhead Faulkner.

Currency options

Introduction

This chapter covers the use of traded currency options to hedge exchange risk. It assumes an understanding of basic option principles as covered in Chapter 14. At the end of the chapter there is a section relating to OTC currency options.

Currency options were first traded on exchanges in Philadelphia, Amsterdam and Vancouver during December 1982. They were traded for a short while at LIFFE/LTOM from 1985, but were discontinued in 1990. Today the main currency options exchanges are in Philadelphia at the Philadelphia Stock Exchange and in Chicago at the Chicago Mercantile Exchange (CME). The Chicago Board Options Exchange (CBOE) tried, but volume was so low that trade was transferred to Philadelphia.

On 20 March 1994 the Marché à Termes des Instruments Financières (MATIF), the French futures and options exchange, introduced two currency options one USD/DEM and one USD/FFR. This went somewhat against the trend in sentiment that says exchange traded currency hedging vehicles, futures and options, are unnecessary where deep and liquid forex markets exist for spot and forward delivery and in OTC currency options. These unregulated markets create flexibility, transaction sizes and delivery terms which exchange traded products cannot match.

The French exchange hopes to capture some of Philadelphia's business, having discovered that a good proportion of it originates in Paris and believes Philadelphia to be an unlikely centre for foreign exchange derivatives. MATIF contracts will be in units of $100,000 and will be traded with spot as the underlying.

In Philadelphia options are traded on spot currencies. At the CME options are traded into the underlying futures contract, here currency options are traded on the Index and Options Market (IOM), itself a division of the IMM, the Merc. The IOM contract sizes are usually twice those in Philadelphia.

The Philadelphia Stock Exchange and the CME trade currency options as in Tables 15.1 and 15.2.

Table 15.1 CME currency options (related to US$)

Currency	Underlying contract	Strike prices	Premium quotations	Tick
Sterling	one BP futures contract (£62,500)	$0.25 intervals, e.g. $1.850, $1.875	US$ per pound sterling	.0002 = $12.50
Deutschmarks	one DM futures contract (DM125,000)	$0.01 intervals, e.g. $.60, £.61	US$ per deutschmark	.0001 = $12.50
Australian Dollar	one AD futures contract (AD100,000)	$0.01 intervals, e.g. $.70, $.71	US$ per AD	.0001 = $10.00
Canadian Dollar	one CD futures contract (CD100,000)	$0.005 intervals, e.g. $.800, $.805	US$ per CD	.0001 = $10.00
Japanese Yen	one JY futures contract (Y12,500,000)	$0.0001 intervals, e.g. $.0072, $.0073	US$ per Yen	.000001 = $12.50
Swiss Francs	one SF futures contract (SF125,000)	$0.01 intervals, e.g. $.75, $.76	US$ per SF	.0001 = $12.50

There is also a cross-currency option DM/JY traded into the DM/JY futures contract (DM125,000).

At the CME options on currency futures are listed for all twelve calendar months. Each option can be exercised into the quarter end futures contract. Thus, January, February and March options are exercisable into the March futures contract. At any point in time it is possible to trade options that expire in the next three calendar months, plus the following two quarter end expirations.

In most option contracts at the CME half strikes may also be listed for the first three consecutive contract months. Trades may also be made in increments of half ticks known as **cabinets**.

Table 15.2 Philadelphia Stock Exchange currency options (related to US$)

Currency	Underlying contract	Premium quote	Average daily volume, contracts
Sterling	spot £12,500	US$ per pound sterling	
Canadian Dollar	spot CD50,000	US$ per CD	
Deutschmarks	spot DM62,500	US$ per DM	15,000
S. Francs	spot SF62,500	US$ per SF	
F. Francs	spot FF125,000	US$ per FF	12,200
Yen	spot Yen 6.25m	US$ per Yen	
Australian Dollar	spot AD50,000	US$ per AD	

Put and call conventions

Options relate rights and obligations to underlying assets. If the underlying asset is a currency and the option is exercised, this involves an exchange of one currency for another. One currency is bought, one is sold at a given exchange rate, the strike. Of course most options will be closed out in reality, rather than be actually exercised. The question naturally arises – how will these obligations/rights be described in terms of puts and calls? Alternatively, which currency is the underlying asset?

If the option relates to the exchange of sterling and US dollars, does a put give the holder the right to sell sterling or sell the US dollar? It is also apparent that the right to sell one currency necessarily conveys the right to buy the other. If you sell sterling you buy the US dollar. Is this a sterling put or a dollar call therefore?

As can be seen from Tables 15.1 and 15.2, most currency options relate currencies to the US dollar, although there are now more cross currency options being traded on exchanges. Taking an option relating sterling and the US dollar, the convention is:

- A buyer of a put on sterling has the right to sell (deliver) a quantity of sterling and buy (receive) US dollars at the strike rate.

Therefore, if exercised:

- The sterling put buyer (long put) sells sterling and buys US dollars.
- The sterling put seller (short put) buys sterling and sells US dollars.
- The sterling call buyer (long call) buys sterling and sells US dollars.
- The sterling call seller (short call) sells sterling and buys US dollars.

Always look at the position from the point of view of the option buyer, the long, and describe their rights in relation to the non-dollar currency, if the option is related to the US dollar.

A sterling/US dollar option is correctly described as a sterling call or put, never a dollar put or call, even though a sterling call is the 'same' as a dollar put.

In general terms, currency options describe rights and obligations in relation to the underlying currency, rather than the base currency. Unfortunately this means that when the option is sterling/US dollar, due to the spot convention, the US dollar is the underlying. Therefore perhaps an easier way to remember how to relate puts and calls for currency options is always to relate the put or call to the non-dollar currency, bearing in mind that most options relate a currency to the US dollar.

One more complication! What if the option is cross-currency, not related to the US dollar, for instance DM/JY? Follow the convention as used in the futures market, refer to p. 118 and the explanation given on p. 189.

As a re-cap and a reminder, the convention for currency options is:

> The US dollar is the base currency, the 'other' currency is the underlying – regardless of the convention in the spot market.

Thus:

- £1 = $1.50, sterling is the underlying;
- $1 = DM1.40, deutschmarks is the underlying.

This convention is followed in all descriptions in this chapter unless otherwise stated. The convention is known as **American terms** or **reciprocal terms**.

American terms is the convention used on all traded currency option exchanges when a currency is quoted against the US dollar, even though in the US, **European terms** are now used in most cases in the spot market. The major exception is of course spot sterling against the US dollar, which is always quoted American-style, i.e. £1 = $2. By using American terms on the traded options exchanges, losses and gains on a given option position can always be expressed directly in US dollar tick values, rather than in the other currency.

Currency option definitions

The definition of a currency option, following the explanation in the previous section relating to calls therefore becomes:

- For a buyer of a currency option it is the right to buy (take delivery of) a predetermined amount of one currency in exchange for a predetermined amount of another at a predetermined date and at a predetermined exchange rate.
- For a writer of a currency call option it is the obligation to sell (deliver if called upon to do so) a predetermined amount of one currency in exchange for a predetermined amount of another currency at a predetermined date and at a predetermined exchange rate.

The definition relating to put options becomes:

- For the buyer of a currency put option it is the right to sell (deliver) a predetermined amount of one currency in exchange for a predetermined amount of another currency at a predetermined date and at a predetermined exchange rate.
- For the writer of a currency put option it is the obligation to buy (take delivery of if called upon to do so) a predetermined amount of one currency in exchange for a predetermined amount of another currency at a predetermined date and a predetermined exchange rate.

Note that these definitions refer strictly to European options, American-style options can of course be exercised at any time until expiration and most currency options are American-style.

Currency options on futures

Reference to Table 15.1 shows that on the CME the underlying asset for currency options is a futures position; they are options on futures. For reasons why an option on a future has advantages over an option on a spot underlying, see p. 208 for a discussion.

When a call futures option is exercised, the holder acquires a long position in the underlying futures contract plus a cash amount equal to the current futures price minus the exercise (strike) price. In reality, cash will not be received as such. The future will be marked to market from the strike price the following day and variation margin received. Initial margin will be payable if the futures position is not closed out. The short call is assigned a short futures position which is then marked to market in the appropriate way.

If a put futures option is exercised, the holder acquires a short position in the underlying futures contract plus a cash amount equal to the exercise price minus the current futures price. As described above, marking to market usually occurs. The short put is assigned a long futures position.

When an American-style currency option on a future is traded, it is referred to by the month in which the underlying futures contract matures, not by the expiration month of the option itself.

The maturity date of the option is usually on or a few days before the earliest delivery date of the underlying futures contract. CME currency futures options expire at least two business days before expiration of the futures contract.

A currency futures option buyer therefore will have the right but not the obligation to take a position in the underlying futures contract.

- Buying a call gives the right to buy the underlying futures contract at a specific price, even if the current futures price is higher. Calls gain value when the futures price rises.
- Buying a put gives the right to sell the underlying futures contract at a specific price, even if the current futures price is lower. Puts gain value when the futures price falls.

Naturally in most cases the option position will itself be closed out and the futures position not taken.

Cross-currency options

The CME option on DM/JY futures is priced in Yen, that is the premium is in Yen and losses and gains are calculated in Yen. This follows the procedure concerning the DM/JY future itself as described on p. 119. Rates are quoted in European terms. The purchaser of the futures contract receives DMs and pays Yen. The seller delivers DMs and receives Yen.

Calls give the option purchaser the right to buy the underlying DM/JY futures contract at an agreed strike rate. The futures position now obtained obligates the receipt of DMs and the paying of Yen, therefore calls gain value if the futures price rises, and this occurs when the DM appreciates against the Yen.

Puts give the option purchaser the right to sell the underlying DM/JY futures contract at an agreed strike rate. The futures position is an obligation to deliver DMs and receive Yen, therefore puts gain value if the futures price falls. This occurs when the DM depreciates against the Yen.

If the option is exercised, rather than closed out, the exchange will assign the relevant DM/JY futures contract, as with US dollar options:

- For a long call a long futures position will be assigned.
- For a long put a short futures position will be assigned.

For the short option position the assigned futures contract will be the reverse of that for the long, therefore:

- For a short call a short futures position will be assigned.
- For a short put a long futures position will be assigned.

Currency option hedging strategies – an outline

Currency options can be used to hedge exchange risk by the use of simple strategies. The basic idea, as seen with other ways of hedging, is that losses/gains in the cash market are off-set by gains/losses from the option position taken.

To hedge against a fall in the value of the US dollar relative to sterling, as required by a UK exporter with dollar receivables at a later date, it is possible to purchase sterling calls or sell sterling puts.

A UK importer with US dollar payments to make at a later date, wishing to hedge against a rise the value of the dollar could purchase sterling puts or sell sterling calls.

As with all option-buying hedges, it can be viewed as purchasing insurance with a deductible clause. The option will protect against losses after a certain exchange rate has been reached. This exchange rate will of course depend upon the strike actually used, in-, at- or out-of-the-money. In turn this will determine the cost of protection via the premium paid. Out-of-the-money strikes will incur lower premium prices because the chance of becoming in-the-money is more remote and there is no intrinsic value.

Option-selling hedges give protection from the consequences of exchange risk up to a maximum of the premium generated, i.e. if exchange rate losses occur these will be off-set up to the receipts from the option sale. Exchange losses greater than the premium income will not be protected. It follows that the sale of in-the-money options generates greater premium income and greater protection through off-set than the sale of out-of-the-money options.

Currency options to hedge contingencies

The classic case where the currency option has the edge in hedging exchange risk is where the risk may not actually arise, as for example, when an exporter is tendering for a sale. If the tender is awarded to the exporter there will be exchange risk. If the tender is not awarded there will be no exchange risk. Should the exporter hedge? Futures or forward contracts leave the possibility of close-out costs of an unknown value if the tender is not won and no currency receivable. If no hedge is placed there is exchange risk if the tender is awarded. An option, however, conveys the right but not the obligation to buy or sell and is therefore ideal for contingent exchange risk.

If a UK exporter is tendering for a US dollar contract and he or she purchases a sterling call and the contract is not awarded, then the exporter knows that the maximum outlay will be the premium paid. There is also a possibility that should the value of sterling rise and the dollar fall, so that the option becomes in-the-money, that the option can be closed out for intrinsic and time value, if any of the latter is left. Should the tender be awarded, then of course the option can be exercised/closed out if it is favourable to do so, or the option can be allowed to expire and spot sterling sold for the purchase of dollars if the option is out-of-the-money.

If the tender is not awarded and the option has not expired, but is out-of-the-money, it will still be possible to recover a little of the expense by selling the option and receiving back remaining time value.

Currency options – what is the best way to hedge currency risk?

Using currency options to hedge, it is not necessarily the case that losses/gains are on a one for one basis as they are in the futures market. Options limit risk, but enable profit participation. Options can never be the best strategy to hedge currency risk – with hindsight either an open position or a forward rate will give the best outcome. The problem is of course that you do not have hindsight, so your choice of an open position or forward rate might turn out to be the worse outcome if you choose incorrectly. Options can never be potentially the best outcome, but they can be better than the worst.

Exporter hedging scenarios

The following sections describe the use of various option strategies to hedge US dollar receivables by a UK sterling-based exporter. Imagine the following scenario in each case:

Current spot is £1 = $1.50.
Anticipated receivables are $1m in three months' time.
Pay-offs are given as if the option position is held to expiration.

Covered at-the-money long call

A UK exporter can purchase long at-the-money calls to hedge exchange risk, to protect falls in the value of the currency receivable. Long calls give the right but not the obligation to buy sterling, sell dollars, at £1 = $1.50 for a premium of, say, 5 cents. The pay-off at expiration is as in Figure 15.1.

Once spot rises above $1.50 it pays to exercise the option. The premium paid is 5 cents, therefore the effective worst rate for the UK exporter is $1.55. At any spot at expiration above $1.50 the cost of the covered position is 5 cents as seen from Figure 15.1. Below spot $1.50 the option is abandoned and sterling bought at spot. However, the premium of 5 cents has been paid, therefore this has to be set against gains in the spot market. Effectively at spot rates below $1.45 gains in the spot market can be fully participated in.

In summary, a covered long at-the-money call provides protection above the breakeven rate and full participation of windfall profit as a result of spot changes, at the expense of the premium paid. A long at-the-money

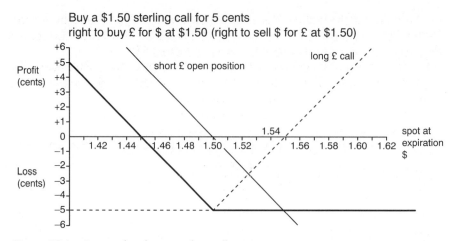

Buy a $1.50 sterling call for 5 cents
right to buy £ for $ at $1.50 (right to sell $ for £ at $1.50)

Figure 15.1 *A covered at-the-money long call.*

call protects against a rise in the exchange rate, i.e. a fall in the value of the US dollar relative to sterling.

Covered long out-of-the-money call

By purchasing an out-of-the-money call the cost of protection for a UK exporter against a rise in the exchange rate is reduced from that of an at-the-money call. However, the level of protection is consequently reduced. You always get what you pay for!

A sterling call could be purchased at, say, $1.55 for 3 cents, with spot at $1.50. As a result the pay-off at expiration would be as in Figure 15.2.

The spot rate has to fall to $1.47 from the spot initially at $1.50 for participation in the increase in the value of the US dollar relative to sterling. However, protection is only given above $1.58 for a fall in the value of the US dollar, which is what the exporter wishes to protect – a fall

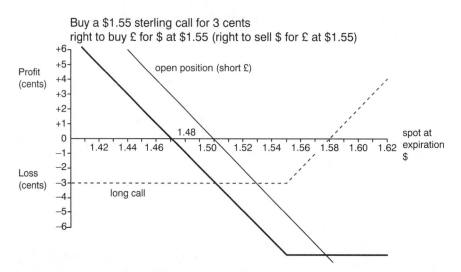

Buy a $1.55 sterling call for 3 cents
right to buy £ for $ at $1.55 (right to sell $ for £ at $1.55)

Figure 15.2 *A covered out-of-the-money long call.*

in the value of the dollar. Here the dollar has to fall in value by 8 cents before there is protection against its further fall. With an at-the-money option protection occurs once the rate reaches $1.55.

An out-of-the-money call is best used by an exporter therefore who wishes to be protected against relatively large falls in the value of the dollar, but feels on balance that the value of the dollar will rise and wishes to participate in the gains arising from this, but with protection against its fall. Protection is of course limited, but its cost is (of course) smaller.

Writing a covered at-the-money put

If a UK exporter writes a covered $1.50 put and the holder exercises the option, then as the put writer he will be obligated to purchase sterling for US dollars and this is what an exporter wishes to do. The premium received, say 8 cents, will off-set the cost of buying sterling.

The option will be exercised by the holder at any rate below $1.50, thus the best rate at which the writer will have purchased sterling will be $1.50 less the 8 cents, or $1.42. Sterling will be purchased at this rate even if the US dollar appreciates considerably. The writer is therefore effectively locking in a rate which can be no better from his point of view than $1.42.

Gains from a large appreciation in the US dollar cannot be participated in. On the other hand, falls in the dollar are not protected. If the spot rate rises above $1.50 the option will not be exercised by the holder. At $1.58 the spot is at its highest before the writer is left unprotected from the losses associated with a fall in the value of the US dollar.

Therefore there is little opportunity to make windfall profits from an appreciation in the value of the dollar and only limited protection from its depreciation. It is a strategy which is useful when the spot rate is relatively stable. Of course this means taking a view of what the spot is going to be. In a sideways market it gives income augmentation at the expense of limited protection from exchange risk and limited windfall profit.

Pay-offs from the covered position are as shown in Figure 15.3.

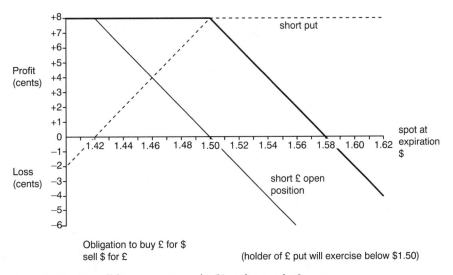

Obligation to buy £ for $
sell $ for £   (holder of £ put will exercise below $1.50)

Figure 15.3 *Pay-off diagram, writing a $1.50 sterling put for 8 cents.*

A covered currency bull vertical call spread

A covered currency bull vertical call spread would involve, for example:

- purchasing a $1.50 call for 5 cents and
- writing a $1.58 call for 2 cents.

Upfront costs are smaller than for a straightforward at-the-money long call. The 5 cent cost of the long call is reduced by 2 cents, the premium income from writing the short out-of-the-money call.

When spot is between $1.50 and $1.58 in net terms spot is taken at a cost of 3 cents in each case. At spot below $1.47, gains arise from the covered position as windfall profits are taken. At spot above $1.58 losses occur as if there were an open position, albeit reduced by 3 cents in each case. See Figure 15.4 for the pay-off diagram.

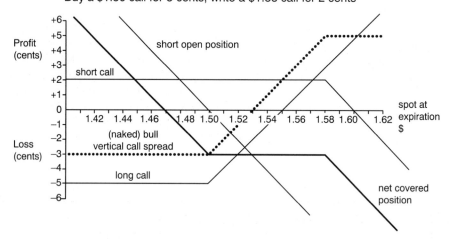

Figure 15.4 *A bull vertical call spread.*

A currency zero cost fence/cylinder option

A **zero cost** fence is so called due to the nature of protection given and because premium received equals premium paid. It is also sometimes called a **cylinder option**. It involves, as an example:

- purchasing a $1.55 call for 3 cents and
- writing a $1.45 put for 3 cents.

The pay-offs from this strategy, coupled with the short sterling (long dollar) position of a UK exporter can be seen from Figure 15.5.

The two option legs in combination produce neither losses nor gains between the strikes of $1.45 and $1.55 since both options are abandoned. As a result a UK exporter short of sterling (long US dollar) can benefit from falls in the spot down to $1.45, i.e. they can gain from gains in the value of the dollars of which he will be long. Once $1.45 is breached no further gains are possible due to the obligations of the short put leg.

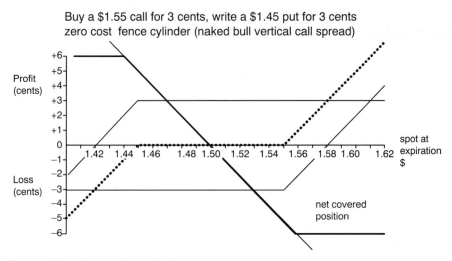

Figure 15.5 *Zero cost fence cylinder option.*

If the spot rises above $1.50, up to a maximum of $1.55, the UK exporter, long US dollars, will lose from a depreciation in the spot value of the US dollar. Once $1.55 is reached no further exchange losses will occur. The option legs do not protect completely, but they do limit loss and limit gains.

It should be clear that between the two strikes of a fence, the hedger will exchange currency effectively at spot and thus make losses and gains as appropriate. The obligation of the short will be cancelled out by the right of the long. Alternatively, if the long is not exercised, its cost will be cancelled out by the income of the short. Limits on gains and losses as a result of exchanges at spot are protected by the fence delimited by the strikes.

Variations on a cost fence

Cost fences can be placed giving slightly different outcomes from that achieved above. The call and put strikes can be altered to widen the exchange rates over which the fence operates and protection is given. The strikes could be, for example, $1.65 and $1.35. This would still probably be zero cost in that premium paid and received would be equal, but the potential for windfall profits would be much wider at the expense of inferior protection for the UK exporter should the spot rate rise substantially. Protection will not 'kick in' until $1.65, any movement in spot above $1.50 to $1.65 will incur loss. Windfall gains can be taken down to $1.35, however.

Strikes can be altered to narrow the fence so that windfall profit potential is low, but downside losses are small due to the greater degree of protection should the spot rate rise. In addition strikes for the call and put can be unequally spaced either side of the current spot, thus producing either a net outlay or net premium income when the hedge is placed. The way the strikes are located either side of current spot gives the pay-off profile. Large windfall gains can be taken with small downside protection should the spot rise, or windfall gains might be limited and small, yet downside risk protected until quite high spot rates.

Currency option premium determination

As discussed in Chapter 14, an option premium may have two components, intrinsic and time value. In-the-money options have intrinsic value and time value before expiration. Intrinsic value will be the difference between strike and spot.

A currency call has intrinsic value when the spot is higher than the strike:

A long call at $1.50, when spot is $1.60, has intrinsic value. The long can buy sterling, sell dollars for $1.50, instead of at $1.60. For example, buying £12,500 at $1.50 requires $18,750, at $1.60 it requires $20,000. Intrinsic value is $1,250. $1,250 would be the intrinsic value of one Philadelphia sterling call at expiration.

A long put has intrinsic value when spot is less than strike:

A long put at $1.50, when spot is $1.40, has intrinsic value. The long can sell sterling, buy dollars for $1.50, instead of at $1.40. For example, selling £12,500 at $1.50 realises $18,750, at $1.40 the sale realises $17,500. Intrinsic value is $1,250.

Alternatively, intrinsic value for a currency call is:

spot minus strike

For a currency put it is:

strike minus spot.

No option can have time value at expiration, only intrinsic value, if there is any. However, an option can have time value before expiry, with or without intrinsic value. The level of time value before expiry depends upon the chance of the option gaining intrinsic value before expiry.

A currency call buyer will pay time value for the chance that the spot of the underlying currency will move higher than the strike. Equally the writer of the call will be demanding the payment of time value due to the risk they are taking that the spot will move higher above the strike and the option will be exercised. This component of the option premium demanded and paid is thus described alternatively as **risk** or **extrinsic premium**.

Thus, prior to expiry, an in-the-money option is worth intrinsic plus time value. An out-of-the-money option will have time value only. As an in-the-money option becomes further in-the-money, its intrinsic value will increase, but the time value component decreases, the reason here is that as the option becomes further and further in-the-money, the likelihood of becoming out-of-the-money diminishes, it will almost certainly be exercised. Thus buyers will not pay risk premium and writers will not be able to charge it.

Out-of-the-money options will only have time value. The longer the time to expiration, the greater will be the time value. Longer time allows the spot of the underlying to change so that the option becomes in-the-money and has intrinsic value.

An option with three months to expiration costs more than a quarter of the cost of a one-year option in relation to time value. A one-year option is not four times the price of a three month option. The cost is based on the square root of time.

$$\sqrt{12} \div \sqrt{3} = 3.464 \div 1.732 = 2$$

A one-year option costs twice as much as a three-month option. The result of this is that time value decays rapidly as at-the-money options approach maturity.

Currency options and volatility

Volatility refers to how much the value of the underlying currency is likely to change over time. The more any underlying changes, the greater will be the effect on the in- or out-of-the-money status of the option. The more volatile the underlying, the higher will be the premium as the risk of the option attaining intrinsic value will be greater.

In relation to currency options, it is an observable fact that some currencies change their values more frequently. It used to be said that currencies within the ERM were less volatile in relation to each other and indeed this was the case. However, since the events of September 1992, this can hardly now be so. During the years that the ERM 'worked' it followed that option premiums say, £/DM would be lower than say £/$, there being a greater risk, to the writer, that the option would become in-the-money with a £/$ option.

There are various ways in which currency volatility can be measured, the idea is to measure the likelihood of changes around the trend. Volatility is usually measured by calculating standard deviations of daily price changes of the underlying currency statistically, and express them on an annualised basis so that comparisons can be made.

Annualised volatility of 20% means that there is a 60% chance of the underlying currency changing its price, up or down, during a year by up to 20%. There is a 32% chance that the underlying currency will have changed value by more than 20%, up or down, during a year.

For at-the-money options, increasing volatility increases the option premium by the same proportion. Volatility increases 10%, the premium increases 10%.

Historically, volatility cannot necessarily be relied upon to predict accurately what volatility will be from now on. What the option market collectively thinks currently volatility is can be calculated from the premiums currently being charged and paid in the options market. For each premium there will be an implied volatility. Implied volatility is often published for each option by information vendors. Volatility and option pricing is discussed at length in Chapter 17.

Currency option premiums and interest rate differentials

Interest rates play a significant role in the determination of option premiums. The issue is discussed also in Chapter 17. When currency options are considered, two interest rates have to be taken into account, that of the base and that of the underlying currency. As will be demonstrated, it is the interest rate differential which is the key factor, as it also is in the determination of forward exchange rates.

Consider a naked long sterling put with:

- strike £1 = $1.50
- spot £1 = $1.50
- dollar interest rate = 5% p.a.
- sterling interest rate = 10% p.a.

(all central rates, bid or offer).

You could sell sterling and buy US dollars at spot. Thus, if the value of the dollar appreciates relative to sterling, gains will be made in the spot market. Such gains will occur if the spot falls, say to $1.40.

A gain is also made by the purchaser of a naked sterling put if the spot falls, the US dollar appreciates. If a sterling $1.50 put is bought, which gives the right to sell sterling at $1.50, the option becomes in-the-money and gains value as the spot falls. You, the holder, will be able to sell sterling for dollars getting $1.50 for every £1, even were the spot to fall to, say, $1.40. You could get your $1.50 for every £1 and then sell the dollars back at spot $1.40 to realise your gain. In reality the option position will be closed out by taking an off-setting position, in this case by selling a sterling put.

Thus, selling sterling for dollars at spot and holding dollars is an alternative to buying a sterling put. Equally, buying sterling for dollars and holding sterling is an alternative to buying a sterling call.

It is for these reasons that currency options are often described as the equivalent of investing in a currency. Buying a call on a currency is the equivalent of investing in that currency as an alternative to investing in another. In the case of a sterling call against the US dollar, the return is the equivalent of the difference between the return for holding dollars and holding sterling, that is, the interest rate differential. Of course the return can be either positive or negative, depending upon the relationship of the interest rates to each other.

If a sterling call is the same as selling dollars, buying sterling and holding sterling on deposit, each alternative strategy achieves a net return equal to the interest rate differential.

A sterling $1.50 call will become in-the-money as the spot rises and will be exercised. If you, with the long sterling call, can buy sterling, sell dollars, at $1.50 instead off say, spot $1.60, then you will gain. You give up $1.50 for £1, then sell back sterling at spot $1.60 for a ten cents profit. The alternative is to hold sterling which appreciates in value relative to the dollar as the spot rate rises.

The question still arises – what is the relevance of the interest rate differential?

In this case $ = 5%, £ = 10% p.a., differential equals 5% (approximately – see p. 34).

Consider again the alternative of a long sterling put and holding dollars. It must be remembered that the dollars were obtained by selling sterling, therefore the financing cost of holding dollars in this case is the cost of borrowing sterling. So, if sterling interest rates rise the alternative strategy of a long sterling put would become more attractive. As a result the premium for the put will also rise, again making the strategies equal in cost. The point, however, is that a rise in the sterling interest rate altering the differential causes the put premium to rise, thus demonstrating the influence of interest rates.

The sterling put premium will rise if the US dollar interest rate falls. Remember the alternative to the put strategy is the holding of US dollars. If dollars are held they can earn interest of 5% p.a. If this interest income falls, the strategy of holding them becomes less attractive and the put option as an alternative becomes more attractive. As a result the put premium increases.

So why in each case is it the interest rate differential which is important? Consider one case: borrow sterling at 10%, exchange the sterling for dollars at spot and hold dollars at 5%. The net cost of this strategy is the interest rate differential between sterling and dollars. The net cost is cost of sterling (10%) minus gain on holding dollars (5%) equals 5%. In all permutations possible it is the interest rate differential which will influence the option premium.

The relationships between interest rate differentials and option premiums (if the spot remains constant and therefore there is no change in intrinsic value to affect premium) are therefore as follows.

If the interest rate differential increases:

● call premiums increase
● put premiums decrease.

If the interest rate differential decreases:

● call premiums decrease
● put premiums increase.

As the interest rate differential changes, so do currency options premiums, but by how much? Is the relationship on a one for one basis? Before this is discussed directly, remember that forward exchange rates are also determined by interest rate differentials as covered in Chapter 6. We will get to the answers to the questions via a discussion in the next section on the price difference in option premiums between American- and European-style currency options.

American- and European-style currency option intrinsic values

The key to a better understanding of intrinsic value for currency options is to appreciate that in reality:

● European-style options give the right but not the obligation to buy/sell the underlying currency at a **forward exchange rate**.
● American-style options give the right but not the obligation to buy/sell the underlying currency at **spot up** to expiration.

The discussion which follows will demonstrate this to be true. It will also show that intrinsic values for European- and American-style options may be different, given the same strikes. If intrinsic values can be different, it must also follow that premiums can also be different. This latter point can be seen to be more intuitively true in that the right to buy /sell up to a later date is a little different from the right to buy/sell at a later date.

Using:

● dollar interest rate = 5% p.a.
● sterling interest rate = 10% p.a.

- spot £1 = $1.50

and the options to be (unrealistically) over one year, it follows that the one-year forward rate is £1 = $1.4546.

The following will apply at various strikes (obviously all are at- or in-the-money and have intrinsic value).

	Intrinsic value	
$1.40 American call	$0.10	spot minus strike
$1.40 European call	$0.0318	strike minus forward
$1.50 American call	zero	
$1.50 European call	zero	
$1.50 American put	$0.0682	strike minus forward
$1.50 European put	$0.0682	strike minus forward
$1.60 American put	$0.1682	strike minus forward
$1.60 European put	$0.1682	strike minus forward

It can be noted that in-the-money calls have different intrinsic values. The American call has intrinsic value of $0.10, whereas the European call has intrinsic value of $0.318.

The at-the-money calls, European- and American-style, have no intrinsic value, as would be expected. However, both at-the-money puts do have intrinsic value and it is the same for both styles. The reason for this is a little less obvious. In-the-money puts, both styles, have the same intrinsic values, unlike their call equivalents.

Arbitrage opportunities are the key to understanding the above apparent inconsistencies.

American in-the-money calls and intrinsic value

The $1.40 American call must have an intrinsic value of at least $0.10. It could be exercised immediately, sterling could be bought, dollars sold at the strike of $1.40. Using a Philadelphia option, £12,500 could be bought at a cost of $17,500. The £12,500 obtained could then be sold at $1.50 spot to obtain $18,750, giving a profit of $1,250. The premium must therefore be at least the intrinsic value, otherwise the arbitrage suggested could take place (£12,500 × $0.10 = $1,250).

Intrinsic value for in-the-money American calls must therefore be:

spot − strike

as discussed earlier (pp. 196, 197).

European in-the-money calls and intrinsic value

European-style options, by virtue of their specification, cannot be exercised prior to their expiration. For this reason the spot is not a relevant issue until expiration. Before expiration the intrinsic value of a European call will be:

strike – forward rate

An arbitrage exercise will illustrate this to be so. Say that the premium (intrinsic value) were less than strike minus the forward rate, the following could be arranged to derive a riskless arbitrage profit:

Buy a $1.40 European call for $0.03 (i.e. less than stated actual intrinsic value of $0.0318). Premium therefore = £12,500 × $0.03 = $375.

Enter into a forward contract to sell sterling, buy dollars at expiration of the option at the forward rate of $1.4318.

At expiration the call will be exercised. This buys sterling, sells dollars at $1.40. Imagine a Philadelphia call, £12,500 could be bought at $1.40 for $17,500.

The £12,500 is taken and sold as per the forward contract at the forward rate of $1.4318 to realise $17,897.50.

Profit is thus $17,897.50–$17,500 = $397.50.

Deducting from this the premium of $375 paid gives a net arbitrage profit of $22.50.

The $22.50 in fact is actually the minimum profit which would be made were the call to be under priced in the way suggested. If at expiration the spot were to be below the strike of $1.40, say, $1.35, then the call will not be exercised. It will be better to sell dollars at spot $1.35 than at the strike of $1.40. Thus the option premium of $375 will have been paid, but it will still be possible, indeed obligatory, to sell sterling, buy dollars at $1.4318 under the terms of the forward contract.

The forward contract will sell £12,500 for $17,897.50. The $17,897.50 can be sold at spot $1.35 for £13,257.41, profit £757.41, less the sterling equivalent of the premium paid of $375 at the then spot of $1.50 = £250. This gives an overall profit of £757.41 minus £250 = £507.41. The minimum profit of $22.50 at spot of $1.35 would be £16.67.

These calculations do ignore the present value of the premium paid and this is dealt with by a different worked example in the next section.

Buying a call and selling at a forward rate has the same profit/loss profile as a long put. For this reason the combined trades are known as a **synthetic put**.

American in-the-money puts and intrinsic value

The $1.60 American put as indicated on p. 200 has intrinsic value of $0.1682, the same as the European $1.60 put, ($1.60 minus $1.4318). This means that an American put must also have intrinsic value of strike minus forward rate, not strike minus spot as for an American call.

If an American in-the-money put were to have a premium lower than a European, as would be the case if it were priced strike minus spot, then an arbitrage profit could be made. The arbitrage would be:

- buy the American in-the-money put and
- sell the European in-the-money put.

At expiration at the latest, rights and obligations on the option legs would cancel each other out. However, if the premium paid for the American put were lower than that received for the European put, then profit would be earned.

Alternatively the following could occur and arbitrage profits could be made if the option were mispriced. It is the 'reverse' of the strategy used on p. 201 for the European in-the-money call.

Buy the American put at $1.60 for $0.1682, buy sterling forward at $1.4318 (assumes central rates).

Say at expiration spot is $1.55, the put would therefore be exercised, sterling would be sold for dollars at $1.60

$$£12,500 \times \$1.60 = \$20,000$$

The $20,000 would provide the means to honour the forward contract. It would be sold to buy sterling at the forward rate of $1.4318, realising £13,968.43.

$$\text{Profit} = £13,968.43 - £12,500 = £1,468.43$$

The premium paid (in relation to intrinsic value) was

$$£12,500 \times \$0.1682 = \$2,102.50$$

At a forward (central) rate of $1.4318 this is £1,468.43.

Thus, profit equals premium paid and demonstrates the American $1.60 put is correctly priced in relation to its intrinsic value element in that it does not allow arbitrage profits.

Intrinsic values, more relationships and a summary

Where interest rates on the underlying currency are higher than those for the US dollar, the relationships given on p. 200 apply, that is:

- All American- and European-style options have the same intrinsic values except for in-the-money calls.

Where interest rates on the underlying currency are lower than those for the US dollar then:

- All American- and European-style options have the same intrinsic values except for in-the-money puts.

In summary therefore:

- For American options the premium must be at least spot minus forward or strike minus spot – whichever is the greater.
- For European options the premium must be at least strike minus forward.

Strictly in each case strike minus the forward rate should be discounted to present value.

Best value – European or American options?

We have seen that some European and American options can have the same intrinsic values, it all depends on the relationship of the interest rate differentials. In the worked examples on p. 200 ff., American and European puts had the same intrinsic value. The question therefore arises, should the American option have a higher premium than the European for reasons other than intrinsic value? Should the American premium be higher because it allows exercise before expiration?

An alternative question is, because the European sterling call had lower intrinsic value in the example given, is there any reason to pay more for the American call?

In most cases it does not make a great deal of difference. You only have to remember that with a traded option you do not necessarily have to exercise to make use of it. You can close out the position before expiration.

If you hold a European option and close out before expiration you should be able to sell it for at least its intrinsic value and exchange at spot. The 'penalty' for closing out before expiration becomes smaller the closer you are to expiration. The reason for this is as follows:

Intrinsic value for a European option is strike minus forward rate. As you approach expiration the forward rate to expiration and spot become closer. Remember the forward rate is an adjustment to the current spot relative to the interest rate differential. The adjustment becomes smaller as the period forward becomes smaller. Thus the further away from expiration, the more different a European is in comparison to the equivalent American, which has intrinsic value equal to strike minus spot.

If you hold an American call you can either exercise it at any time up to expiration and take delivery of sterling at the strike rate, or the option can be sold and the position closed out. This means that the option can be sold for at least its intrinsic value and sterling bought at spot. The outcome in either case will be the same, effectively sterling will have been purchased at the strike rate.

If the option is closed out rather than exercised it will also be possible to recover time value. For this reason an American option should never be exercised early, by so doing any remaining time value is lost. The time value can of course be recovered by closing out the position. The only qualifications to this conclusion are:

- An American option should be exercised early, rather than be closed out, if it is trading for less than intrinsic value due to market imperfection.
- A hedger may require the currency before expiration. If the position is closed out the currency will still have to be exchanged at spot and this will incur transactions costs, a comparison by each hedger should be made to see which is the cheaper.
- When an option moves deep in the money it will have no time value, it will trade only for its intrinsic value, thus closing out and getting time value is not possible so exercise is preferable. Transactions costs are probably smaller and continuing to hold the option position means forgoing the return on holding actual currency itself.

It must be appreciated that interest rates on either the underlying or base currency may well change whilst the option position is held. This will alter the interest rate differential and thereby intrinsic values when they are determined by the differential.

OTC currency options

The OTC currency options market is highly liquid. Actual turnover is difficult to estimate, but it is probably at least that on the exchanges. Strike rate, time to expiration, the actual currencies to be exchanged, exercise procedures, amount of premium and how it is to be quoted and the unit amounts are all subject to negotiation between the parties. By definition there is no standardisation, flexibility to tailor-make each option to the specific needs of the buyer is of the essence.

Inter-bank trades are as high as $100m. In contrast Barclays Bank offer their customers options down to a unit of £5,000. Expirations vary from hours to ten years, most liquidity is, however, in the one month to a year maturities.

There is no clearing house which takes over and virtually eliminates credit risk. However, for the option buyer dealing with a top rated bank the credit risk is small. For the bank the premium paid up front means default risk is eliminated, although they will be subject to some delivery risk of currency if the option is actually exercised, rather than closed out.

With option writers banks will usually allow exposure up to the customer's overall credit limit. Effectively the risk is equivalent to that of the bank's when entering into a forward contract where exposure is to that of close-out.

There is no commission payable as such, profit for the bank is on its spread.

Summary

- Exchange traded currency options are not as liquid as other exchange traded derivatives due to the depth of liquidity in the forex markets for spot and forward delivery and the flexibility found in the OTC market.
- The CME has the greatest volume of currency options, followed by the Philadelphia Stock Exchange. Most other exchanges which have introduced currency options, including LIFFE, have delisted them due to lack of volume. However, the MATIF in May 1994 introduced two new US dollar contracts against the deutschmark and French franc.
- The quote convention for the US dollar against other currencies is for calls and puts to relate to the non-dollar currency. Thus a sterling/US dollar call gives the right to buy sterling and sell dollars. A sterling/US dollar put gives the right to sell sterling and buy dollars. In other words the non-dollar currency is the underlying, as for currency futures.
- Currency options at the CME have a currency futures contract as the underlying, i.e. they are options on futures. At Philadelphia the underlying is a spot currency.
- If a long call exercises, a long futures position is assigned by the exchange. The short call acquires a short futures. If exercised a long put is assigned a short future and a short put acquires a long future. Each future is marked to market appropriate to the relationship of the strike rate for the option

and the settlement rate for the future. The long (formerly in the option) will receive margin and the short will pay. Alternatively the futures position acquired can be closed out and profit or loss taken.

- Exchange risk can be hedged using appropriate strategies as described in Chapter 14. A UK importer can purchase sterling puts or sell sterling calls. A UK exporter can purchase sterling calls or write sterling puts. Options are useful to hedge contingencies, as in the case of an exporter tendering for a contract. The commercial contract may or may not be awarded. If awarded the option can be used if in-the-money. If not in-the-money, it can be walked away from, with a known cost from the outset, the premium. If the contract is not awarded and the option has intrinsic value, the option can be closed out and value taken. If there is no intrinsic value it may still be possible to recover some of the premium by selling its time value.
- Multi-option strategies can be used and different strikes can be used to alter pay-off and cost of a hedge.
- Apart from the volatility of the underlying, an important variable for a currency option premium is the interest rate differential between the two currencies of the option.
- European options can be viewed as rights and/or obligations to buy/sell the underlying currency at a forward rate of exchange, whereas American-style options relate to spot up to expiration, due to the fact that they can be exercised at any time until expiration.
- In general terms an American-style option should never be exercised early because this way any time value remaining will be lost. The long should close out and thereby recover any time value left. There are a few important exceptions to this general rule.

Key terms

- American terms (p. 188)
- cabinets (p. 186)
- cylinder option (p. 194)
- interest rate differentials (p. 197)
- options on futures (p. 188)
- reciprocal terms (p. 188)
- synthetic put (p. 201)
- zero cost fence (p. 194)

Questions

15.1   You hold a long sterling call, the underlying is a US dollar futures contract, it has intrinsic value, you decide to exercise it. Which futures position will you be assigned by the exchange? What alternative action can you take once you have acquired the future?

15.2   Why is it usually not optimal to exercise an American option early? Are there any exceptions?

15.3   If you are a UK exporter expecting to receive US dollars, what option positions could you take to hedge?

15.4   Sketch a pay-off diagram for an ATM $1.60 covered long sterling call.

15.5   If you write a naked American option, what are the risks?

15.6   If interest rate differentials increase, what will happen to call premiums?

Further reading

Sutton, William (1990) *The Currency Options Handbook*, 2nd edn, Woodhead Faulkner.

16 Interest rate options

Introduction

In this chapter we discuss the use of traded options to hedge interest rate risk. It is assumed that basic option principles as covered in Chapter 14 are understood.

Interest rate options are traded on a number of exchanges including:

- CBOT/Chicago Board Options Exchange (CBOE)
- Chicago Mercantile Exchange (CME)
- LIFFE/London Traded Options Market (LTOM).

With some interest rate option contracts the underlying is a cash market instrument, e.g. an actual bond. In other options the underlying is a futures contract which in turn can be closed out or taken to delivery. Of course in the case of options on short-term interest rate futures cash settlement is made if the futures position is held to expiration. As with all exchange traded options, the option need not be taken to expiration and then exercised into the underlying cash or futures contract if there is intrinsic value. It can be closed out by taking an off-setting position.

On LIFFE /LTOM the following option contracts are traded:

Options on short-term interest rate futures

- three-month sterling future
- three-month Eurodollar future
- three-month Euromark future
- three-month Euroswiss future.

Options on long-term bond futures

- Long (UK) gilt future (introduced 1986)
- German Government Bond (Bund) future (introduced April 1989)
- Italian Government Bond future.

On the CBOT/CBOE the following are traded:

Options on long-/medium-term bond futures

- US T-bond future (introduced October 1982)
- ten-year US T-note future (introduced May 1985)
- five-year US T-note future (introduced May 1990).

Options on short-term interest rate bonds

- two-year US T-note future (introduced May 1992)
- Flexible options on a number of US bond and note futures are to be introduced subject to CFTC approval.

At the CME the following are traded (all are short-term interest rate contracts):

- one-month US dollar LIBOR future
- 13-week US T-bill future
- three-month Eurodollar future.

Why interest rate options on futures?

Interest rate options deliverable into an underlying futures contract is now the norm. Formerly the CBOE traded an option where the underlying was cash market T-bonds. This contract is now discontinued. Briefly, its demise is due to the fact that an option on futures is easier. An option on cash market T-bonds requires compensation for accrued interest on the bond, this does not apply to a futures contract. Futures contracts are more liquid than the cash market. There is the fear that if an option were exercised the short call may have difficulty in obtaining sufficient actual bonds to meet their obligations, except of course at a high price. The cash bond market is a dealer market. Price on futures contracts is always available, this is not necessarily so in the cash market. It is of course necessary that the price of the underlying is accurately known at all times in order to correctly price the option.

Futures and options are traded on the same floor and use the same clearing system, thus accounting entries are simpler. Exercising into a cash market underlying requires full payment or delivery, whereas with a future as the underlying, margin applies and thus leverage is retained. If a writer of an American-style option is assigned a futures position because the long has exercised, rather than having to buy or sell a cash underlying, the futures position assigned can be easily closed out without difficulty.

Puts and calls on underlying futures

First a reminder of some material covered in Chapters 14 and 15.

Options relate rights and obligations to an underlying asset. Where the underlying is a futures contract the following applies:

- A long call has the right but not the obligation to buy from the writer a given futures contract at a strike price, at or over a given period of time.
- The long call, if exercised, will acquire a short futures position.
- The short call, if the long exercises, will acquire a short futures position.
- A long put has the right but not the obligation to sell to the writer a given futures contract at a strike price, at or over a given period of time.
- The long put, if exercised, will acquire a short futures position.
- The short put, if the long exercises, will acquire a long futures position.

For quick reference here are the relationships again:

Option	Underlying into which exercisable
long call	long futures
short call	short futures
long put	short futures
short put	long futures

Logic dictates the above relationships. For example a long call gives the right to buy an underlying physical, therefore a long futures position is necessary to enable this right to be ultimately achievable if the option is on a future rather than a physical directly.

When a long call is exercised, the holder acquires a long futures position plus a cash amount from the short equal to the current futures price minus the exercise price of the future.

In reality cash will not be received as such. The future will be marked to market from the strike. If the futures position is closed out 'return' of margin will be made. If the futures position is held it will of course be marked to market every day until it is closed out or exercised. Initial margin will also be payable if a futures position is held.

If the long call exercises, the short call will be in the opposite position to that just described above for the long. The short call will acquire a short futures position. In addition they will have to pay to the long the cash amount equal to the current futures price minus the exercise price of the option. Again, in reality cash will not be paid as such direct to the long. The futures position will be marked to market from the strike, in this instance variation margin will be payable. The futures position can then be either held to its expiration or closed out.

Long calls have intrinsic value when the strike is below the futures price, the future can be bought cheaply, therefore calls gain value as the futures price rises.

Long puts have intrinsic value when the strike is above the futures price, the future can be sold at a higher price than the current futures price. Puts gain value when the futures price falls.

A numerical example should illustrate:

A long call is purchased at strike 90.

A long call with a strike at 90 will be exercised if the futures price exceeds 90, say 95.

When exercised the long call is assigned a long futures position at the strike of 90.

The writer is assigned a short futures position at 90.

Both the short call and the long call have their futures position marked to market.

Current futures price is 95, therefore:

Long call's futures position realises a gain of 5
(long future gives the right and obligation to buy at 95, but only 90 has been paid).

Short call's futures position sustains a loss of 5
(short future gives the right to sell at 95, but position has been taken on receipt of 90).

Marking to market the futures positions entails the long call receiving variation margin of 5 and the short call paying variation margin of 5.

The long call can receive 5 by closing out the futures position. As an alternative the position can be held, in so doing the risk then becomes that of any futures position. In this case the long futures position itself will lose value should the underlying asset on which the future is based fall in value. If the futures position is held then initial margin on the futures position must be paid of course, in turn this can come from return of initial margin on the option position if the option is traded futures style (p. 211).

As an alternative consider a long put with a strike of 80 and the underlying future currently trading at 75.

Once the price falls below the strike, the option becomes worthwhile exercising. The option gives the right to sell at 80, instead of at 75.

When exercised the long put is assigned a short futures position and the writer is assigned a long futures position.

The former short and long puts now have their futures positions marked to market.

Current futures price is 75, therefore:

Long put's short futures position realises a gain of 5
(short future gives right and obligation to sell at 75, but option position gives right to sell at 80).

Short put's long futures position sustains a loss of 5
(long future gives the right and obligation to buy at 75, but the position has been assigned at 80).

Marking to market the futures positions means that the (former) long put will receive variation margin and the (former) short put will pay variation margin.

  Again the margin can be actually received by the long put or paid by the short put by closing out the futures positions. Alternatively, the futures positions can be held with the pay-off possibilities of holding the relevant futures positions. Incidentally, the long and short futures positions can of course be closed out independently of each other in the normal way in the futures market.

Contract highlights – LIFFE option on three-month sterling

The contract highlights of the LIFFE option on three-month sterling (short sterling) interest rate future are as follows:

Unit of trading	One three month sterling futures contract (i.e. £500,000)
Delivery/expiry months	March, June, September, December
Delivery/exercise/expiry day	Exercise by 17.00 any business day Delivery on first business day after exercise day Expiry at 12.30 on last trading day
Last trading day	11.00 last trading day of the three month sterling futures contract
Quotation	Multiples of 0.01 (i.e. 0.01%)
Minimum price movement	0.01
Tick size and value	£12.50
Exercise price intervals	0.25 (i.e. 0.25%), e.g. 94.25, 94.50, 94.75, 95.00 etc.
Introduction of new exercise prices	Thirteen exercise prices will be listed for new series. Additional exercise prices will be introduced on the business day after the three-month sterling futures contract settlement price is within 0.12 of the sixth highest or lowest existing exercise price

The underlying, the three-month short sterling interest future itself, has a unit of trading of £500,000 and is cash settled. Reference to pp. 94–7 may be useful to remind you how this and other similar futures contracts are traded.

Briefly it should be remembered that short-term interest rate futures are priced 100 minus the implied rate of interest. If 3m LIBOR is 5.5% then the futures price becomes 100.00 minus 5.5, 94.50.

Remembering the inverse relationship between bond prices and interest rates/yields, it becomes that as prices fall interest rates rise. Thus, for example, a fall in interest rates 'gives' a rise in bond prices. A fall in interest rates leads to a rise in futures prices. Interest rates falling to 5.0% gives a futures price of 95.00.

A particular feature of this interest rate option, and all LIFFE options, is that it is traded **futures style**. This means that the premium is not paid by the long at the time of purchase to the writer via the clearing house. The long, not just the short option position, is subject to initial margin and then each option position, short and long, as with futures, is marked to market daily resulting in variation margin payments and receipts. If the option is closed out, exercised or simply let to expire worthless by the long they are required to pay the original premium to the short via the clearing house. The premium payment for purchasing the option by the long paid to the short is guaranteed because it is set against the value in the equity account and the balance returned to the long. Options traded futures style therefore mean no carry costs related to the premium for the long.

All LIFFE options are American-style.

Price quotes and intrinsic value for LIFFE Short Sterling options

As described in Chapter 14, the option premium comprises two components, intrinsic and time value.

- Intrinsic value for an option on a future will be the relationship between strike and the underlying futures price.
- Intrinsic value of a call option will be:

    futures price – strike

- Intrinsic value of a put option will be:

    strike – futures price

- A long call gains intrinsic value as the futures price rises and interest rates fall.
- A long put gains intrinsic value as the futures price falls and interest rates rise.

Consider the LIFFE Short Sterling option on February 2 1994 when the following rates applied:

Strike	Calls			Puts		
	Mar	Jun	Sep	Mar	Jun	Sep
94-50	0.18	0.38	0.47	0.04	0.06	0.13
94-75	0.05	0.20	0.30	0.37	0.27	0.33
95-00	0.01	0.09	0.17			

Three-month LIBOR 5.5%–5.375%.
March future = 94-64.

A March 94-50 call cost 0.18, i.e. 18 ticks at £12.50 per tick, therefore the premium is 18 × £12.50 = £225. With a short sterling March future trading at 94-64, intrinsic value is:

    94-64 – 94-50 = 14
    14 ticks equals £12.50 × 14 = £175

Time value will therefore be £225 minus £175 = £50, i.e. 4 ticks (4 × £12.50). Intrinsic value of a March 94 - 50 put is of course zero.

    strike – futures
    94-50 – 94-64 = –14

Because an option cannot be less than zero, its intrinsic value will be zero, all the option premium for this put is represented by time value. Time value of course will be the sum demanded by the short and paid by the long relative to the volatility of the interest rate implied in the futures price and time remaining to expiration.

Time value for the March 94-50 put is only 0.04 because time to expiration is small (the option expires on March 16) and due to the fact that it has some way to go before it becomes in-the-money during this small time window. Intuitively, implied volatility of the future is low, were interest rates implied to be more volatile then there would be a greater chance that the put would become in-the-money due to high swings in interest rates

Put/call parity – LIFFE Short Sterling option

(Refer also to pp. 168–9.)

The put/call parity relationship for options on futures trading American-style and with futures style margining is:

$C = P + F - X$
C = call price
P = put price
F = futures price
X = strike price

Due to futures style margins, with no upfront premium to be paid, there are no carrying costs for LIFFE type options. Inserting the data for the short sterling option for February 2 into the formula gives:

$C = 0.04 + 94\text{-}64 - 94\text{-}50 = 0.18$

Indeed, 0.18 is found to be the price for the call. Further note that the time value for the 94-50 call and put is the same, 0.04, as would be expected.

Hedging short-term interest rates with options – an outline

As discussed in earlier chapters, options allow a number of basic hedging strategies to be used and these same strategies can be employed in hedging interest rate risk by taking an appropriate option position so that its pay-off compensates for changes in the underlying. As the underlying loses value the option gains and vice versa. However, as always with an option, gains in the underlying can be participated in fully except at the expense of the option premium if an option is purchased.

For the cost of the premium the long can obtain a guaranteed fixed rate of borrowing or lending at a later date, coupled with the opportunity to benefit from favourable movements in the underlying. Maximum rates can be set for borrowing and minimum rates can be set for lending/depositing. The more extensive the protection in insurance type terms, the greater will be the premium which will have to be paid. Short-term interest rate options can be used to hedge short-term deposits and borrowing at a later date, as well as enabling hedges for contingent exposures, FRAs and OTC caps, floors and collars, in the latter case perhaps written by a bank or other financial institution.

Long-term interest rates can be hedged by using options such as the LIFFE Long Gilt or CBOT US T-bond contracts.

To return to short-term interest rate hedges:

- A long call hedges a minimum deposit/lending rate and allows an increase in interest rates to be participated in, albeit at the expense of the premium. This is a floor and gives protection against falls in rates for lenders.

- A long put hedges a maximum borrowing rate and allows a fall in rates to be participated in, again adjusted by the premium paid. This is a cap and gives protection against rising rates for borrowers.
- Lower cost hedges can be achieved by taking option positions whose legs create a collar, or strikes can be selected whose premium is lower. Naturally in these cases the level of protection and participation in gains is reduced.
- Collars hedge interest rate increases for borrowers at lower cost by the strategy of selling calls and buying puts.
- Collars hedge interest rate falls for depositors/lenders at low cost by buying calls and selling puts.

A number of these option strategies are described in the following sections.

Caution: when hedging with options it is important to know that the value of the option position and that of the underlying do not change in the opposite direction in equal amounts as time to expiration approaches. The reason why this is so, the option's delta, is fully covered in Chapter 17. Here we need to recognise that hedge weighting needs to be adjusted over time if hedges are to be fully protective. The number of options/underlying held needs to change over time and be adjusted dynamically – a **dynamic hedge** – for a hedge to be fully effective using options. This issue is ignored in the examples in this chapter unless otherwise indicated.

Buying a cap to hedge short-term borrowing – a long put

If there is a need to borrow £5m in three months' time for a period of three months, this can be hedged by purchasing a LIFFE at-the-money short sterling put. For the purposes of illustration assume that the hedge matches LIFFE option contract dates, December 16 1993 to March 16 1994.

A long put hedge will protect against a rise in interest rates, but allow the benefit of participation in their fall. A long put will gain intrinsic value as the futures price falls and interest rates rise. A gain from the option position will off-set the loss which occurs if money has to be borrowed at higher rates.

Example Assume the following:

December 15

3m LIBOR = 5.5% p.a.

March futures price = 94-50

March 94-50 put premium = 0.04

March 16

3m LIBOR = 6.00% p.a.

futures price 94-00

The hedger should purchase 10 short sterling put options which will gain intrinsic value, become further in-the-money, if interest rates increase.

The maximum borrowing rate will be 5.5% p.a. as implied by the strike of 94-50. The premium for each option contract is 0.04, therefore the maximum effective borrowing rate will be:

5.50% strike

\+ $\underline{\text{0.04\% put premium}}$

    5.54%

If three-month LIBOR on March 16 is 6.00% p.a. then:

Borrow in the cash market at 6.00% p.a.

Futures price will be 94-00 (100-6.00), therefore

sell 10 March 94-50 puts for 0.50.

0.50 received minus premium paid originally of 0.04 gives a gain of 0.46.

6.00 minus 0.46 gives an effective borrowing rate of 5.54% p.a., i.e. the maximum effective target rate.

An alternative possibility is for the rate of interest to have fallen to say 5.00% p.a. at 16 March, in which case the outcome will be as follows:

Purchase 10 short sterling puts as before, strike 94-50, premium 0.04.

If 3m LIBOR on March 16 is 5.00% p.a. then the put will have no intrinsic value and can expire worthless. (The put gives the right to sell the futures contract at 94-50 but the futures price at 5.00% will be 95-00, so it will be better to sell at 95-00.)

The £5m can be borrowed in the cash market at 5.00% p.a., to which must be added the cost of the premium paid, 5.00 plus 0.04, to give a net effective cost of borrowing at 5.04% p.a.

Thus the strategy has allowed participation in the benefit of a fall in interest rates, only at the expense of the premium which protected its rise above 5.54% p.a.

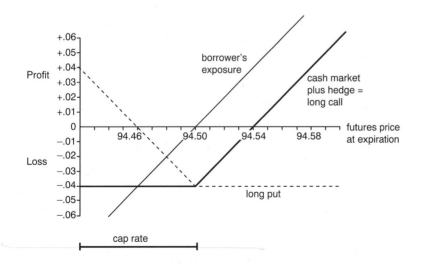

max. = 94.50, i.e. 5.5%. However much the futures price falls, i.e. interest rates rise, the hedger will always pay 5.5% less the cost of the hedge

Figure 16.1   *Profit and loss diagram for short sterling long put.*

Note that the underlying is the futures price, therefore as rates rise the futures price falls and vice versa. The overall pay-off of cash market plus hedge is that of a long call.

Buying a floor to hedge short-term lending – a long call

If there is a need to deposit/lend in the future over a short period of time a floor can be arranged by purchasing a long call. The long call will gain intrinsic value as interest rates fall and futures prices rise. Thus a fall in interest rates is protected and any rise in interest rates can be participated in, albeit in both instances, at the expense of the premium paid.

Example If £10m is to be lent in three months' time for a period of three months, the lending can be hedged by purchasing 20 LIFFE short sterling calls. Assume the hedge matches LIFFE contract dates, December 16 to March16.

Say December 1993:

3m LIBOR = 5.75% p.a.

March futures price = 94.25

March 94-25 at-the-money call premium = 0.15

A hedger should purchase 20 short sterling calls which will gain intrinsic value, become in-the-money should interest rates fall.

At March 15 1994 let:

3m LIBOR = 5.25% p.a. giving a futures price of 94-75.

The minimum effective lending rate will be the strike less premium paid, i.e.:

	5.75%
less	0.15% call premium
	5.60%

On March 16, when 3m LIBOR is 5.25% p.a., the sum involved, £10m, will actually be lent in the cash market at 5.25% p.a.

The long call will be closed out by selling at 94-75 (100–5.25).

The call was bought at 94-25, therefore profit is 94-75 minus 94-25, i.e. 0.50.

The profit of 0.50 when reduced by the call premium paid gives a net option profit of 0.50 minus 0.15, i.e. 0.35.

When the net profit realised from the call is added to the return in the cash market the total return becomes 5.60% (5.25 + 0.35) – 5.60% p.a. is of course the target minimum rate of return on the lending, i.e. the floor.

Of course should lending rates in the cash market exceed the strike of 5.75% p.a. then the option will be abandoned, being out-of-the-money and

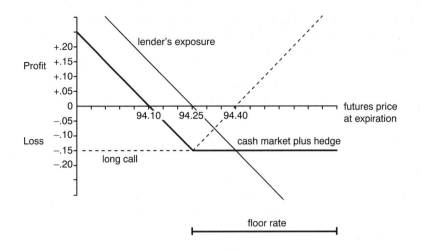

minimum lending rate (floor) will be equal to futures price of 94.25 (5.5%),
plus cost of hedge at 0.15. 94.25 + 0.15 = 94.40 (5.60%)

Figure 16.2 *A short sterling lending floor – a long call.*

worthless. The rise in rates will be participated in, subject only to the
premium paid of 0.15.

A further possibility is that the lending does not occur at all, in which
case if the call is out-of-the-money it again will be abandoned at the cost of
the premium. Should it be in-the-money, it can be sold for its intrinsic
value at least, the proceeds of which can be set against the premium paid.

If it becomes apparent that the lending will not occur before the option
expires it can be sold for remaining time value, unless it is deep out-of-the-
money. Figure 16.2 illustrates the possible outcomes at expiration.

An interest rate cap over more than one option contract period

LIFFE option contract periods last for three months. The situation may
arise when it becomes necessary to borrow for, say, a six month period in
three months' time. Today is 18 December 1993, you wish to borrow £10m
for a period of six months beginning in three months' time on 16 March.
You will not wish to see interest rates rise, but will wish to participate in
their fall. A hedge using options can be organised in the following way:

18 December	
3m LIBOR	5.50%
6m LIBOR	5.375%
March futures price	94-67
June futures price	94-82
March 94-50 put premium	0.04
June 94-50 put premium	0.06

The hedger will need to buy 10 short sterling March puts and 10 June puts. Each option position will increase in value should interest rates rise.

The strikes set a maximum borrowing rate, which when the premiums are taken into account, give an effective maximum three-month rate in each case.

	March	June
94-50 strike	5.50%	5.50%
put premium	0.04%	0.06%
	5.54%	5.56%

Compounding theses two three-month rates gives an effective six-month rate of:

$$[\{(1 + 0.0554/4) \times (1 + 0.0556/4)\} - 1] \times 2 =$$
$$[(1.01385 \times 1.0139) - 1] \times 2 =$$
$$[1.0279425 - 1] \times 2 = 0.0559 = 5.59\%$$

If six-month interest rates were to rise to 6.00% by 16 March when the borrowing is actually to occur, the £10m will be borrowed in the cash market for six months at 6.00%.

Premiums paid to purchase the March and June 94-50 puts were 0.04 and 0.06.

On March 16 both puts will be sold.

The March EDSP will be 94-00 (100 – 6.00). It is settled at 94-00 and the position realises a gain of 0.50 (94-50 – 94-00).

If the June futures price is 93-97, the June put can be sold for 0.53 (94-50 – 93-97).

The net outlay on these two option positions is therefore:

cost to purchase March 94-50 put	(0.04)
June 94-50 put	(0.06)
gain on sale of March 94-50 put	0.50
June 94-50 put	0.53
net options gain	0.93

Related to the six-month borrowing period in percentage per annum terms the gain is:

$$0.93 \div 2 = 0.465$$

The £10m was borrowed in the cash market at 6.00%, the gain on the option positions therefore makes the net borrowing rate achieved to be 5.535%. This is below the maximum rate of 5.59%.

As an alternative the outcome can be examined if interest rates in the cash market were to fall during the life of the hedge.

Imagine six-month LIBOR were to fall to 5.00% p.a. by the time the hedge is lifted in March.

This makes the EDSP for March futures 95-00 and the June futures price, say, 95-10.

The £10m is borrowed in the cash market at 5.00%.

The March 95-50 puts expire worthless	0.00
sell June 94-50 puts for	0.03 (time value only)
less cost of March put	(0.04)
June put	(0.06)
	(0.07)

Related to the six-month borrowing period the loss on the option positions is:

0.07 ÷ 2 = 0.035

The effective cost of borrowing therefore becomes 5.00% + 0.035% = 5.035%.

The borrower is able to benefit from the favourable movement in rates with an adjustment for the net cost of the hedge.

A short sterling lending collar

If you buy a floor and sell a cap you create a lending or investor's collar. It is described as selling a collar. This is the cylinder hedge we have seen in Chapters 14 and 15. A minimum lending rate is achieved for a later date at a reduced cost.

Cost is reduced because the premium received from the short position offsets some or all of the premium paid for the long. However, profit potential is reduced should lending rates rise. A collar is created between which lending rates will be effectively experienced.

- The purchase of the call creates a minimum lending rate, the floor.
- The sale of the put creates a maximum lending rate, the cap.
- Cap and floor create a collar.

Today is February 7. You wish to lend £5m on March 15 for three months.

Three-month LIBOR = 5.50% p.a.

March futures price = 94-59

A short sterling March 94-75 call can be bought for	(0.03)
A short sterling March 94-50 put can be sold for	0.04
Net premium outlay, net credit	0.01
Interest rate implied by call	5.25%
Net premium outlay (credit)	0.01%
Effective minimum lending rate (floor)	5.24%
Interest rate implied by put	5.50%
Net premium outlay (credit)	0.01%
Maximum effective lending rate (cap)	5.49%

The collar is thus 5.49% to 5.24%, the £5m will be lent between these effective rates.

The actual outcome will materialise as follows:

3m LIBOR at March 15 is 5.25%.

The sum of £5m will be lent in the cash market at this rate.

The options will be closed out as follows:

March 94-75 calls expire at-the-money and realise zero.

Buy March 94-50 puts for 0.25.

Option outlays and receipts are therefore:

Purchase March 94-75 call	(0.03)
Sell March 94-75 put	0.04
March 94-75 expires at-the-money	0.00
Purchase March 94-50 put	(0.25)
	(0.24)
Cash market lending	5.25
Net options outcome (cost) add on	0.24
	5.49

The 5.49% is the maximum allowable within the collar. Had the hedge not been placed then the lending would have been at an inferior 5.25% in the cash market alone.

A short sterling borrowing collar

If you sell a floor and buy a cap you create a borrower's collar. It is described as buying a collar. You buy puts and sell calls. A borrowing cap is set with a minimum borrowing floor.

Today is February 8 and 3m LIBOR is 5.1875% p.a. You wish to borrow £10m on March 16 and hedge the interest rate risk by way of an interest rate collar.

Buy March 94-75 put for	(0.03)
Sell March 95-00 call for	0.01
Net outlay	(0.02)

The put will gain value as the futures price falls and interest rates rise.

Interest rate implied by the put is	5.25
plus net outlay	0.02
Effective cap	5.27
(maximum effective borrowing rate)	

Interest rate implied by the call is	5.00
plus net outlay	0.02
Effective floor	5.02

(minimum effective borrowing rate)

The collar is thus 5.27% to 5.02%, the £10m will be lent between these two rates, whatever the cash market LIBOR is on March 16.

Say 3m LIBOR at March 16 is 6.00%, the outcome will materialise as follows:

Sell March 94-75 put for	0.75
March 95-00 calls expire worthless	
to the long, no need for short to close out	0.00

Therefore:

Borrow £10m at cash market 3m LIBOR	6.00
less net return realised at close out of option positions	(0.75)
	5.25

Money has been borrowed at the cap rate because interest rates increased. The maximum rate for the borrower is 5.25% p.a., regardless of how high cash 3m LIBOR goes.

The floor part of the collar can be seen in operation from the next example.

The hedge is placed in the same way, with a long March 94-75 put and a short March 95-00 call.

Imagine that at March 16 3m LIBOR in the cash market is 4.5% p.a.

The March 94-75 is allowed to expire worthless	0.00
Buy the March 95-00 to close out, cost	(0.50)
Borrow £5m at cash market 3m LIBOR	4.50
Add loss realised at close out	0.50
Add net cost of placing hedge	0.02
	5.02

Thus the floor part of the collar is in operation if interest rates fall. The hedged borrower using a collar cannot borrow for less than 5.02% p.a. in this example, no matter how low the cash market rate falls. The close-out cost will always match the gain in the cash market.

LIFFE Long Gilt futures option contract highlights

The contract highlights of the LIFFE Long Gilt futures option are as follows:

Unit of trading	One Long Gilt futures contract
Delivery/expiry months	March, June, September, December
Exercise day	Exercise by 17.00 on any business day, extended to 18.30 on the last trading day
Delivery day	Delivery on the first business day after the exercise day
Expiry day	Expiry at 18.30 on last trading day
Last trading day	16.15 six business days prior to first day of delivery month
Quotation	Multiples of 1/64
Minimum price movement (Tick size and value)	£1/64 (£7.8125)

- Contract standard assignment of one Long Gilt futures contract for the delivery month at the exercise price.
- Exercise price intervals £1 e.g. £106-00, £107-00.
- Introduction of new exercise prices – 13 exercise prices will be listed for new series. Additional exercise prices will be introduced on the business day after the Long Gilt futures contract settlement price is within $£^{16}/_{32}$ of the sixth highest or lowest existing exercise price.
- As with all LIFFE options it is traded futures style.

Price quotes – LIFFE Long Gilt option

Example Most bond futures are priced in ticks of $1/_{32}$nds as in the actual bond market. Thus one tick for the LIFFE Long Gilt future is £15.625. For the LIFFE Long Gilt option one tick is £7.8125, i.e. half that for a future. Option price quotes are thus $1/_{64}$th increments. A price of 2–26 for an option premium is thus 154 ticks (2 × 64 + 26) and is £1203.13 (154 × £7.8125).

On June 27 the following prices were marked to market:

UK gilt futures (LIFFE)

	Sett
Sep	101-09
Dec	100-09

UK gilt futures options (LIFFE)

Strike price	Calls		Puts	
	Sep	Dec	Sep	Dec
101	2.26	3.07	2.08	3.53
102	1.57	2.43	2.39	4.25
103	1.29	2.19	3.11	5.01

Taking the September 101 calls, these are in-the-money 9 futures ticks, 18 option ticks. You can buy for 101 instead of the current futures price of 101.09. The option is priced at 2.26. Intrinsic value is 18 option ticks, 2.26 minus 0.18 gives time value of 2.08, which is of course the premium for the out-of-the-money September 101 put, due to the put–call parity relationship.

Hedging long-term interest rates/bond prices with options – an outline

Long-term interest rates and bond prices can be hedged by using a number of option strategies. The contract we will use to illustrate will be the LIFFE Long Gilt option, highlights of which were reproduced earlier (pp. 221–2).

In the same fashion that applied to short-term interest rate options, the option relates to an underlying futures position, in this case the Long Gilt future.

If the option is exercised by the long, the following positions will be assigned (as previously described):

- long put   short Long Gilt future
- short put   long Long Gilt future
- long call   long Long Gilt future
- short call   short Long Gilt future

As always with hedging strategies, the aim is to take an option position whose pay-off will compensate for adverse movements in interest rates/bond prices. Additionally with options gains can be participated in at the expense of any premium paid as the long.

Option strategies

Where there is further discussion of the strategy, the page numbers are given.

Hedge requirement	Option strategies	Page numbers
1. Protection against rising interest rates/falling bond prices for a borrower/bond issuer	long puts short futures + long calls a bear call spread a bear put spread	224
2. As in (1), but wish only limited protection, believe only moderate risk of rise in interest rates/decline in bond prices	short futures + short puts short calls	226
3. As (1) but believe on balance rates/prices will be stable	neutral calendar spread short put – call straddle	
4. Protection against falling interest rates/rising bond prices for a lender/bond investor	long calls long futures + long puts a bull call spread a bull put spread	226

5. As (4) but wish only limited protection, believe moderate risk of rate falls/rise in bond prices	long futures + short calls short puts	228
6. As (1) but believe interest rates/bond prices to be highly volatile and could move either up or down.	long put – call straddle	

In general terms long calls fix maximum purchase price of bonds (caps or ceilings) and long puts fix minimum selling price (floors).

Strategies 1 and 4 are hedges, whereas 2, 3, 5 and 6 are for income enhancement. Option buyers purchase protection against unfavourable interest rate/bond price changes from their perspective, but they can still enjoy favourable movements.

It must be remembered that bond futures contracts have as their underlying a basket of deliverable bonds, in the case of the LIFFE Long Gilt contract it is UK gilts with fixed interest coupons, and maturity of 10–15 years. The notional gilt coupon is 9%, thus bonds deliverable into the basket will be subject to a conversion factor (refer to p. 102).

A long put to hedge falling bond prices

A corporate which intends to issue bonds at a later date will not wish to see the price of bonds falling due to rises in interest rates. Equally a current holder of bonds will not wish to see bond prices falling so that they realise a loss on their intended sale at a later date.

To simplify matters we will concentrate upon the second example and assume that a portfolio of gilts is held which are deliverable into the Long Gilt contract. Assume UK Treasury stock 8.50% redemption 2007 is held.

A long put will hedge falling bond prices. Its immunisation strategy gives unlimited protection against a fall in bond prices at the expense of the premium, whilst enabling rises in bond prices to be fully participated in – at the expense of the premium. It protects unlimited downside risk by providing a floor price.

The floor price in principle will be the strike chosen, adjusted by the premium paid. High in-the-money strikes will naturally attract high premiums due to intrinsic values. Low out-of-the-money strikes give 'deductible' insurance at a lower cost.

The minimum floor for a long put on a Long Gilt is in fact:

(strike × conversion factor of bonds in portfolio) – premium

Example UK Treasury stock 8.50% 2007, the conversion factor is 0.9607523 (LIFFE conversion tables).

On February 14 the gilt identified was priced in the cash market at 114 $^{17}/_{32}$.

The premium for a March put with a strike of 115 was 0.14 (i.e. $^{14}/_{64}$, 14 ticks, 14 × £7.8125 = £109.375).

Thus a long March 115 put would have an effective floor price of:

$$(115 \times 0.9607523) - {}^{14}\!/_{64}$$
$$110.4865145 \qquad - {}^{14}\!/_{64}$$
$$110\ 15.57/32 \qquad - {}^{14}\!/_{64} = 110{}^{7}\!/_{32}$$

At worst the gilt could be sold for $110{}^{7}\!/_{32}$.

Expressed another way, if the gilt portfolio consisted solely of 8.50% 2007 Treasury stock, for each multiple of £50,000 nominal stock held its value in the cash market on February 14 would be:

$$£50,000 \times 114{}^{17}\!/_{32} = £57,265.63$$

This value would be fully protected in net terms to the floor price of:

$$£50,000 \times 110{}^{17}\!/_{32} = £55,109.38$$

£109.38, the premium, gave the portfolio this net, minimum value until expiration of the option.

The actual floor value may be a little higher than that shown if the identified gilt is not the cheapest to deliver into the futures contract.

If interest rates were to rise, bond prices fall, or even anticipated to change in this way, the gain which would follow from a fall in the futures price below that of the strike should off-set the fall in the cash market price of the bonds once this falls below that of the effective net strike of $110{}^{7}\!/_{32}$.

In order to examine outcomes from the hedge imagine that the yield on the gilt in the cash market were to increase by expiration of the option so that the gilt would then trade in the cash market at $110{}^{3}\!/_{8}$.

If 100 gilts were held, each with a nominal £50,000 value, this would make their total cash market value £5,518,750. The original value at the placement of the hedge would have been £5,726,563.

The number of puts needed to be purchased is:

$$100 \times 0.9607523 = 96.07, \text{ i.e. 96 contracts}$$
$$\text{(conversion factor)}$$

Total cost of hedge premium:

$$96 \times £109.375 = £10,500$$
$$(96 \times 14 \text{ ticks at } £7.8125)$$

The gilt at $100{}^{3}\!/_{8}$ in the cash market has a futures price of 111-29. With actual strike of 115 the put has an intrinsic value of:

$$115 \text{ minus } 111\text{-}29 = 3{}^{3}\!/_{32} = 3{}^{6}\!/_{64} = 198 \text{ ticks}$$
$$(111{}^{29}\!/_{32})$$
$$(\text{Each tick} = {}^{1}\!/_{64}{}^{\text{th}} \text{ of } £50,000)$$

$$198 \times £7.8125 \qquad\qquad = £1,546.875$$
$$(\text{no. of ticks} \times \text{value of tick})$$

Therefore 96 contracts gain in value £148,500 (£1,546.875 × 96). Hedge outcome:

Cash market value of portfolio Feb 14	£5,726,563
Cash market value of portfolio at expiration of option	£5,518,750
Loss in cash market	£207,813

| Gain from option position | £148,500 |
| Net overall loss | £59,313 |

However, note the effective floor price of £55,109.38 per contract has not been breached.

96 × £55,109.38 = £5,290,500

An outlay of total premium, £10,500, has reduced the overall loss and led to a gain on the option position of £148,500, net of the premium, £138,000.

A long call to hedge rising bond prices

Long calls hedge falling interest rates/rising bond prices. A potential investor in long-term bonds does not wish to see bond prices rise before they are purchased at an anticipated later date.

A long call will gain intrinsic value as a bond price and its futures price rise above the strike rate. Gains realised will off-set wholly or in part extra cost incurred in purchasing the bonds.

Intrinsic value is thus:

current futures price – strike

If an in-the-money call is purchased with a strike of 110 in a LIFFE Long Gilt futures option for 2 – 28, with a current futures price at 111-29, then as and if the bond and futures price rises, the call will gain value.

Suppose that the futures price rises to 114-50, intrinsic value will be:

114-50   – 110 = 4-50
(current futures – strike)

4-50 is 306 ticks (4 × 64 + 50, make sure you can see why this is so, refer to contract highlights if unsure).
Premium paid was 2-28 = 156 ticks (2 × 64 + 28).
Net gain on the option position is therefore:

306 ticks – 156 ticks = 150 ticks
150 × £7.8125 = £1,171.875

The gain off–sets the 'loss' in the cash market due to the rise in bond prices.

Writing a call

If you hold a gilt portfolio and believe that interest rates and bond prices will be fairly stable and that if there is to be any movement it will be in an upward direction in rates and consequently a fall in bond prices, then premium income can be earned by writing a call. This will increase the return on the portfolio held. Assume the gilts are deliverable into the underlying Long Gilt futures contract.

Naked calls can be written without fear of disruptions to the portfolio should the long exercise the option. Any obligations to sell can be 'avoided' by closing out the futures position assigned immediately, taking the associated losses, another advantage of options on futures.

If expectations prove correct and rates and prices remain stable, then the option will expire worthless and all premium income will be retained. If interest rates rise and gilt prices fall, again the option will not be exercised by the long and all premium income will be retained. Only if bond prices rise as a result of a fall in interest rates will the long call exercise. They will be able to buy at the strike instead of at higher cash/futures prices. It will be as well to decide the point at which the short should close out their position to minimise losses should bond prices start to rise. Premium income will of course be earned until the breakeven point is reached.

As in the examples in on pp. 224, 225, assume that UK Treasury Stock 8.50% redemption 2007 is held, conversion factor 0.9607523. This stock is deliverable into the LIFFE Long Gilt futures contract.

On March 24 the gilt identified was priced at 106 in the cash market. The premium for a June 107 call was 2-01 (i.e. $2\frac{1}{64}$, 129 ticks at £7.8125 per tick). The futures price was 107.

If the portfolio is 100 gilts, each with a nominal value of £50,000, then the number of calls to be sold should be (using weighting via the conversion factor):

> 100 × 0.9607523 = 96.07, i.e. 96 contracts

> Total premium income received =
> 96 × (129 ticks at £7.8125) = £96,750

On April 22 the cash market price of the gilt falls to $104\frac{3}{4}$. June 107 calls are 1-06 and the futures price is 106-16. The long will not exercise a call which gives the right to buy a futures contract at 107, the strike, when futures can be bought for the lower futures price of 106-16. Thus all the premium income earned will be retained provided that the futures price does not exceed the strike of 107 (important qualifications to this statement are made shortly, you may wish to refer back to it).

Assume that on April 22 the short closes out, purchases back therefore, at 1-06 (70 ticks). The outcome can be assessed as follows:

Premium received March 25 to sell		
(96 contracts at 2-01, i.e. 129 ticks at £7.8125)	=	£96,750
Premium paid April 22 to purchase and close out		
(96 contracts at 1-06, i.e. 70 ticks at £7.8125)	=	52,500
Net premium earned		£44,250
Value of gilt portfolio March 25		
(100 × £50,000 × 106)		£5,300,000
Value of gilt portfolio April 22		
(100 × £50,000 × $104\frac{3}{4}$)		£5,237,500
Loss		£62,500

In summary, net premium income earned is £44,250 and the value loss to the portfolio is £62,500. It can be seen that the premium income does not match the loss in portfolio value. It can be readily appreciated that the loss in portfolio value would have occurred with or without the writing of the option. The fact that an option was written in this instance does, however, mitigate the loss.

The question still arises, why does the net premium earned only amount to £44,250 and not £96,750? The option was not exercised by the long because it is not in-the-money. The earlier statement that 'the long will not exercise a call which gives the right to buy a futures contract at 107, the strike, when futures can be bought for the lower futures price of 106-16' clearly holds good. So why does the statement which follows that just quoted from above not hold good that 'all the premium earned will be retained provided that the futures price does not exceed the strike of 107'? Clearly all premium income is not retained even though the strike does not exceed 107. What is going on here? It's all to do with option delta, something we have come across before and which is dealt with more fully in Chapter 17.

Delta is important when weighting a hedge with options, if it is ignored an outcome as illustrated is inevitable. In our example a better approach would be to take a short call position with regard to the number of contracts sold in relation to the option's delta.

Briefly here, delta measures the amount by which an option premium changes due to changes in the price of the underlying, changes do not occur on a one for one basis and therefore hedges need to be weighted relative to the option delta. If this is done, then a more accurate hedge will occur. The net premium income would cover the loss in portfolio value in this case if more options were written.

Let us say that the delta of the June 107 call is 0.60. This means that the option premium moves 60% of a tick for each one tick move in the underlying futures price. Therefore 160 (96 × 0.6) calls should be sold.

As a result the outcome is as follows:

Premium received by selling 160 calls March 25	£161,250
Premium paid by buying 160 calls April 22	£187,500
Net premium earned	£73,750

Loss in the value of the portfolio will be as previously shown, £62,500. The reason that there is overcompensation is because the delta is greater in the example than it is in reality.

Writing a put

If you hold a portfolio of gilts and believe that interest rates and bond prices will be fairly stable, but that if there is to be a movement it will be moderate and that interest rates will fall a little, bond prices rise a little, then income can be augmented by writing puts. As with writing calls, naked puts can be written and any obligations to buy can be 'avoided' by closing out immediately the futures position assigned, taking the associated losses.

If the put writer is correct in their expectation, then the puts written will expire worthless and the premium income earned will be retained. This will increase the return on the portfolio held, or alternatively can be viewed as highly leveraged profit on the initial margin, which is returned anyway with interest.

If a naked put is written, then a limit to tolerated loss should be set, as loss is unlimited in theory and will be large should interest rates rise and bond prices fall by large amounts. Therefore a stop loss futures price should be set at which the short put will be closed out.

Example On June 22 the following prices were reported for the LIFFE Long Gilt futures and option contracts:

UK gilt futures (LIFFE) £50,000 32nds of 100%:

	Sett
Jun	101-01
Sep	99-25
Dec	98-25

Long gilt futures options (LIFFE) £50,000 64ths of 100%:

Strike price	Calls Sep	Calls Dec	Puts Sep	Puts Dec
99	2-48	3-33	1-62	3-47
100	2-13	3-05	2-27	4-19
101	1-48	2-43	2-62	4-57

We will follow the outcome of writing puts over a few day, ignoring the marking to market on the intervening days.

June 22

Sell Sept 101 put at 2-62 (i.e. $2^{62}/_{64}$).

premium income received 190 ticks at £7.8125 per tick =£1484.38

As long as the futures price is 101 or above the put will expire, being worthless to the long. Note here that the 101 put has intrinsic value because the future is trading at 99-25, i.e. $99^{25}/_{32}$. Intrinsic value is thus $101-99^{25}/_{32} = 1^{7}/_{32}$, i.e. 39 ticks at £15.625 per tick = £609.38. Time value is therefore £1484.38 – £609.38 = £875.(Futures in the long gilt priced in $^{1}/_{32}$nds, options $^{1}/_{64}$ths.)

June 27 the following prices were reported:

UK gilt futures (LIFFE) £50,000 32nds of 100%:

	Sett
Jun	102-16
Sep	101-09
Dec	100-09

Long gilt futures options (LIFFE) £50,000 64ths of 100%:

Strike price	Calls		Puts	
	Sep	Dec	Sep	Dec
99				
100				
101	2-26	3-07	2-08	3-53
102	1-29	2-19	3-11	5-01

Note here that strikes of 102 and 103 are now being traded due to the movement in bond prices in the cash market and bond futures prices.

Therefore between June 22 when the put was written and June 27, September 101 put prices have changed from 2-62 to 2-08, a change of 54 ticks at £7.8125 per tick, equals £421.88. This is obviously a gain having sold for 2-62, then bought back at 2-08.

Futures prices have changed from 99-25 to 101-09. Above 101 the long put will not exercise, at these prices selling at 101-09 is clearly better than selling at 101.

If the put writer were to close out by purchasing a September 101 put, not only the original premium income of £1484.38 can be retained, but also the additional gain as a result of the movement in the option price of £421.88.

The option premium has to change 190 ticks for the option writer to break even, i.e. the premium needs to go to 5-24 and the futures price to 98-01.

In the example, an in-the-money put is written and thus income is high. More safety for the short, traded against a lower income, could be achieved by writing an out-of-the-money put, for example a Sep 99 put for 1-62, i.e. 126 ticks at £7.8125, £984.375, compared with £1,484.375 for the in-the-money Sep 101 put.

However, it follows that the futures price has to go to 97-01 before any loss is incurred, compared with 98-01, thus the greater safety margin.

Hedging uncovered futures with options

By taking an uncovered futures position a highly leveraged profit or loss can be made, depending upon the direction of futures prices relative to the position taken. As an example a long futures position will gain from a fall in interest rates and an increase in bond and therefore bond futures prices. Going long in anticipation of such a price movement involves unlimited risk, prices may move in the opposite direction.

Risk can be limited by the simultaneous taking of an appropriate position, a long put, in the example given above. Other risk limiting strategies involving simultaneous futures and option positions are outlined on pp. 223, 224.

Summary

- Most exchange-traded interest rate options and all LIFFE option contracts have a futures contract as the underlying because of the advantages this brings should the option be exercised. Futures prices are more transparent than prices in the cash market. A cash market position has to be paid for in full or delivery made. A futures position only requires a returnable initial margin. A futures position can be closed out easily, on the same trading floor, and not be held at all.
- LIFFE option contracts are all traded futures style, both long and short are margined. It means that the long does not pay for purchasing the option outright at the beginning, but deposits initial margin.
- When using options to hedge it is important to know that the value of the option and that of the underlying do not change in the opposite direction in equal amounts as expiration approaches due to the decay in time value. The relationship between underlying and premium changes is the option delta (covered in detail in Chapter 17).
- A price quote of 0.38 for the LIFFE Short Sterling option costs £475, each tick being £12.50, as it is with the underlying future.
- LIFFE Long Gilt option prices are quoted in price increments of 1 tick equals 1/64th, not 1/32nd as in the futures and bond markets. Thus a price of 2-39 is 167 ticks ($2 \times 64 + 39$) at £7.8125 per tick, i.e. half that for a tick in long gilt futures at £15.625 per tick. Strike prices are, for example, 101, 102, 103 intervals.
- Intrinsic value for a call will be futures price minus strike.
- Intrinsic value for a put will be strike minus futures price.
- A long call gains intrinsic value as the futures price falls and interest rates rise.
- A long put gains intrinsic value as the futures price falls and interest rates rise.
- If an option on futures is exercised by the long the following futures position will be assigned by the exchange:

long put   short future
short put   long future
long call   long future
short call   short future

Key terms

- borrowing collar (p. 220)
- lending collar (p. 219)
- options on futures (p. 207)
- options traded futures style (p. 211)

16.1 What are the advantages of options on futures in contrast to options on a cash market underlying?

16.2 What are the advantages of trading options futures style?

16.3 Which futures position is a long put exercisable into?

16.4 What alternative action can be taken if a futures position is assigned?

16.5 You are the short put in a LIFFE Short Sterling option. Interest rates rise, do you gain or lose?

16.6 Examine the following price information and fill in the gaps:

Three-month sterling futures (LIFFE)

	Sett
Sep	94.34
Dec	93.74
Mar	—
Jun	92.35

Short sterling options (LIFFE)

Strike price	Calls			Puts		
	Sep	Dec	Mar	Sep	Dec	Mar
94.25	0.21	0.15	0.09	—	0.66	1.33
94.50	—	0.09	0.09	0.25	0.85	1.54
94.75	0.02	0.05	0.03	0.43	1.06	1.77

16.7 Examine the following price information and fill in the gaps:

Long gilt futures (LIFFE)

	Sett
Jun	101.22
Sep	100.14
Dec	—

Long gilt futures options (LIFFE)

Strike price				
100	—	3.07	2.04	3.43
101	2.00	2.43	2.36	4.15
102	1.36	2.18	—	4.54

16.8 How would you create a lending collar? A borrowing collar?

16.9 How would you create an interest rate cap over more than one option contract period?

16.10 Which option positions could you take to hedge a fall in bond prices?

16.11 Which statement is true and why?

(a) A bond put option locks in the implied repo rate at worst.

(b) The purchase of an out-of-the-money option is a more conservative hedge than that of an in-the-money option.

(c) Buying a put option against a cash instrument allows the retention of much of the upside potential.

(Securities Institute, Financial Futures and Options, December 1992.)

16.12 The rate of interest is 10% and the prices of 3-month options on a bond which has no interest payments in the next three months and whose price is 100 are as follows:

Exercise	Call	Put
90	15	3
100	11	6
110	5	10
120	1	18

(a) Identify three arbitrage opportunities involving the bond and its options.

(14 marks)

(b) What principles of option pricing are violated in each case?

(6 marks)

(Securities Institute, Financial Futures and Options, December 1992.)

16.13 Discuss the specific problems involved in valuing interest rate and bond options.

(Securities Institute, Financial Futures and Options, December 1992.)

16.14 Which statement(s) about the nominal value of a T-Bond futures contract is true and why?

(a) Its value is the same as the nominal value of a Eurodollar futures contract.

(b) Its value depends on the maturity and coupon of the bond delivered.

(c) Its value depends on the conversion factor.

(d) Its value is independent of the coupon, maturity and conversion factor.

(Securities Institute, Financial Futures and Options, July 1993.)

16.15 Assume that it is now 2 April and that you wish to hedge a $50m loan commencing on 15 May with three-month rollovers. The 3 month interest rates are 9.500–9.625 and the only quoted futures are

June	90.18
Sep	89.93
Dec	89.63

How would you construct the appropriate hedge?

(Securities Institute, Financial Futures and Options, July 1993.)

16.16 LIFFE December Euromark futures are trading at 94.66. March futures are trading at 94.45. Both periods are 91 days.

(a) What is the implied rate of interest for the six-month period?

(b) What are the starting and ending months of the period in question?

(Securities Institute Financial Futures and Options, December 1994.)

Further reading

Antel, B. *Management of Interest Rate Risk*, Euromoney.

Bookstaber, R. (1991) *Option Pricing and Strategies in Investing*, 3rd edn, McGraw Hill.

Fabozzi, Frank (1993) *Bond Markets*, 2nd edn, Prentice Hall.

Ross, Derek (1990) *International Treasury Management*, 2nd edn, Woodhead Faulkner.

17 Option pricing

Introduction

The first part of this chapter is concerned with determining what is a 'fair premium' for a given option. We look at the factors which we have discussed in earlier chapters, the relationship between the strike rate and the price of the underlying and time to expiration. We look at the role of the short-term, risk-free interest rate and then introduce volatility of the underlying and the Black and Scholes Option Pricing Model (BSOPM).

Some readers may feel that the sections on the BSOPM are not for them, in which case the relevant sections can be quite easily passed through without loss of continuity. Just think of the calculations as a 'black box' into which the values of the variables can be inserted and the answer produced. With the large number of software programs now available this can be done quite easily and indeed is done by virtually everyone. It is, however, useful to have some understanding of what is going on. To have a good appreciation of volatility and its importance to option pricing is desirable, along with the concept of implied volatility. Readers are urged to follow this material.

The end sections of the chapter are concerned with **sensitivities**, which are measures of the sensitivity of an option price to changes in the value of one of its pricing variables. One of the problems in using options to hedge is that the underlying and the option do not change value at all times at the same rate. Some examples:

Premiums of deep-in-the-money options which are very near to expiration move more or less on a one for one basis in line with changes in the price of the underlying, they have little or no time value. In contrast, premiums of deep-out-of-the-money options with a short period of time to expiration will not change very much at all if the price of the underlying changes, they are still out-of-the-money and the chance of becoming in-the-money is small. Time value is therefore also small.

If option premiums and prices of the underlying do not have a one for one relationship, it follows that if, for instance, you wish to hedge against a rise in 3m LIBOR because you wish to borrow £10m at a later date, you cannot necessarily do this by purchasing 20 LIFFE Short Sterling puts (contract is on one short sterling futures which is for £500,000 nominal). The problems become more apparent when option positions are not taken over a whole contract period, i.e. from the first day of the contract to expiration, or when a hedge covers more than one contract period, or when the hedge covers one part of a contract period and part or the whole of another. You must also remember that many options are American-style and thus can be exercised at any time up to expiration. Shorts can find themselves being assigned as a counterparty to a long who has exercised and find themselves with a pay-off different to that which would have occurred at expiration. However, this is not particularly likely. It is not optimal for a long in an American option to exercise early, it is better to close out and sell. The reasons for these phenomena should become clear after working through this chapter.

Re-cap on intrinsic and time value

We have seen in Chapter 14 that American-style options must always sell for at least their intrinsic value if they are in-the-money. If this is not the case then the options can be purchased and exercised immediately at a profit. Taking the LIFFE Short Sterling option as an example:

On 9 May the following prices applied:

| Strike price | Calls | | | Puts | | |
	June	Sep	Dec	June	Sep	Dec
94-50	0.12	0.13	0.09	0.06	0.40	0.92
94-75	0.03	0.06	0.05	0.22	0.58	1.13
95-00	0.01	0.03	0.02	0.45	0.80	1.35

The three-month short sterling future is the underlying, prices 9 May:

June	94.56
Sep	94.23
Dec	93.67
Mar	93.08

The June 94-50 calls are in-the-money by 0.06 (94-56–94-50). Time value must therefore make up the remainder of the option price, i.e. 0.06. Note the same time value of 0.06 for the June put which is out-of-the money and therefore has no intrinsic value.

June 94-75 calls are out-of-the-money and therefore the premium of 0.03 is all time value. The time value of the June 94-75 call at 0.03 is different to that of the 94-50 call at 0.06. Further note that the 95-00 call is priced at 0.01.

A call whose strike differs by 25 ticks, 94-50 compared to 94-75, has a time value difference of 0.03, whereas in another case a 25 tick difference in the strike, 94-75 compared with 95-00, only changes the time value by 0.02.

All the June calls obviously have the same expiration, yet time values differ, 0.06, 0.03, 0.01 respectively.

The same kind of relationships apply to the June puts. We have already noted that the June put is out-of-the-money and has time value therefore of 0.06. The June 94-75 is in-the-money 0.19 (94-75–94-56), time value 0.03 (i.e. as time value of 94-75 call in-the-money). June 95-00 puts are deep-in-the-money, intrinsic value 0.44 (95-00–94-56). Time value is thus 0.01.

These price relationships are all internally consistent and further demonstrate that time value is not just related to time. As previously indicated, time to expiration is the same, yet time value is different.

On 10 May prices are now as follows:

Short sterling options (LIFFE)

Strike price	Calls			Puts		
	June	Sep	Dec	June	Sep	Dec
94-50	0.14	0.14	0.09	0.04	0.36	0.87
94-75	0.04	0.07	0.05	0.19	0.54	1.08
95-00	0.01	0.03	0.02	0.41	0.75	1.30

Three-month sterling futures

	10 May	9 May	Change
June	94.60	94.56	+0.04
Sep	94.28	94.23	+0.05
Dec	93.72	93.67	+0.05
Mar	93.14	93.08	+0.06

The 94-50 June call on 9 May was 0.12. On 10 May it is 0.14. The option has changed 0.02, the underlying has changed 0.04.

The 94-75 June call on 9 May was 0.03. On 10 May it is 0.04. The option has changed 0.01, yet the underlying has changed 0.04. Similar differences in the change in value of the option can be observed in relation to the change in the underlying at other strikes and expirations of both calls and puts. We see that changes in the value of the underlying do not always change the value of options by the same amount.

In the introduction to Chapter 17, we stated that 'premiums of deep-out-of-the-money options with a short period of time to expiration will not change very much at all if the price of the underlying changes'. Look at June 95-00 calls, they are deep out-of-the-money with the underlying at 94.56 on 9 May. On 10 May the underlying has changed 0.04 to 94.60, but the premium is unchanged at 0.01.

A position in an option is held at the cost of the premium, the option can only be exercised until or at expiration, depending on whether it is American or European, and therefore the premium will never be as high as the price of underlying. As the price of the underlying changes, so will the value of the option, but in percentage terms the option price will always move more than that of the underlying, once the option is in-the-money.

Option price variables

From earlier sections in this and other option chapters it is apparent that option prices are dependent upon:

- the strike (K) (some notations use E for Exercise rate)
- spot price of the underlying (cash) security (S) or
- price of the underlying future (F)
- time to expiration (T).

In addition option prices are dependent upon:

- expected price volatility of the underlying (σ)
- the short-term, risk-free interest rate over the life the option (r) NB this does not apply when the underlying is a futures contract and the option position is margined futures style as at LIFFE
- coupon payments (if the underlying is a bond for example).

Taking the price of a European call as c, prior to expiration c is a function of S, T and K if the second set of variables is ignored for the time being, i.e.

$$c = c\,(S, T, K)$$

T, time to expiration and S, price of the underlying security can both change whilst an option position is held. K, the exercise price always remains fixed once the option position is taken. It can of course be different for different option positions.

At expiration a European call is either worth zero, i.e. $c = 0$, if it is out-of-the-money or its intrinsic value if in-the-money. Intrinsic value will be the price of the underlying minus the exercise price, i.e. $c = S - K$. As the price of the underlying (S) increases the value of the call (c) will also increase by at least this amount at expiration. As the price of the underlying increases, the option price gets nearer the intrinsic value. When K is greater than S at expiration, the call expires worthless, it is better to buy the underlying at its lower price.

If you imagine that an option can have a negative value, which of course it cannot, it can be seen that as S rises the value of c approaches zero, its 'negative value' becomes smaller and smaller. Once S is greater than K it pays to exercise the call at its realisable intrinsic value.

e^{rT} continuous compounding/e^{-rT} continuous discount factor

A sum of money, A, placed on deposit at a rate of interest r for T years will be worth in T years' time:

$$A(1 + r)^T$$

If $A = £10$

$r = 10\%$

$T = 1$ year

then $£100\,(1 + 0.1) = £110$

If A is placed on deposit and interest r is paid semi-annually then the compounding factor becomes:

$$A (1 + r/m)^{mT}$$

where $m = 2$, i.e. interest paid semi-annually.

$$£100 (1+0.1/2)^{mT} = £100 \times 1.05 \times 1.05 = £110.25$$

The more often interest is paid the larger the compounded sum becomes. If A were compounded every day for one year, at the end of the year £100 would be worth:

$$£100 (1+0.1/365)^{365 \times 1}$$
$$£100 (1+0.0002739726027)^{365} = £110.5155539$$

If the number of compounding intervals becomes infinite, then this is continuous compounding. If A is continuously compounded over time T at interest rate r, A becomes:

$$Ae^{rT}$$
where $e = 2.71828$
If $r = 10\%$,
$T = 1$ year
$$£100 \times 2.71828^{0.1 \times 1} = £110.5170844$$

- e is the mathematical constant used to continuously compound. Using e gives the 'same' result as compounding daily, i.e. £110.52 when rounded two decimal places.
- e^{-rT} therefore becomes the continuously compounded discount factor.

We need to use these rates when pricing options as will be soon revealed.

Present value of the exercise rate

We have seen that:
- e^{-rT} is the discount factor when continuously compounding, as shown above.
- $c = c(S, T, K)$ (p. 238).
- The value of the call cannot be greater than that of the underlying (p. 237).
- If the value of an option is represented only by intrinsic value at expiration, then $c = S - K$ (p. 238).

If first of all we imagine that the underlying is a bond, we can see that its present value can be discounted by the factor e^{-rT}.

The price of a call on the bond will be

$$c = c(S, T, K)$$

whose value must be at least equal to and possibly be greater than its intrinsic value, $S - K$.

However, if we see that its intrinsic value must be discounted to present value to determine the value now, it can be seen that

$$c = c(S, T, K) \geq S - e^{-rT} K$$

$e^{-rT} K$ being the present value of the exercise price.

To make it clear, if a call is in-the-money we can say, so far, that its value at any given time, before expiration can be seen to be:

$$c = S - e^{-rT} K$$

This assumes that the price of the underlying at expiration is known and certain. It must also be realised that there may be no intrinsic value, i.e. when $e^{-rT} E$ is greater than S, in which case the value of the option cannot be less than zero for reasons previously stated above.

r is the risk-free rate of interest. An additional element should be added as a risk premium, the notation for this is I.

Thus the value of a European call at expiration will either be zero if out-of-the-money or if in-the-money:

$$c = S = e^{-rT} K + I$$

American calls

So far we have discussed European calls which of course have to be taken to expiration. We have discussed in Chapter 14 that it is optimal for a long American call to sell the option before expiration rather than exercise before expiration. We can demonstrate this to be so from what we have here so far.

We saw in Chapter 14 that an American call must be at least as costly as a European call, with same strike and expiration. If C is an American call then

$$C(S, T, K) \geq c(S, T, K)$$

At expiration both American and European calls will be worth their intrinsic value (or nothing at all if out-of-the-money). If in-the-money, their intrinsic value at expiration is

$$S - K$$

Before expiration, when the American call could still be exercised the value of the American call will be (if in-the-money):

$$S - e^{-rT} K$$

Because $e^{-rT} K$ discounts K, $e^{-rT} K$ must be smaller than K, therefore intrinsic value must be greater before expiration, i.e.

$$S - e^{-rT} K > S - K$$

Thus it is better for the long to sell an American option than to exercise it before expiration.

Option prices and interest rates

We have seen (p. 238) that the value of a European call prior to expiration will be not less than zero and at least its intrinsic value if it is in-the-money, when the intrinsic value is brought to present value by the continuously compounded factor. It follows that the higher the rate of interest the lower will be e^{-rT}. It therefore must be that the higher the rate of interest, the higher will be the price of a call.

Put valuations

A European put, p, at expiration is worth:

$p = K - S$, or zero if out-of-the-money

Further refinements and manipulation of formulae enable us to state that a put option on a bond at expiration will be worth:

$p = c + e^{-rT} K - S$

This is in fact the put–call parity relationship reformulated as described in Chapter 14.

Note – rewritten for a call this becomes:

$c = S - e^{-rT} K + p$

The extra term p in the identity replaces that of I, the risk premium interest rate as described on p. 240.

Prices of options on futures

Many options have a futures contract as their underlying as described in Chapters 15 and 16. We therefore need to take account of this in our formula.

So far we have related option prices to the underlying as a physical security S. We now need to relate the option price to a futures price F. A futures price will be spot plus cost of carry as described in Chapter 10. Cost of carry will relate to interest rate cost, thus if the continuous compound rate is applied to the security this will give the futures price. Thus:

$F = e^{rT} S$

Alternatively, if the futures price is discounted to present value, this will give the price of the security. Thus:

$S = e^{-rT} F$

$e^{-rT} F$ can thus be inserted everywhere S occurs in place of S to give option values which relate to futures.

Thus before expiration a European call on a future will either be zero or:

$c = e^{-rT} F - e^{-rT} K$

assuming for the moment that the value of F is known and certain at expiration. This relationship also only applies when the option is not margined futures style, as at the CBOT or CME for example. For options margined futures style there will be zero cost attached to holding the options position and the discount factor for the future as the underlying can be removed from the identity. More on this later.

Option price and volatility of the underlying

We have seen to date that the value of a call is a function of the price of the underlying, the exercise rate, the interest rate and expiration. We have dealt with the effect of interest rates and the exercise rate related to expiration, we now need to consider the effect of the price of the underlying in more detail. As the price of the underlying changes, so does the value of the call, as readily seen from $c = S - e^{-rT} K$. Change S and c changes. The fact is that S does change, were this not so then there would be no need to hedge and no value in having options and other derivative instruments whose pay-off changes as a result of the underlying changing.

$c = S - e^{-rT} K$ assumes that the value of S at expiration is known and certain. Clearly this is not the case in reality. We do not know what the value of the underlying will be at expiration.

We do know that some underlying securities have more volatile prices than others. It is this price volatility which in fact creates greater value for a given option. The greater the volatility of the underlying, the greater the value of the option. Options are assets where volatility is a 'good thing', it creates value for the option. This is in contrast to the situation with other financial assets where volatility is a 'bad thing'. Volatility gives uncertain values and therefore risk of loss. Investors are usually assumed to be risk adverse and therefore place a lower value on highly priced volatile assets. So why are options different? The reason is that purchasers of options have only upside potential, not downside risk, and this is where options differ. Other financial assets have both risks. Options allow you to benefit from upside potential and provide protection for downside risk.

There is in fact an exception to this general principle. Average price options, Asian options, have pay-offs generated by the average price of the underlying up to expiration. This averaging will have the effect of reducing volatility and therefore reduces option prices.

If the underlying were to have a known, certain value at expiration there would be little difficulty in pricing options correctly. At expiration the price for European calls would be, as we have seen:

$$c = S - K \text{ or } c = F - K$$

if they were in-the-money, or zero if they were out-of-the-money.

We could price the call at any time prior to expiration by applying an appropriate discount factor to the strike and also the futures price if the underlying were a future and the option were not margined futures style, i.e.

$$c = S - e^{-rT} K \text{ or } c = e^{-rT} F - e^{-rT} K$$

Puts could also be priced in a similar appropriate way.

The option price would simply be related to the interest rate and time to expiration, with a known price of the underlying. The reality is, of course, the underlying does and will change. Its value at expiration is uncertain. We therefore have to find a way of reliably estimating its value at expiration so that this can be discounted by the prevailing interest rate and time, to give a reliable, 'correct' price of the option before expiration. We need to be able to assess the volatility of the underlying.

Volatility (σ) is a measure of an asset's potential for deviating from its current price. The measure actually used is the variability of an asset's past, historical price behaviour. It is assumed therefore that historical volatility is a good predictor of future price volatility.

To measure historical price volatility, prices are observed at given time intervals, either daily, weekly, monthly or yearly and their standard deviations calculated. The reason that volatility can be measured by calculating the standard deviations of price observations is taken from portfolio theory whereby, for example, an expected return of 10% can be said to represent the average, arithmetic mean return on an investment. However, because this is an average expected return, outcomes can be greater or less than the average, e.g. 15% or 5%. We need to look at the probability of different actual outcomes with regard to their range from the average 15%–5% and how this range is dispersed around the expected average. Thus price volatility of an asset can be measured by the standard deviation of possible returns around the expected average.

Annualised price volatility is obtained by taking the calculated standard deviation relating to the observation interval and adjusting. Thus for daily observed data:

$$\sigma \text{ (annual volatility)} = \text{standard deviation of prices per trading day} \times \sqrt{252}$$
(i.e. volatility per trading day)

(252 is the number of trading days in a year).

For monthly data:

$$\sigma = \text{volatility per month} \times \sqrt{12}$$

In practice daily observed data is most frequently used.

The answer comes out as the average percentage probability that the price of the underlying will change in either direction on an annualised basis. Note that the direction of price changes is not the issue. Prices trending upwards can be equally variable as prices trending downwards or trending flat. Volatility is a measure of an asset's potential for deviating from its current price. Reference to the values given by the calculation will show that volatility also changes with time. Volatility of an asset over one month will be greater than volatility of the same asset over a year. A **volatility cone** can be constructed which illustrates this principle.

Actual volatility for an option is therefore not directly observable, as it is for other variables, but historical volatility is directly observable and is used to forecast future price volatility.

Option quotes can be made in volatility terms instead of price. Traders will talk about selling an option at '18% volatility'. The market price of an option can be described as **rich** or **cheap in volatility**. Being rich or cheap means when the price of an option is evaluated, as in the next section, it may be found that its theoretical value differs from that of the market value. Such a difference between fair value and actual price of the underlying might be due to the fact that the price of the underlying has been much more stable, or volatile, than its historical volatility.

High volatility means high price changes in either direction, up or down, therefore as volatility increases so must the option price. At or out-of-the-money options, as we have seen in earlier chapters, have no intrinsic value, they are all time value. Time value, it can be seen therefore, is a price for such options that can be expected to give a breakeven position to the buyer and seller of either a put or a call at expiration as a function of a given volatility related to time and interest rates, if the underlying is a physical and not a future.

Black and Scholes Option Pricing Model

The most commonly used method of pricing options follows the **Black and Scholes Option Pricing Model (BSOPM)**, developed in 1973 for options on dividend paying stocks. It was later modified by Black and others (1976) for options on futures.

The model recognises and handles the volatility of the underlying as a pricing variable. Formally the BSOPM makes a number of assumptions:

- The price of the underlying follows a log normal distribution, returns are therefore normally distributed.
- The value of returns is known and is directly proportional to time.
- Interest rates are constant.
- Options are European, therefore cannot be exercised before expiration.
- No dividends or coupon payments are paid on the underlying.
- There are no transactions costs.

We will have the underlying being a physical security, this makes the formula simpler with fewer terms. It can be easily adapted for a future as the underlying by substituting $e^{-rT}F$ wherever S occurs in the formula. For options traded futures style as at LIFFE the formula used is covered on p. 247.

The Black and Scholes formula for a European call is:

$$c = SN(d_1) - Ke^{-rT}N(d_2)$$

r	=	risk-free interest rate
S	=	price of underlying (cash) security
T	=	time to expiration of the option
K	=	strike/exercise rate
$N(.)$	=	cumulative normal distribution function of d_1 and d_2 respectively
e	=	exponential, 2.71828
d_1	=	$\dfrac{\ln(S/K) + (r + \sigma^2/2)\,T}{\sigma\sqrt{T}}$
d_2	=	$d_1 - \sigma\sqrt{T}$
$\ln$	=	natural log
σ	=	standard deviation of changes in price of the underlying, i.e. volatility as described earlier (pp. 242, 243), therefore:
σ^2	=	instantaneous variance of the price of the underlying, i.e. the measure of the return volatility of the underlying.

Earlier we described how it would be if the underlying had a known certain value, when the price would relate to the strike and the known price of the underlying at expiration, i.e.

$$c = S - K$$

Prior to expiration the option value would merely discount the strike rate to give:

$$c = S - e^{-rT}K$$

If a known certain value is given to the underlying and input into the BSOPM, then σ^2, the variance of the return on the security, is zero. The formula then equates to $c = S - e^{-rT}K$.

In reality of course the price of the underlying does vary, it will have a degree of volatility and therefore such volatility must be input into the formula in terms of σ and σ^2. The formula weights S and e^{-rT}. The weights are determined by probabilities given from a normal distribution. We will see how this is done when we work through an example in the next section.

BSOPM, a worked example

All inputs into the model can be observed by reference to the option in question or can be ascertained by reference to statistical tables, except volatility. We have seen (pp. 242, 243) how volatility can be measured, for our purposes here we will assume a volatility of 20%. Therefore let:

S = 102
K = 100
T = 90 days = 90/365 = 0.2465 years
σ = 20% p.a.
r = 5% p.a.

$$d_1 = \frac{\ln(102/100) + (0.05 + 0.20^2/2)0.2465}{0.20\sqrt{0.2465}}$$

The value of $\ln(102/100)$ can be ascertained from the relevant statistical tables or by the use of a calculator with the relevant function.

Using the Casio fx-7000G calculator, $\ln(102/100)$ is 0.0198026273. Table 3 in Murdoch and Barnes' *Statistical Tables for Science, Engineering, Management and Business Studies*, 3rd edn, Macmillan, gives a value of 0.01980.

When 0.01980 is placed into the formula d_1 evaluates as:

$$\frac{0.01980 + 0.07 \times 0.2465}{0.0993} = 0.3732$$

$d_2 = 0.3732 - 0.20\sqrt{0.2465} = 0.2739$

$N(d_1)$ equals $N(0.3732)$ and $N(d_2)$ equals $N(0.2739)$.
In turn $N(0.3732) = 0.6455$ and $N(0.2739) = 0.6079$.
To get these figures we need to consult Table 3 in Murdoch and Barnes. This table gives the value of the shaded area under the normal distribution curve as in Figure 17.1.
From the table, 0.3732 gives the value 0.3545. However, we need the value of the unshaded area under the curve and therefore need to deduct 0.3545 from 1 to give the final figure of 0.6455. 0.2739 leads to a final figure of 0.6079.
Plugging these values back into the BSOPM formula gives:

$c = 102 \times 0.6455 - 100 \times 2.71828^{-0.05 \times 0.2465} \times 0.6079 = 5.80$

Therefore if S at 102 is £102 and K at 100 is £100, then the 'fair value premium' for a call is £5.80. Note with the strike at £100 and the underlying at £102 the call has some intrinsic value, as well as time value. Because the call is European-style, we cannot say that intrinsic value is £2, the call is only exercisable at expiration and this is 90 days away. During

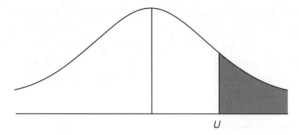

Figure 17.1 *Value for U of shaded area under the normal distribution curve.*

the 90 days the price of the underlying will change, to give a different intrinsic value, or possibly none at all. The pricing formula handles the volatility of the underlying over time to expiration. We can see intuitively, however, that a call with a strike of £102 should currently be priced below the premium for a £100 call at £5.80, but not £2 below. An at-the-money option, with strike at 102, should give the value of the option as £4.67. Confirmation of the correct working of the formula can be given by inputting the strike at 102, keeping other variables as before.

$$d_1 = \frac{\ln (102/102) + (0.05 + 0.20^2/2)0.2465}{0.20\sqrt{0.2465}} = 0.1738$$

$d_2 = 0.1738 - 0.20\sqrt{0.2465} = 0.0745$

$N(d_1) = N(0.1738) = 1 - 0.4310 = 0.5690$

$N(d_2) = N(0.0745) = 1 - 0.4703 = 0.5297$

$c = 102 \times 0.5690 - 102 \times 2.7128^{-0.05 \times 0.2465} \times 0.5297 = 4.67$

£4.67 is below the premium of £5.80 for the £102 call, but clearly not £2 below. An American-style option, which is of course exercisable at any time up until expiration, would price an option currently in-the-money to include 'current' intrinsic value. The LIFFE option pricing model (below) does this.

Different values for the variables obviously create different option prices. If the option is not priced 'correctly', then arbitrage strategies ensure that it is. It should be appreciated that such activity can of course alter the value of the variables, as well as the option price. Arbitrages will alter the demand for the underlying and thus alter its price. A change in demand for funds to finance positions in the underlying will alter interest rates. In this respect it is possible to argue that it is the underlying which is mispriced relative to the option. However, we generally say that it is the option which is incorrectly priced.

The formula uses historical volatility of the underlying, not its expected future value. Expected future value cannot be measured directly, therefore having such a variable in a pricing formula would be of little practical use.

LIFFE option pricing model

The BSOPM is slightly adapted to price options traded at LIFFE to reflect the fact that they are options on futures and traded futures style. An option position can be taken by both long and short by deposit of initial margin, thus no outlay is necessary by the long to pay for the premium up front. For this reason the risk free interest rate is not a variable. In addition the underlying is of course a future and not a physical.

The following formula is used for short-term interest rate options, note the different notation.

$$C = R_x \times N(-d_2) - R_f \times N(-d_1)$$

where:

$$d_1 = \frac{\ln(R_f/R_x) + \frac{1}{2} \times S^2 \times T}{S \times \sqrt{T}}$$

d_2 $= d_1 - S \times \sqrt{T}$
$N(-d_1)$ $= 1 - N(d_1)$
$N(-d_2)$ $= 1 - N(d_2)$
C $=$ Call premium (American-style, thus capital C)
F_f $=$ rate implied by futures price (i.e. 100 minus futures price), equivalent to S in BSOPM
R_x $=$ rate implied by strike price (i.e. 100 minus strike price), equivalent to K in BSOPM
S $=$ volatility of three-month rates measured by annual standard deviation, equivalent to σ in BSOPM
T $=$ time to expiration in years
$N(.)$ $=$ cumulative function of normal distribution

Thus the price of short-term interest rate options traded at LIFFE is a function of time to expiration, rates implied by the futures and strike prices and the volatility of interest rates.

Implied volatility

For every actual market price of an option it is possible to calculate the implied volatility of the underlying by iteration, all other variables which determine the option price are directly observable.

If $c = (S, T, K, r, \sigma)$ it is only σ which is unknown. Solving for the value of σ gives the volatility implied by the market price of the option. Look at our examples of the BSOPM calculations, if we know the market price of a call to be £4.67, then we can solve by iteration for the value of σ, all other variables being known.

Caution must be exercised in using the measure of implied volatility, which is helpfully calculated for you by vendors of market information such as Datastream. Volatility of a given value does not affect all option premiums in the same way.

Options at or very near-the-money are most sensitive to changes in volatility of the underlying and are more so the nearer they are to expiration. Sensitivity to changes in volatility are measured by **Vega/Kappa** (p. 250). It is therefore possible to find different implied volatilities for the same option where strike differs. If this is found to be the case then a spread strategy can be undertaken to profit. In practice a profit is not always possible, transaction costs have to be taken into account. Higher volatility means higher price, therefore sell this and buy the lower priced, lower implied volatility option on the principle of selling that which is expensive and buying that which is cheap.

If options at or very near-the-money and near to expiration are most affected by volatility, it follows that they will have a large component of their total value being time value. For this reason they will be attractive to call writers, they will give them higher incomes.

The use of volatility cones and **cheapness indices** are useful analytical tools which enable rich or cheap prices to be identified. See further reading list at the end of the chapter.

Sensitivity of option price to changes in key variables

We have seen that relevant key variables affect the price of an option. It follows that as the variables change, so does the option price in response. There are various measures, derived from the BSOPM, which calculate the sensitivity of the option price to changes in the variables. If a key variable changes by a given percentage amount, by how much does this make the option price change in percentage terms? This is always an important matter because options are rarely taken to expiration to take advantage of any time value remaining. Thus the pay-off from a given option position will be different to that at expiration. Figure 17.2 gives the pay-off related to time before expiration using a long call as an example.

Measures which relate the sensitivity of an option price to changes in the underlying include **delta** and **gamma**, the measure which relates sensitivity to changes in time is **theta** and to volatility it is **vega**.

Delta (Δ)

Delta is the rate of change in the price of an option following a change in the price of the underlying. It can be calculated for small changes as:

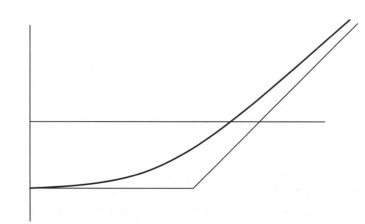

Figure 17.2 *Pay-off from a long call before expiration.*

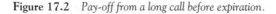

$$delta = \frac{\text{change in option price}}{\text{change in price of underlying}}$$

It can be thought of as the speed with which an option price changes related to the underlying. It is the probability that an option will be in-the-money at expiration. It is the option's pay-off.

- If an option is deep-in-the-money its price will be virtually all a reflection of intrinsic value. Premium and underlying will change on an almost one for one basis and delta will be near to 1.
- A deep out-of-the-money option premium will be near to zero. Small changes in price of the underlying will not alter the premium. Delta will be near to zero.
- At-the-money options will have a delta of approximately 0.5.

The delta of a call will decline as the price of the underlying falls. For a put the delta will increase as the price of the underlying falls. Therefore deltas of calls are positive, deltas of puts are negative. Delta changes in a non-linear way.

If the delta of a call is 0.5 and the price of the underlying changes by £1, then the option will change in price by 50p. If the underlying goes up £1, the option premium goes up 50p. If the underlying goes down £1, the option falls by 50p, other variables constant.

A **delta hedge ratio** to ensure that a position in the underlying is fully hedged therefore requires sufficient options whose pay-off will compensate for changes in the price of the underlying. Such a hedge, option combined with the underlying, is said to be **delta neutral** and requires option contracts in proportion to the delta.

If delta is 0.50, then 100 option contracts will hedge 50 contracts in the underlying future or its spot market equivalent. The delta hedge ratio is therefore the reciprocal of the delta. A delta of 0.50 gives:

$$\text{delta hedge ratio} = \frac{1}{0.50} = 2$$

i.e. two option contracts for every one in the underlying future or cash market nominal value. An alternative term for the delta hedge ratio is the **delta risk**.

Delta must change as the underlying changes price and time to expiration declines. Thus the hedge ratio has to be re-balanced from time to time. Such rebalancing is known as **dynamic hedging**. It is the opposite to **hedge and forget** which applies to hedging with futures and other derivatives.

In terms of the BSOPM:

- $\Delta = N(d_1)$ for a call and
- $\Delta = N(d_1) - 1$ for a put

Gamma (Γ)

Delta changes in a non-linear way, gamma measures the change in delta when a small change in the underlying occurs. If delta measures the speed with which an option price changes then gamma can be said to measure the acceleration in the change in the option price as the underlying changes.

If gamma is small then a dynamic hedge ratio need only be adjusted occasionally because delta will not be changing quickly. The opposite of course applies if gamma is large.

Gamma will be large when an option is at-the-money and near to expiration. Gamma will be small, approaching zero, when either an in- or out-of-the-money option is nearing expiration. Delta does not change much when expiration is near for in-the-money options, changes in the premium will be almost wholly a reflection of changes in intrinsic value. Options which are out-of-the money have little chance of getting intrinsic value as expiration nears, thus the premium changes little.

Options with high gammas will be attractive to option buyers, but less attractive to option sellers. High gammas mean fast, accelerating changes in delta, thus options going in-the-money accelerate sellers' losses and purchasers' gains.

Theta (Θ)

Theta measures an option's loss in value due to time decay, thus it is almost always of negative value. An option premium will not fall in value if it relates to a deep-in-the-money European option. As an example, if an option has a theta of -0.05 it will lose 5 ticks in price for each day that elapses.

Vega (kappa, lambda or sigma)

Volatility of the underlying can and does change, this is especially so for currencies. Thus vega is a measure of change in option price as a result of change in volatility of the underlying. It is actually calculated as change in option premium for a 1% change in implied volatility.

If an option has a vega of 0.05 and implied volatility is 10%, then if volatility were to change to 11%, then the premium would change 5 ticks.

Vega has values between zero and infinity and falls as expiration nears. Vega will be high for at-the-money options with long times to expiration.

Summary

- In determining what an option price ought to be, what is a fair price to charge or pay, is related to a number of variables, all of which can be observed in the case of strike (K), price of the underlying (S), time to expiration (T) and the short-term, risk-free interest rate (r), or can be estimated from historical data in the case of volatility (σ).
- By inputting appropriate values into the Black and Scholes Option Pricing Model, a fair price for a European call (c) can be calculated. Small adaptations to the model can be made to price American calls (C), puts (p and P) and options on futures.

- In practice the market may be a little different to that calculated. The market price will have imbedded in it a level of volatility implied by its price. This implied volatility can be used to see whether it differs from your own analysis of what volatility is or will be. As a result prices can be said to be either rich or cheap.
- Volatility is a measure of an asset's potential for deviating from its current price in either direction. Prices are observed at given time intervals and their standard deviations are calculated and related to the time interval of the observations so that an annualised figure in percentage terms is obtained. It is assumed that historical volatility treated statistically in this way will deal adequately with actual volatility over the life of the option. High volatility creates value for an option because for the purchaser there is only upside potential, no downside risk.
- Option prices and the price of the underlying do not change on a one for one basis over the life of an option, except in a few circumstances. An option's price is of course sensitive to changes in the value of the variables which are used to calculate it. An obvious variable which changes over the life of an option is time. The common sensitivity measures are delta, gamma, theta and vega.

Key terms

- Black and Scholes Option Pricing Model (BSOPM) (p. 244)
- cheapness indices (p. 248)
- continuous compounding e^{rT} (p. 238)
- continuous discount factor e^{-rT} (p. 238)
- cumulative normal distribution function (N.) (p. 244)
- delta (Δ) (p. 248)
- delta hedge ratio (p. 249)
- delta neutral (p. 249)
- delta risk (p. 249)
- dynamic hedging (p. 249)
- gamma (Γ) (p. 249)
- implied volatility (p. 247)

- kappa (p. 250)
- lambda (p. 250)
- lognormal distribution (p. 244)
- normal distribution (p. 244)
- observations (p. 243)
- option price variables (S, T, K, r, σ) (p. 244)
- re-balanced (p. 249)
- rich/cheap in volatility (p. 243)
- sensitivities (p. 235)
- sigma (p. 250)
- standard deviation of price (p. 243)
- theta (Θ) (p. 250)
- vega (p. 250)
- volatility cones (p. 243)

17.1 Explain the term delta.

17.2 If you hold a deep out-of-the-money option near to expiration, will delta be high or low?

17.3 What are the variables which determine the fair value of an option?

17.4 Calculate the continuously compounded discount factor when the risk-free rate of interest is 5.5% p.a. and time to expiration is 45 days.

17.5 K = £25, S = £25, r = 6% p.a., T = 90 days, σ = 12%. Calculate the fair price for a European call using the BSOPM.

17.6 Why does volatility increase the value of an option, but reduce the price of other financial assets?

17.7 In what way is the fair value of an option affected in relation to the basic BSOPM if the option is on a future and margined futures style?

17.8 What is meant by an option being cheap in volatility? Give reasons why this might be so.

17.9 Calculate delta if an option price changes 3 ticks when the underlying changes 5 ticks.

17.10 Estimate delta for an ATM option.

17.11 If the price of the underlying future falls, will the delta of the option rise or fall as a result?

17.12 If delta is 0.8, what will the delta hedge ratio be?

17.13 Why does a hedge need rebalancing when using options?

17.14 What does gamma measure? In what way is the measure useful when hedging?

17.15 Which sensitivity measure calculates an option's change in value due to time decay?

17.16 Which two of the following statements are true, and why?

(a) The sensitivity of the delta of an option to a change in the price of the underlying is called theta.

(b) The delta of a put is negative.

(c) For a call option, delta increases as the price of the underlying rises, until it reaches unity.

(d) The delta of an option measures its sensitivity to interest rates.

(Securities Institute, Financial Futures and Options, July 1994.)

📖 ▷ Further reading

Eades, Simon (1991) *Options, Hedging & Arbitrage*, McGraw Hill.

Gemmill, Gordon (1993) *Options Pricing*, McGraw Hill.

LIFFE Money Market Review, Futures and Options, 2nd quarter, 1994.

LIFFE Short-term Interest Rates, *Futures and Options* (LIFFE Publication).

Natenberg, Sheldon (1991) *Option Volatility & Pricing*, Probus.

Ritchenken, Peter (1992) *Options*, HarperCollins.

Interest rate swaps

This chapter deals with the development of swaps and focuses especially upon interest rate swaps. The next chapter is devoted to currency swaps in detail.

Interest rate swap definitions

Interest rate swaps have been defined variously as:

- an agreement between two or more parties to swap obligations on two or more debt instruments or benefits on assets so that all can gain;
- an arrangement whereby one party exchanges one set of interest payments for another, e.g. fixed for floating rate;
- a transaction in which two parties agree to exchange a predetermined series of payments over time;
- an exchange between two parties of interest obligations (payment of interest) or receipts (investment income) in the same currency on an agreed amount of notional principal for an agreed period of time. 'In the same currency' makes this a definition of an interest rate swap.

    Where there is an exchange of interest obligations, i.e. interest to be paid on a debt, the swap is a **liability swap**.

    Where there is an exchange of interest receipts, i.e. interest received from an investment, then this is an **asset swap**.

Plain vanilla

The basic interest rate swap is often called a **plain vanilla**. Alternatively it is a **coupon swap** or **generic swap**. It involves exchanging fixed rate interest obligations for floating rate obligations over a given period of time relative to a **notional principal** sum of money. It is commonly used and described here to illustrate basic swap features.

There are two counterparties to the swap agreement, A and B, and a dealer arranges the swap taking a margin or spread.

	Fixed	Floating
A can borrow funds at	5.0%	6m LIBOR + 50 bp
B can borrow funds at	7.0%	6m LIBOR + 100 bp

The above rates refer to the borrowing of a notional principal of £100m over 15 years.

Note that the difference between the rates in the different markets for A and B is different! This difference, the **quality spread** is:

fixed market   7.0%–5.0% = 2.0% (200 bp)
floating market 100 bp–50 bp = 50 bp

A has an **absolute advantage** in fixed and floating markets. B has a **comparative advantage** in the floating rate market. This issue is discussed later (pp. 259, 260).

Clearly A is the better credit rated organisation, it can borrow at lower rates in both markets compared with B – its absolute advantage. By swapping interest rate obligations both A and B can borrow at lower rates.

A wishes to borrow at floating rates and becomes the floating rate payer in the swap arrangement. However, A actually borrows fixed rate funds in the cash market. It is the interest rate obligations on this fixed rate borrowing which are swapped.

B wishes to borrow at fixed rates and becomes the fixed rate payer in the swap. B, however, actually borrows at floating rates in the cash market and swaps the interest rate payable on this floating rate borrowing for fixed.

Under the swap arrangement:

A, the floating rate payer,

- pays floating rate 6m LIBOR
- receives fixed rate of 5%.

B, the fixed rate payer,

- pays fixed rate of 5.5%
- receives floating rate 6m LIBOR.

The rates apply if the dealer takes a spread of 50 bp. Here the dealer receives 5.5% fixed and pays 5% fixed. The flow of swapped interest payments can be illustrated as in Figure 18.1.

The net cost of funds to A and B using the swap arrangement can be seen by examining their cash flows.

A: – 6m LIBOR	+5%	– 5%	= – 6m LIBOR
paid to dealer	received from dealer	paid to fixed rate lender in cash market	i.e. net cost
B: – 5.5%	+ 6m LIBOR	– (6m LIBOR+100 bp)	= – 6.5%
			i.e. net cost
paid to dealer	received from dealer	paid to floating rate lender in cash market	

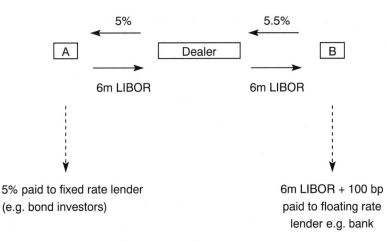

Figure 18.1 *Swapped interest flow – plain vanilla.*

If A achieves floating rate at 6m LIBOR, this is better by 50 bp than without the swap.

If B achieves fixed rate at 6.5%, this is 50 bp better than without the swap.

The dealer has also made a margin of 50 bp (5.5% received less 5% paid).

The quality spread differential in the fixed cash market was 2%, in the floating rate market it was ½%.

$$2\% - \tfrac{1}{2}\% = 1\tfrac{1}{2}\%$$

The gain which can be shared out between the swap counterparties and the dealer is $1\tfrac{1}{2}\%$. In our example they both gain $\tfrac{1}{2}\%$ each. You will be able to see how these rates are obtained later (pp. 256–8).

The amount of money borrowed has to be the same, but this underlying, notional principal is not swapped – there is no need – it is the same currency and amount. A single net difference payment is all that is needed in relation to the interest payment flows.

Both A and B must meet their original obligations to the actual lender of the funds. Each remains responsible for servicing their own debt, this must be so. If B were to become liable for A's debt, then logically A would not be able to raise funds at rates applicable to their credit rating in the first place.

Floating rates used as the bench mark or **index** can be Treasury bills, bankers' acceptances or bank CDs, in addition to the almost standard use of LIBOR. Each swap's documentation will specify how the index is to be determined. Most swaps use either ISDA (International Swaps and Derivatives Association) standard terms or BBAIRS (British Bankers Association Interest Rate Swaps). The latter only covers swaps up to two years, although 'Extended BBAIRS' is sometimes used. The general preference is for ISDA standard terms, however.

Swaps terminology

We have already used the terms fixed rate payer and floating rate payer. The description describes their obligations in the swap and not what they do outside of it.

The fixed rate payer in the swap:

- pays fixed rate
- receives floating rate.

They are said to be:

- short the fixed rate bond market
- long the floating rate bond market
- long a swap
- purchaser of a swap.

The fixed rate payer can be described as the provider of floating rate funds, even though no funds are actually provided in the swap as such because the principal amount is not exchanged.

The floating rate payer in the swap:

- pays floating rate
- receives fixed rate.

They are said to be:

- long the fixed rate bond market
- short the floating rate bond market
- short a swap
- seller of a swap.

The floating rate payer can be described as the provider of fixed rate funds.

We can see how it is that the fixed rate payer is short the bond market and the floating rate payer is long the bond market by reminding ourselves of the inverse relationship between bond price changes and interest rate changes.

Floating rate payers:

- gain when interest rates fall (they will pay lower rates when the interest rate is reset);
- lose when interest rates rise.

Fixed rate payers:

- lose when interest rates fall (they remain locked into the fixed rate);
- gain when interest rates rise.

If you are long in the bond market you will gain if interest rates fall – bond prices will rise. From the above relationships it can be seen that floating rate payers gain when interest rates fall and therefore can be said to be long in the bond market.

If you are short in the bond market you will gain if interest rates rise – bond prices will fall, making them cheaper. Again from the above relationships, it is the fixed rate payer who will gain from a rise in interest rates and is therefore short in the bond market.

Later (p. 258), when we discuss swaps as a string of FRAs or futures, the long and short swap terms will be made clear.

Dealers and swap quotations

The **trade date** is the date the counterparties agree on the swap conditions.

Discussion is usually over the telephone and verbal agreement is binding. Confirmation is then made by fax and letter.

A potential swap user telephones a number of swap dealers who make a market in swaps and asks for a quote. Those with the best quotes are then contacted again to see if they wish to quote even lower. In general the lower bidder will be chosen, although the swap counterparties must be aware of credit risk in relation to the dealer, it is the dealer who will be required to pay compensation. Many dealers operate as **special purpose vehicles**. This allows them to make a market in derivatives and enjoy a higher credit rating within the special purpose vehicle than that enjoyed by the parent company. The special purpose vehicle is separately capitalised from the parent so that the relevant assets and liabilities are isolated from those in the parent.

Many dealers are **assignment brokers**. They are prepared to make a market in swaps, but as soon as a suitable swap counterparty is found the swap contract is redrafted so that each counterparty is obligated directly to the other, rather than to the swap dealer. This is known as **warehousing**.

> The **effective date** is the date that the swap becomes effective, i.e. when interest obligations start to accrue.
> The **maturity date** is the date the swap stops accruing interest.

It must be appreciated that the interest flows may occur at different times. Floating linked to LIBOR will usually be every six or three months, depending upon the index used. Fixed will usually be paid annually (sterling swaps). Care must always be taken by participants to be aware of the different day count conventions for different currencies, 360 or 365 day years, 30 day months or actual (as discussed in Chapter 8).

Swaps have been quoted in a number of ways, but that most commonly seen is for the swap dealer to set the floating rate equal to a bench mark/index rate (e.g. 6m LIBOR, p. 255) free of the margin actually payable in the cash market by the relevant counterparties. The rate is said to be quoted **flat**. Having set the floating rate flat, the fixed rate is then set appropriate to it. It is because of this that the market is said to 'talk the fixed rate'. In the sterling swap market the fixed rate is always taken to be quoted against 6m LIBOR unless otherwise agreed.

By quoting in this way the dealer can quote bid–ask (or bid–offer) terms. Different swap quotes can be evaluated on a comparable basis if quoted in this way.

A dealer in sterling interest rate swaps will therefore quote a bid–ask spread of, for instance, 5.00%–5.5% fixed against 6m LIBOR flat as the floating rate.

It means that the dealer is willing to:

- pay (bid) 5.0% fixed and receive 6m LIBOR;
- receive (ask/offer) 5.5% fixed and pay 6m LIBOR.

The dealer will make 0.50% – obviously the spread on 5.00%–5.5%. He pays 5.0% having received 5.5% and pays and receives 6m LIBOR.

Swaps are not actually executed as quoted. Net flows are determined and then paid or received as appropriate. Note that the above terms would be taken up by A (bid) and B (ask) as described on pp. 254, 255 and illustrated in Figure 18.1

In contrast, with US$ interest rate swaps a suitable bench mark rate applicable to maturity of the swap is taken, e.g. US T-bonds, to enable the fixed rate to be set a given number of basis points margin to it. The margin will be as the bid–ask rates. Therefore, if the bid is 50 bp and the ask 100 bp and the 15 year benchmark T-bond yield is 4.5%, a dealer will quote an ask price of 100 bp versus receiving LIBOR flat to the fixed rate payer (B), i.e. 4.5% plus 100 bp = 5.5%.

To the floating rate payer (A) the dealer will quote the bid price of 50 bp versus paying LIBOR flat, i.e. 4.5% plus 50 bp = 5%.

Reference to Figure 18.1 will see that the dealer is asking for 5.5% from the fixed rate payer and bidding 5% to the floating rate payer. Different quote conventions, same outcome in interest rate terms.

Asking is therefore placing the fixed rate payer into a position analogous to purchasing the swap or long the swap.

Bidding to the floating rate payer is analogous to the floating rate payer selling the swap or short the swap.

This is the explanation for the swap terminology given on p. 256.

The dealer is at risk that one or both of the counterparties to the swap will not pay. The dealer is not at risk in relation to the repayment of the notional principal, that is a matter for the actual lenders. If the fixed rate payer does not pay, the actual loss to the dealer, if any, will be the difference between the fixed rate the dealer does not receive and the floating rate they would have paid. Needless to say, the obligation to the floating rate payer must still be honoured. Payments by the dealer to either counterparty are not conditional upon receipt from the other counterparty.

Swaps – a string of FRAs or futures

A swap can be interpreted as a strip of FRAs or futures contracts. To see that this is so consider that every time the floating index is reset an interest rate payment goes from one counterparty to the other in just the same way that compensation is payable/received under an FRA. In a similar way, as interest rates change so the value of a futures position changes.

Consider a long futures position and a short FRA position – remember these denote the same obligations. Each position gains if interest rates fall and loses if interest rates rise. This risk/return profile is that of a swap floating rate payer.

For a swap fixed rate payer the position is the same as that for a short futures position and a long FRA position. Each will lose if interest rates fall and gain if interest rates rise.

A swap cannot be replaced by an appropriate FRA strip because liquidity in the FRA market does not go further than one year, whereas in the swap market it goes out to at least 15 years; however, quotes for FRAs with maturities up to two years are made. In addition a swap is one contract, not a package of separate contracts.

Swaps – a package of cash market bonds

To an interest rate swap counterparty, the swap can be viewed as being long in one bond and short another. Even though the notional principal value is not exchanged in practice, a swap can be viewed, in terms of the original counterparties A and B and the dealer (refer to Figure 18.1), as:

- A has borrowed £100m for 15 years at 6m LIBOR from the dealer.
- The dealer has borrowed from A £100m for 15 years at 5% p.a. fixed.
- B has borrowed £100m for 15 years at 5.5% p.a. fixed from the dealer.
- The dealer borrowed from B £100m for 15 years at 6m LIBOR.

Taking A and B:

- A has sold a floating rate bond (short)
- A has purchased a fixed rate bond (long)
- B has sold a fixed rate bond (short)
- B has purchased a floating rate bond (long)

(Check this out with the conclusions on p. 256.)

In each instance the counterparties are short one type of bond and long the other.

The value of an interest rate swap spread with a maturity of 15 years, and any swap with a maturity greater than 5 years will be the difference in the value of fixed rate and floating rate corporate bond spreads.

Comparative advantage

The reason that interest rate swaps 'work' is said to be due to the principle of comparative advantage. In our earlier examples we have seen that A had an absolute credit advantage in both fixed and floating rate markets, but that B had a comparative advantage in the floating rate market. The quality spread in the fixed was larger than the quality spread in the floating.

As long as the quality spread is not the same in both markets, arbitrage gains via an interest rate swap are possible. Without this quality spread there will be nothing to be gained by either of the counterparties in swapping. Each borrower raises funds where they have a comparative advantage and then swaps obligations for the type of finance, fixed or floating, that they really seek.

That a quality spread differential exists, it is argued, is that investors in fixed rate instruments are more sensitive to the credit rating of the borrower (i.e. issuer) than floating rate bank lenders. As a result, issues of fixed debt instruments with lower credit ratings have to issue such debt at premium rates. Low credit rated issuers of debt instruments, by entering into a swap, can get long-term fixed rate funds. Two kinds of risk can be identified when funds are lent, credit risk and interest rate risk. Credit risk is the risk that the borrower will default. Interest rate risk is that interest rates will change and so cause changes in the value of the debt instrument (i.e. bond).

The bond market is able to bear interest rate risk on long-term debt. Investors in long-term bonds will be typically pension funds and life assurance companies, both of which have long-term liabilities which can be matched with bond maturities. In this way fluctuations in bond prices do not matter to them. Banks, however, cannot manage interest rate risk well. They have short-term liabilities on which they pay variable interest rate or rates which can be altered in the short term.

Banks are able to assess credit risk. The borrower is their customer with whom they may enjoy **relationship banking** and therefore have better information. They can monitor performance of loans. The bond market cannot do these things well, thus the premium demanded.

Swaps allow credit risk and interest rate risk to be separated. Take B as an example. If they default on their cash market loans say from a bank, the bank loses – credit risk. However, the bond investors in A bear interest rate risk and it is B that is paying interest on the bonds via the swap arrangements.

It could be argued that B, the fixed rate payer in the swap, only pays fixed at 6.5% net in the example on p. 254 if B can continue to borrow at LIBOR + 100 bp. Remember, every six months the loan has to be rolled over. If LIBOR changes there is no problem, but if the margin above LIBOR is increased by the lending bank in the cash market, then this will effectively increase the fixed rate payable by B under the swap.

It could be argued that the reason why B has to pay so much more in the fixed rate cash market than A is because it is perceived that its credit rating is falling and thus its margin over LIBOR will widen in the floating rate market. Therefore comparative advantage does exists, but it may be difficult to arbitrage it to advantage over the life of the swap.

It is often argued that comparative advantage does not exist any longer. Swaps being an arbitrage activity, like all such activity will erode the quality spread differentials. This is certainly the case, up to a point, quality spread differentials are much smaller than before interest rate swaps began. However, swaps do act as a mechanism for arbitraging segmented markets.

Arguably the floating and fixed markets are completely separate and competitive within themselves. Each market sets price relative to risk which is different in each market, one is long-term the other short-term, but each market will have its own users who cannot access the other market. The example often given is that of financial institutions, e.g. insurance companies, which can only or mainly invest in domestic instruments. As a result domestic issuers will be favoured. Additionally, it seems likely that domestic issuers will always have an advantage in their own market, investors will be more familiar with their performance and therefore credit risk. Tax differences in different geographical markets may also create market imperfections which can be arbitraged in the swap market.

An important reason to explain the existence of the interest rate swap market is the volatility of interest rates and the increased need for borrowers and lenders to hedge. As discussed earlier, the risk/return characteristics of an interest rate swap are those of a package of futures or strip of FRAs. Futures are not as liquid as swaps once maturities exceed one year. Swap maturities are liquid up to 15 years and cost less than a series of FRAs whose liquidity also does not reach anywhere near 15 years.

Origin and development of the swap market

The interest rate swap market has really only existed in its present form since 1981. Early forms of currency swap existed before this date in the shape of back-to-back loans. A Swiss franc/deutschmark/US dollar currency swap between the World Bank and IBM really created interest and activity in swap arrangements. Initially deals were on a matched basis whereby a bank would bring two counterparties together with the same, matched requirements.

Later, 1984, especially in the US dollar interest rate swap market, banks started to develop **warehousing** whereby a single counterparty would approach them and without another counterparty the bank would enter into a swap arrangement with them. A temporary hedge would be taken in the bond or futures market until a suitable counterparty could be found. Today banks act as dealers and make a market in swaps. Most activity is in US dollar interest rate swaps. Swaps on less actively traded currencies are still on a matched basis, although interest rate swaps in yen, sterling and deutschmarks are gaining in importance.

Liquidity in the US dollar interest rate swap market is generally agreed to be due to, straightforwardly, the demand for them and the ease of hedging swaps in the US Treasury repo and futures markets. Standard terms introduced by the ISDA and BBA in 1985 also assisted growth in the swap market. Product innovation in interest rate swaps also sustains growth, however the secondary market in swaps is still illiquid.

In January 1991 the Law Lords ruled that UK local authorities do not have the power to enter into swap arrangements. As a result existing swaps were declared null and void. These amounted to notional values of about £70bn and interest payment of about £1bn. These rulings have somewhat clouded the legality of other swap arrangements with, for instance, pension funds and building societies. The total legal position is far from clear and further court decisions are awaited.

Interest rate swap users

The main users of interest rate swaps are:

- supranational bodies like the World Bank
- public sector institutions like ECGD
- multinational corporations
- medium size companies
- banks, both as dealers/market makers or end user

Secondary market in swaps

Swaps are mutual obligations, even though it is usual for the swap counterparties to be unaware of each other's identity because of the role of the swap dealer/market maker. It is difficult in many respects to think of swaps being traded in a market. The primary market became more of a market once warehousing became prevalent and standardised terms and standard documentation became common. However, the secondary market still remains thin, due to mutuality.

There are three ways in which a swap can be unwound. The counterparty wishing to unwind can ask the market maker for a **cancellation**. This is also known as a **close-out** or **swap buy-back**. Here the counterparty must pay (or receive) a sum representing the present value of the future income streams generated by the swap to the other counterparty. If the counterparty is in fact the market maker, then the swap can be cancelled.

With a **swap reversal** the counterparty which wishes to unwind will have to find a counterparty for another swap via a dealer where the principal amount is the same as the original swap, but where the maturity is that remaining in the original and where the interest rate obligations are the reverse of those in the original swap.

An example:

A originally enters into a 10-year swap with B, notional principal amount is £100m. A pays 10% fixed and receives LIBOR.

After 5 years A wishes to unwind their position. They will have to enter into another swap, via a dealer, with another counterparty, C. Notional principal amount is £100m, maturity of swap is 5 years and A pays LIBOR and receives fixed. The fixed rate will depend upon current rates for floating rate receivers for the second swap arrangement.

In net terms A has neutralised their swap obligations, however, they must appreciate that there are now two credit risks, that of B and C.

A **swap sale** or **assignment** overcomes this problem. Here A will find another counterparty, D, who is willing to take A's obligations over in the original swap, i.e. pay 10% fixed and receive LIBOR for the years left until maturity. A will have to compensate D to take over his obligations, or perhaps D will be willing to pay A to do so, it will all depend upon current swap terms 5 years into the swap.

If interest rates have increased, A being a fixed rate payer of 10% would expect to be compensated by D. If interest rates have fallen, D would expect to be compensated by A.

All these arrangements are difficult, they do not create speed and certainty. They almost certainly mean the primary swap market is smaller than it otherwise would be. There are proposals from time to time to introduce a swap clearing house as for futures and options, with daily marking to market to reduce counterparty credit risk.

Swaps as a hedging vehicle

We have seen how swaps can be used to lower the cost of funding, it should also be apparent that they can also be used as a way of hedging interest rate risk. Reference to p. 256 will show how the value of swap position can change in response to changes in interest rates. If interest rates change and swaps gain/lose value as a result it follows they can be used as a hedging vehicle.

Earlier (p. 256) we described how it is that:
a floating rate payer:

- gains when interest rate fall
- loses when interest rates rise.

a fixed rate payer:

- loses when interest rate fall
- gains when interest rates rise.

Changes in the value of a swap position can be arranged so that it is the opposite to changes in value on a cash market position, thus a position neutral to interest rate changes in net terms can be achieved.

Imagine you hold a portfolio of long-term bonds, your concern is that interest rates will rise causing a resultant loss in the capital value of the portfolio. If you become a fixed rate payer in a swap you will gain if interest rate rise. Effectively you have converted your fixed rate bonds into floating rate bonds. Floating rate bonds will not experience a change in their capital value as a result of interest rate changes. You will have immunised your fixed rate portfolio from the consequences of interest rate rises. If interest rates rise the value of the portfolio will fall, but this fall will be offset by a gain in the value of the swap position. This is an example of an asset swap. Equally you will have minimised the portfolio against interest rate falls. The portfolio and swap position gains and losses will cancel each other out should interest rates fall. The portfolio will rise in value, but the swap position will fall in value.

Another example of interest rate risk would be that to a life assurance company. It will have long-term, fixed rate liabilities. A fall in interest rates will increase the value of the liabilities. By becoming a swap floating rate payer the interest rate risk could be hedged. Reference to the change in swap values above to a floating rate payer will confirm that as interest rates fall the floating rate payer gains. The gain from the swap will offset the losses to the insurer as its liabilities increase in value.

One further example is that of a medium-sized company with say a BBB credit rating. It wishes to borrow £5m over five years. Cost of borrowing fixed it regards as too high, it can, however, currently borrow at a lower floating rate relative to fixed. The risk of course is that interest rates will rise over the term of the loan to make the project for which they require the funds uneconomic.

If the company enters into a swap agreement as a fixed rate payer it can probably achieve fixed rate obligations lower than it could achieve without the swap. However, with regard to a hedge, if interest rates rise in the cash market it pays higher rates to service its loan. This extra cost, however, can be offset by the gain in value of the swap position, its value will rise as interest rates rise as a fixed rate payer. A more straightforward view is that as a fixed rate payer in the swap, interest rate payments, net, are fixed.

Other interest rate swaps

Other types of interest rate swaps include:

- basis swaps
- forward swaps
- callable swaps
- putable swaps
- extendible swaps
- call swaptions

- put swaptions
- rate-capped swaps
- zero coupon swaps
- amortising swaps
- accreting swaps
- rollercoaster swaps
- deferred rate setting swaps.

Basis swaps

In a plain vanilla swap fixed rate is swapped for floating. In a basis swap the counterparties both swap floating rate payments where the two floating rates are determined by different indexes.

A 'classic' example would be a bank entering a basis swap exchanging interest rate income from UK base rate determined loans for LIBOR determined funds. The risk is that the spread between base rate and LIBOR will change, i.e. basis risk. The bank swaps to become a floating rate payer of base rate linked payments and a receiver of LIBOR based floating rate, in this way the floating rate earned on the asset (i.e. loan) is determined in the same way as the funds to lend are obtained.

The Bank (C), raises LIBOR based funds and lends the money linked to base rate. The interest flows are as indicated in Figure 18.2. By means of the basis swap, LIBOR based flows into C match LIBOR based outflows. Base rate flows into C match outflows.

The dealer is able to receive 'base' and pay LIBOR due to swap arrangements they have with other swap counterparties. Figure 18.3 shows how the basis swap is engineered alongside two fixed for floating swap arrangements with D and E.

LIBOR flows from LIBOR borrowers to D, then from D via the dealer to C and then to the depositors with funds at C.

Base flows from borrowers of funds from C to C, then via the dealer to E and then on to base rate depositors at E.

Fixed flows from fixed rate borrowers from E to E, then via the dealer to D, who in turn pays their fixed rate depositors.

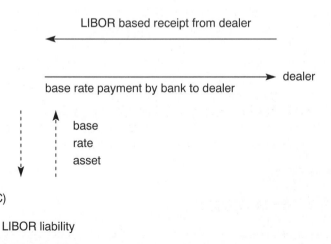

Figure 18.2 *Basis rate swap.*

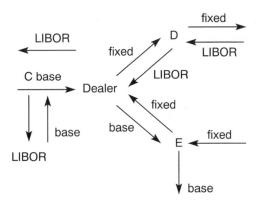

Figure 18.3 *Basis swap and the dealer.*

Basis swaps will swap floating rate indexes as previously identified, i.e. LIBOR, Treasury bills, bank CDs, commercial paper.

Forward swaps

A forward swap is any appropriate swap whose commencement date is sometime in the future, i.e. set forward, in this way it is possible to lock into swap rates and use them at a later date, when required. Forward swap rates and current swap rates will not necessarily be the same.

Deferred rate setting swaps

A deferred rate setting swap differs from a forward swap in that it allows the fixed rate payer to enter into the swap at any time up until a given future date. As a result the fixed rate payer can defer the fixed rate payable in the swap arrangement. Should rates fall a lower rate would become payable, fixed at the rate structure at the deferred date and not that at the commencement of the deferred swap arrangement itself.

Callable swaps

A callable swap gives the fixed rate payer the option to terminate the swap before its maturity. The holder of a callable swap therefore might wish to terminate the swap if interest rates fall. As a fixed rate payer they would otherwise be obligated to pay higher rates than available now at floating.

As with everything, the right to terminate comes at a price, as does every purchase of an option. The premium paid is not a sum of money in this case, however, but is reflected in the higher fixed rate which is paid in the swap than would otherwise be the case. Some callable swaps also incur a termination fee. The purchaser of a swap is the fixed rate payer – thus this is a callable swap.

Putable swaps

A putable swap gives the floating rate payer, the seller of a swap, the option to terminate the swap before its maturity. The right to terminate would be exercised in the event that interest rates rise. The option premium is reflected in higher floating rates and possible termination fee. Callable and putable swaps are sometimes referred to as **terminable** or **cancellable** swaps for self-evident reasons.

Extendible swaps

In an extendible swap the fixed rate payer has an option to extend the swap maturity date. Such a swap extension would be exercised if interest rates had increased during the period of the swap and were expected to remain high, or go even higher. A new swap arrangement could be made had an extendible swap not been purchased, but the new swap would obviously be in terms reflecting the higher interest rates, not those prevailing when the extendible swap would have been entered into.

The additional flexibility given by the extendible feature is again reflected in the fixed rate payable and possibly an extension fee if the right is exercised. Callable, putable and extendible swaps are all swaps with embedded options.

Call swaption

A call swaption gives its purchaser the option of entering into a swap as the fixed rate payer. The writer of the call swaptions is therefore the floating rate payer, if the option is exercised.

The strike rate is the fixed rate that is swapped for the floating rate. A maturity date is specified which can be either on European or American option terms.

The purchaser will pay the writer an appropriate premium up front, or this will be incorporated into the swap terms.

Put swaption

The purchasers of a put swaption has the option of entering into a swap as the floating rate payer. The writer of the put swaption becomes the fixed rate payer if exercised.

Call and put swaption uses

Call and put swaptions can be used appropriately to hedge uncertain cash flows, either as interest on liabilities or interest income on assets. An example of an uncertain income would be if you held callable bonds. You would not know if the bonds would be called, purchased from you, and therefore continue to be held by you producing an income flow.

Rate-capped swaps

If you are the floating rate payer in a swap the risk is that interest rates will rise causing you to have to pay more. The floating rate payable could be capped. The cap feature will cost. A fee will be paid up front to the fixed rate payer who will require such compensation to reflect the fact that the floating rate they will receive cannot exceed a given amount.

Zero coupon swaps

Zero coupon bonds by definition pay no coupon interest and therefore a bond issuer pays no interest and a bond holder receive none. All the return is in a single payment at the redemption of the bond when the bond is repaid in full. In a zero coupon swap the fixed rate payer makes a single fixed payment at the maturity of the swap from the proceeds of being repaid the bond. The floating rate payer makes periodic floating rate payments as is usual, they are therefore exposed to the credit risk that they will not be paid at all, having made payments in full over the life of the swap.

By entering into a swap the fixed rate payer benefits from any rise in interest rates. Their counterparty to the swap will of course lose out should rates rise, they will pay higher floating rates.

Amortising swaps

With an amortising swap the notional principal amount reduces during the life of the swap. With a plain vanilla the amount stays the same. A plain vanilla swap is suitable where loan interest is repayable periodically, but the principal amount being borrowed is repaid in one lump sum at the end of the period. It is a bullet repayment and its swap, the plain vanilla, is sometimes called a **bullet swap** for this reason.

With other types of loan, interest and part of the principal is repayable periodically, thus the next interest payment, along with repayment of principal, will be for a reduced sum because the principal outstanding will be less. This is an amortised loan. If the loan is **level payment** an equal amount of the principal is repaid periodically. It is a fully amortised loan.

A bank might make fully amortised loans to its customers on a fixed rate basis. The income generated from these loans would be used in a swap arrangement by the bank as a fixed rate payer in a swap arrangement. Because the loans are fully amortised an amortising swap would be necessary.

Accreting swaps

With an accreting swap the notional principal amount increases during the life of the swap. Such a swap could be used by a bank which has agreed to lend increasing sums over time to its customers so that they may fund projects.

Rollercoaster swaps

With a rollercoaster swap the notional principal amount is allowed to either increase or decrease in line with the needs of the swap counterparty.

Summary

- An interest rate swap is an arrangement whereby one party exchanges one set of interest rate payments for another, e.g. fixed for floating rate. Swaps can be either asset or liability swaps. Only interest payments are swapped, there is no need to exchange the notional principal.

- A swap is arranged through a dealer who will quote a bid/ask spread. For sterling swaps the quote is for the fixed rate and is usually quoted against six-month LIBOR flat as an index. The bid rate is the fixed rate paid by the dealer in exchange for receiving floating. The ask rate is the fixed rate paid to the dealer in exchange for receiving fixed.

- Quotes for US dollar swaps quote a margin related to a benchmark fixed rate, usually US T-bonds. In reality only net interest payments are exchanged in interest rate swaps.

- The swap is an arrangement completely separate from those connected to the actual borrowing of funds and indeed the fund lenders will know nothing of the swap. Each swap counterparty still remains responsible for servicing their own debt.

- Plain vanilla swaps 'work' when there is comparative advantage enjoyed by one of the counterparties in the cash market. The swapping of interest rate flows due to this quality spread lowers the interest rate cost to both parties. The difference between the quality spreads in the fixed and floating rate markets is the gain which can be allocated between the parties to the swap, including the dealer. Swap documentation uses either ISDA or BBAIRS standard terms.

- The swap purchaser is the fixed rate payer and receives floating. The swap seller pays floating and receives fixed rate.

- Swaps are quoted for a period of up to about 15 years. The market is liquid due to the system of warehousing, whereby a dealer will act as a temporary counterparty to a swap until a suitable permanent party can be found.

- Positions can be closed out by cancellation, also known as a close-out or swap buy back, or by a swap reversal or a swap sale, also called an assignment.

- In addition to interest rate advantages, swaps can also be seen as a hedging vehicle. Changes in the value of a swap position can be arranged so that it is the opposite to that of the cash market position. As an example, a fixed rate payer gains when interest rates rise. A fixed rate bond portfolio holder will lose as rates rise. The simultaneous holding of the two positions gives a net position neutral to interest rate changes.

- In addition to the plain vanilla, fixed to floating swap, other interest rate swaps include: basis swaps, forward swaps, callable and putable swaps, extendible swaps and call and put swaptions.

Questions

18.1

	Fixed	Floating
X can borrow at	6.5%	6m LIBOR + 75bp
Y can borrow at	8.0%	6m LIBOR + 135bp

Notional principal sum – £50m over 10 years.
Dealer's margin 20bp.
Quote the dealer's bid/ask rates.

18.2 Refer to Question 18.1. Which is better credit rated, X or Y? Which has comparative advantage? Which has absolute advantage?

18.3 Which is said to be long a swap, the fixed or floating rate payer?

18.4 If interest rates rise, who gains from the swap position, the fixed or floating rate payer?

18.5 What is meant by warehousing?

18.6 What is the difference between a swap reversal and a swap sale?

18.7 In what ways do callable swaps and call swaptions differ?

18.8 What is the more common term for a bullet swap?

18.9 Manling PLC has £14 million of fixed rate loans at an interest rate of 12% per year which are due to mature in one year. The company's treasurer believes that interest rates are going to fall, but does not wish to redeem the loans because large penalties exist for early redemption. Manling's bank has offered to arrange an interest rate swap for one year with a company that has obtained floating rate finance at London Interbank Offered Rate (LIBOR) plus $1\frac{1}{8}$%. The bank will charge each of the companies an arrangement fee of £20,000 and the proposed terms of the swap are that Manling will pay LIBOR plus $1\frac{1}{2}$% to the other company and receive from the company $11\frac{5}{8}$%.

Corporate tax is at 35% per year and the arrangements fee is a tax allowable expense. Manling could issue floating rate debt at LIBOR plus 2% and the other company could issue fixed rate debt at 11¾%. Assume that any tax relief is immediately available.

Required
(a) Evaluate whether Manling PLC would benefit from the interest rate swap
     (i)   if LIBOR remains at 10% for the whole year
     (ii) if LIBOR falls to 9% after six months.
(b) If LIBOR remains at 10% evaluate whether both companies could benefit from the interest rate swap if the terms of the swap were altered. Any benefit would be equally shared.

(ACCA, June 1990.)

18.10 Company A wishes to borrow £10m at a fixed rate for 5 years and has been offered either 11% fixed or six-month LIBOR + 1%. Company B wishes to borrow £10m at a floating rate for 5 years and has been offered either six-month LIBOR + 0.5% or 10% fixed.

(a) How may they enter into a swap arrangement in which each benefits equally?

(12 marks)

(b) What risks may this arrangement generate?

(8 marks)

(Securities Institute, Financial Futures and Options, December 1992.)

18.11 An investor purchases a newly-issued five-year bond yielding 7.5% and simultaneously enters into a five-year interest rate swap contract with matching terms under which she pays 6.75% and receives six-month LIBOR.

(a) What is the investor's combined return?
(b) Supposing the value of the bond to be £10 million, what cash flows would take place on the day of purchase?

(Securities Institute, Financial Futures and Options, December 1994.)

18.12 ABC Ltd. enters into a sterling interest rate swap under which it pays 8% fixed semi-annually against six month LIBOR on £10 million to XYZ Bank. The first LIBOR fixing is 6% for a period of 182 days.

(a) What sum of money is due at the end of the first period?
(b) To whom is it payable?

(Securities Institute, Financial Futures and Options, July 1994.)

 Further reading

DeCovny, S. (1992) *Swaps*, Woodhead Faulkner.

Currency swaps

Introduction

Currency swaps appeared on the scene before interest rate swaps, which have now overtaken them in importance. The main reason for this is that due to capital adequacy requirements, currency swaps are very expensive for banks and therefore expensive to use for potential counterparties. They developed from parallel or back to back loans which are difficult to arrange because funds are actually borrowed and re-lent, thus default risk is high. The loans also appear on-balancesheet. Documentation needs to be lengthy and complicated, largely due to the problems concerning right of set-off. As a result currency swaps developed.

The first example of a currency swap occurred in 1981 and as this did not involve an exchange of principal, it could also be off-balancesheet. The swap was between IBM and the World Bank and involved Swiss francs, deutschmarks and US dollars.

Currency swap definitions

The term swap in relation to currency is used here in a particular way. Swap is used in the currency futures market as an alternative to basis (Chapter 12). In the spot currency market it is a spot sale and a forward purchase of currency (Chapter 5).

Here we are using a currency swap to be a contract to exchange payments in one currency for payments in another.

In its simplest form this involves exchanging fixed interest payments on a loan in one currency for fixed interest payments on an equivalent loan in another currency. This is a **fixed to fixed currency swap**. It is not necessary that the actual principal be swapped, although it sometimes is. As an alternative currency can be exchanged at spot into the desired currency. Whichever is the case the principal amounts are always re-exchanged at the maturity of the swap.

Types of currency swaps

The following types of cross-currency swaps are found:

- fixed to fixed swap, as introduced in the previous section and further covered below;
- fixed to floating swap, sometimes called a circus swap or currency coupon swap, covered on p. 275.

Currency swap basics

Currency swaps involve three steps, although the first may be notional. The steps are:

1. Initial exchange of principal amount
2. Exchange of interest
3. Re-exchange of principal at maturity.

The principal amounts are agreed at the outset. The principal amount is agreed in one currency along with an exchange rate which will be used to determine the equivalent amount in the other currency. The principal amounts may be physically exchanged on the commencement date of the swap or may be notionally exchanged as with an interest rate swap. The exchange rate will usually be the spot, but an off-market rate could be used, which would, in turn, alter the subsequent interest rate flows.

A notional swap of principal has an outcome the same as a physical exchange. Funds raised in the spot market instead of being exchanged as part of the swap arrangements are simply exchanged into the desired currency in the foreign exchange market.

Interest rate obligations having been swapped, result in interest payments and receipts on agreed dates based upon the swapped principal amounts. Interest will be either fixed or floating as appropriate to the type of swap and each counterparty's obligations. Naturally the two interest rate flows will be in different currencies.

At maturity the principal amount is always physically re-exchanged. At this time spot will differ from that on the commencement date. In order to determine the actual sums involved the usual arrangement is that the original spot rate is used, as a result it follows that one party will then not make an exchange gain and the other a loss.

Fixed to fixed currency swap

The counterparties to a fixed to fixed currency swap may wish to enter the swap because of comparative advantage, the same kind of motivation as with interest rate swaps. The comparative advantage may be in either direction.

Company A is an American company and in this instance is able to access its own domestic bond market at low fixed rates because it is a familiar name. It can thus raise US dollars at low cost, lower than, for example Company B, a UK company, is able to raise US dollars by issuing its dollar bonds. Company B on the other hand is able to raise sterling at lower fixed cost than the US company. The situation is that the US company really wishes to raise sterling and the UK company really wishes to raise US dollars. Each enjoys a comparative advantage in their own domestic market. By using a fixed–fixed swap each is able to lower the cost of their funds.

An opposite scenario may also be observed. The American company may have a number of bond issues in its own domestic market and is unable to make further issues except at higher rates because the market has become saturated with its bonds. To take more bonds into portfolios, would represent a greater concentration of risk to investors, they therefore would require a greater return.

The UK company may also be in a similar position in its domestic market. Bond holders' appetites may be somewhat satiated with their bonds and they too can only make further issues at higher rates.

Company A in this second example access the sterling market at lower rates than B, even though it is a US company, B can access the dollar market at lower rates than A, even though it is sterling-based.

Company A and Company B can become matched swap counterparties in an appropriate fashion depending in which market they have the comparative advantage. We will take the following rates as an example:

Fixed borrowing rates

	US dollars	Sterling
Company A	5.0%	7.5%
Company B	7.0%	8.0%

A has a better credit rating than B as can be seen from the above rates. A has a comparative advantage in US dollars – 2% lower than B. B has a comparative advantage in sterling, A is only 0.5% lower.

A really wishes to borrow sterling and B really wishes to borrow US dollars. Each actually borrows in the market where they enjoy a comparative advantage, i.e. A borrows US dollars, B borrows sterling. Each swaps with the other so that A effectively borrows sterling and B effectively borrows US dollars. Each will need an income flow to service the effective interest liability they now have. The US dollar interest rate differential is 2%, the sterling differential is 0.5%. The gain shared between the parties to the swap, including the dealer, will be 2.0% minus 0.5%, i.e. $1\frac{1}{2}$%.

If the exchange rate is £1 = $1.50 and B wishes to borrow £10m, then A will borrow $15m. The principal is then exchanged. A borrows the dollars at 5% and B the sterling at 8%.

A and B during the life of the swap will service each other's debt. The arrangements so far are as illustrated in Figure 19.1.

A receives US dollar interest at 5% matching coupon payments of 5%. Sterling at 7% is paid, this is 0.50% less than they would pay in the cash market.

B receives sterling interest at 8% matching coupon payments of 8%. Dollar interest at 6.5% is paid which is 0.5% less than they would pay were they to issue US dollar bonds.

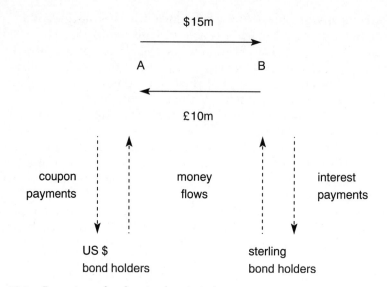

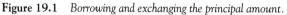

Figure 19.1 *Borrowing and exchanging the principal amount.*

A and B are thus both 0.5% better off.

The dealer makes a 1% loss on sterling flows and a gain of $1\frac{1}{2}\%$ on dollars. Therefore the net gain is 0.5%.

During the life of the swap the dealer is therefore exposed to exchange risk. The risk is that, here, US dollars will depreciate and sterling will appreciate. This exchange risk therefore needs to be hedged in the forward market.

The swap interest rate obligations given in Figure 19.2 can be altered so that some of the exchange risk can be borne by either A or B. Figure 19.3 gives an example.

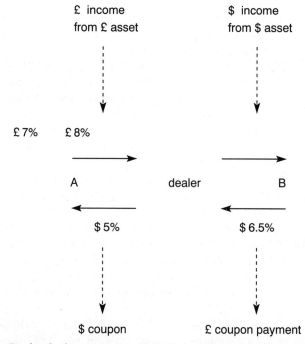

Figure 19.2 *Fixed to fixed currency swap, dealer bears exchange risk.*

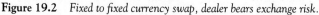

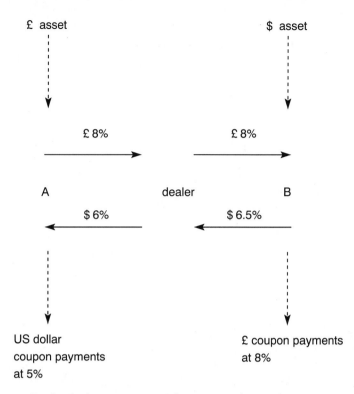

Figure 19.3 *Fixed to fixed currency swap, A bears some exchange risk.*

In Figure 19.3, A is paying 1% more sterling and receiving 1% more dollars. The risk is that dollars will depreciate and sterling appreciate.

A fixed to floating cross-currency swap

With a fixed to floating cross-currency swap, fixed rate obligations in one currency are swapped for floating rate obligations in another currency. Such swaps are described as coupon or circus swaps.

A is able to borrow US dollars advantageously at fixed rates and B is able to borrow sterling advantageously at floating, 6m LIBOR-based, rates.

By entering into the appropriate swap A and B can reduce the overall cost of borrowing each other's currency. A really wishes to borrow floating rate sterling and B US dollars fixed.

The US dollars at fixed rates are priced in the swap at a number of basis points above the index conventionally used, i.e. US T-bond rates of the appropriate maturity, e.g. five-year swap–five-year T-bond yields. The dealer might quote 71-78. If five-year T-bonds are currently yielding 7.50% p.a. then the fixed rate payer in the swap will pay 7.50 + 78 bp = 8.28% against 6m sterling LIBOR received flat. The counterparty will receive 71 bp over T-bond yield, i.e. 7.50 + 71 bp = 8.21% fixed and pay 6m LIBOR sterling flat. The spread of 7 bp will be retained by the dealer.

In terms of A and B the position will be as in Figure 19.4.

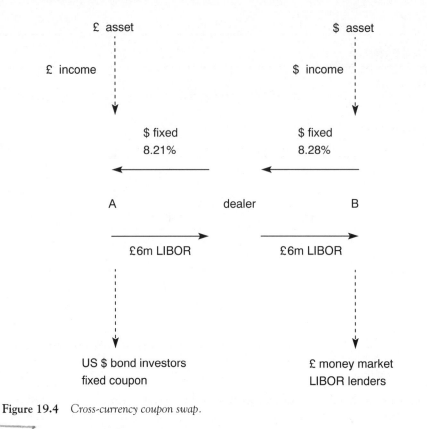

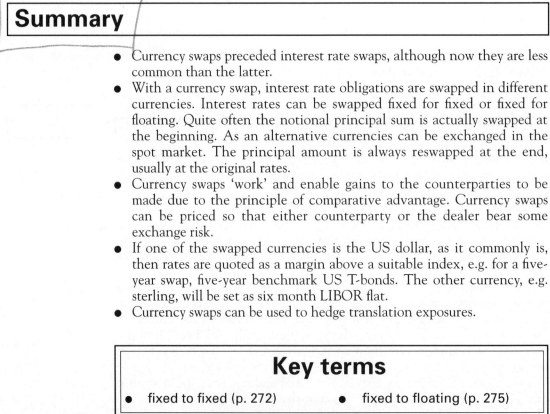

Figure 19.4 *Cross-currency coupon swap.*

Summary

- Currency swaps preceded interest rate swaps, although now they are less common than the latter.
- With a currency swap, interest rate obligations are swapped in different currencies. Interest rates can be swapped fixed for fixed or fixed for floating. Quite often the notional principal sum is actually swapped at the beginning. As an alternative currencies can be exchanged in the spot market. The principal amount is always reswapped at the end, usually at the original rates.
- Currency swaps 'work' and enable gains to the counterparties to be made due to the principle of comparative advantage. Currency swaps can be priced so that either counterparty or the dealer bear some exchange risk.
- If one of the swapped currencies is the US dollar, as it commonly is, then rates are quoted as a margin above a suitable index, e.g. for a five-year swap, five-year benchmark US T-bonds. The other currency, e.g. sterling, will be set as six month LIBOR flat.
- Currency swaps can be used to hedge translation exposures.

Key terms

- fixed to fixed (p. 272)
- fixed to floating (p. 275)

Questions

19.1 Using the following information, giving the dealer a profit of 10 bp, give the dealer's quote.
10-year term, fixed borrowing rates.

	USD	GBP
Company X	6.5%	7.0%
Company Y	8.0%	7.4%

19.2 With your quote in answer to Question 19.1, identify the parties who bear exchange risk. Suggest ways in which this risk can be hedged.

19.3 Company X finds itself overhedged on its US$ exposure and wishes to correct the situation. The simplest way of achieving this would be to unwind a sterling/dollar swap it has which matures in exactly five years' time. In the swap the company pays fixed rate US$ at 10% p.a. and receives floating rate sterling.

However, the swap is very much out-of-the-money at present. The cost of unwinding as a percentage of the notional principal of the swap would be 11.2%. This is considered to be too expensive.

Company X reluctantly accepts that it must continue with its overhedged position but wishes to reduce the carrying cost. As the company's banker you perceive that this can be achieved by converting the fixed rate of US$ interest paid by the company into floating rate interest. In the new swap your bank would pay 10% fixed rate interest against receiving six-month LIBOR (currently 3.5% p.a.) plus 275 basis points p.a.

Required:

Explain and illustrate how, by entering into the proposed second swap, Company X would reduce its costs. What else must it do in order to ensure that it maintains a cost advantage until both swaps mature in five years' time?   [20]
(CIOB Multinational Corporate Finance, May 1993.)

Further reading

DeCovny, S. (1992) *Swaps*, Woodhead Faulkner.

20 ► Summary/conclusions

Introduction

This final chapter seeks to bring together a number of issues. We discuss corporate treasury losses incurred when using derivatives and try to find some common errors practised by end users. We look at reporting and accounting for derivative risk in corporates and finally we discuss new developments at LIFFE, in particular the introduction of serial options and single transaction strategy trades.

Corporate treasury losses

During 1994 there was a steady trickle of press reports concerning large losses made by companies which had made use of derivatives. In turn this led to articles which discussed the possibility that derivative markets might undermine the whole global financial system. Other articles dealt with accounting issues, bank regulation and supervision. To quote the title of an article by John Plender in the *Financial Times*, 27 May 1994. 'Is the fear that derivatives are a multi-billion accident waiting to happen justified?'

The year 1994 certainly seems to have seen an acceleration in corporate treasury losses. At the beginning of the year Coopers and Lybrand were quoted as saying 'There is almost one [large corporate treasury loss] a year ... and they all seem to involve the use of derivatives' (*Financial Times*, 26 January 1994). Earlier, well-documented treasury losses at Allied Lyons and Showa Shell were cited. However, during the first half of 1994 the following treasury losses were the most notable:

- Metallgesellschaft (Germany) $1.4 bn (£933m) loss by its subsidiary MG Corp using oil futures and OTC options in conjunction with forwards.
- Balsam (Germany), loss not quantified, but currency options were entered into concerning underlying values of DM10–DM14bn (£4–£5.6bn) compared with the much smaller total company sales

turnover of DM460m, a clear sign of trading derivatives far in excess of that needed for hedging purposes.

- Codelco (Chile) lost an estimated US$100m in derivatives trading, compared with estimated profits for the previous year at $115m. Copper futures traded on the London Metal Exchange were the cause of the losses.
- Kashima Oil (Japan) lost ¥150bn ($1.5bn) in foreign exchange derivatives trading, enough to wipe out its capital completely.
- Proctor & Gamble lost $102m on interest rate swaps.

Losses using derivatives 'seem to have the common theme that senior management did not have full knowledge or full understanding of what was being transacted' (Brian Quinn, Bank of England's Executive Director of Banking Supervision speaking at a conference organised by the Futures Industry Association and the Futures and Options Association, reported *Financial Times*, 26 May 1994).

In some instances there is also alleged to be an element of fraud, as in the Balsam case where forged documents were used to obtain cash to finance Balsam's currency options business. Interestingly, Balsam was quite successful in many of its derivatives trades, profits in this area had disguised losses in other business areas for a number of years. However, the value of the receivables from the options trades was fraudulently inflated on many occasions and illustrates that little transparency exists in the case of OTC products which were usually used by Balsam and it is end users, the corporate hedgers which use OTC derivatives the most heavily.

In the case of Metallgesellschaft and its subsidiary MG Corp, the strategy they used was not overelaborate and complicated, it was understood by their top managers. It appears that the company's risk models were ignored when it told them of problems. The company was carrying such large positions in derivatives that they became unmanageable. A further problem is that its hedges suffered from timing mismatches.

MG Corp sold oil forward then hedged their forward contracts by going long in oil futures and oil swaps. Their problems arose because the forwards were for between five and 10 years maturities but their off-setting futures and swaps were for three months where there was good liquidity. The short-term hedges generated profit as long as short-term oil futures prices were above those for 5–10 year delivery and at maturity each three-month contract was rolled over into the next three months. The risk model could quite easily predict that if short-term prices fell below long-term prices large losses would be incurred. If prices should move in this way the hedge would need to be restructured. It was not and generated losses at roll over of about $30 m per month. It is believed that the enormous size of the future and swaps prevented restructuring. Estimates were made that MG's trades at Nymex represented about 10% of open positions on that exchange, thus putting a question mark over the amount of liquidity really available.

Clearly the attraction of the hedge actually placed was the short-term profits it generated so long as short-term prices were above long-term. This price relationship had held ever since the early 1980s and it was believed in the market that the relationship would always hold, or if it changed it would only be temporary.

The maturity mismatch seriously calls into question whether this is loss due to hedging. It certainly is loss due to derivatives trading. It crosses the line between management of exposure and speculation. Corporates which speculate expose their shareholders to risks of which they most certainly are unaware. Metallgesellschaft shareholders were aware of their exposure to oil price risk, but unaware they were exposed to the risk that short-term oil prices would fall below long-term and certainly unaware of the magnitude of the risk due to the leveraged position.

A key element in corporate loss is the lack of enforcement of controls. Often suitable controls are put in place which should ensure that losses cannot be made above a certain level and cannot be disguised, yet losses do occur which are kept from senior management. Perhaps corporates should not employ staff with high trading instincts? The psychology of trading is well known, that when a trader gets it wrong 'it's just a matter of timing' and often the position will be doubled up to make good the 'temporary' loss. There is every incentive to cover things up because it will all right itself eventually. Unauthorised trades will probably always occur, but controls should bring them to light at the end of the working day so that they can be closed out to minimise losses. Positions can be marked to market daily, even if not exchange traded, so that positions can be monitored. However, it must be acknowledged that in many OTC markets liquidity can easily evaporate, so that there is no market price and no certain value for positions.

In contrast, too much control can be a danger, it can look impressive but may disguise serious weaknesses. Information overload can just as easily confuse as the complexity of some strategies themselves.

Corporates need to have two levels of control upon their treasury operations – managerial and operational. Management controls should define what the treasury can do, give authorisation to personnel to undertake given operations with authorised counterparties, set limits as to authorisations and put in place operational controls to see that policy is implemented. Most large corporate losses are due to either lack of management controls or lack of adequate operational controls, or both.

Clear, written, formal objectives for dealing activity need to be given which reflect the company's attitude to risk. Specific authorities need to be given to individual staff specifying dealing limits, approved instruments and positions in them (can we write options?) along with maximum maturities.

Formal management controls have to be carefully drawn. If stated policy is 'there should be no exchange risk exposure, net positions should be fully hedged', dealers may fully hedge, but attempt to speculate through timing mismatches unless timing mismatches are prohibited within the policy. Dealing limits on individual transactions can be circumvented by splitting deals into small units, therefore operation controls should monitor, policy daily cumulative transaction limits.

Day time limits can be larger than overnight limits due to the easier close-outs during the day if positions deteriorate or go outside loss limits, if set.

Dealing should be separated from reporting, accounting and settlement to prevent fraud.

New developments at LIFFE

Strategy variations using derivatives are probably almost limitless. It is useful if some of the more popular strategies which involve taking simultaneous multiple futures and/or option position can be executed as a single trade on the exchange. Some examples are identified in the following sections.

Single transaction strips

On 21 March 1994 it became possible to trade in a single transaction a strip in either any four or six consecutive delivery months (refer to pp. 138–9 for an explanation of strips). This single trade strategy is available in all LIFFE three-month interest rate futures contracts. Contract specification is summarised in Table 20.1.

- Buying a strip involves the simultaneous purchase of one futures contract in each of four or six consecutive delivery months.
- Selling a strip involves the simultaneous sale of one futures contract in each of four or six consecutive delivery months.

Pricing and quotation

The price of a strip is quoted, in line with current market quotes, as the sum of the differences between the current price for each delivery month and its previous settlement price.

Table 20.1   Four month/six month strip

Short Sterling	Bid/offer	Previous settlement
March 94	94.60/61	94.58
June 94	94.86/87	94.84
Sep 94	94.97/98	94.91
Dec 94	94.90/91	94.86

Market quote:

'What's there in the March–Dec Short Sterling Strip?'
'It's 14 for 20/20 at 18'

Seller (trades at bid price):

		Previous settlement	Bid minus settlement
94.60	Mar 94	94.58	2
94.86	Jun 94	94.84	2
94.97	Sep 94	94.91	6
94.90	Dec 94	94.86	4
		Total	14

20 is 20 lots (contracts).
Bid is 14 for 20.

Single transaction butterfly

On 21 March 1994 it became possible to trade a butterfly in a single transaction in all LIFFE short-term interest rate futures contracts.

A butterfly involves futures contracts of three consecutive delivery months in the same future.

To buy (sell) a butterfly:

- Buy (sell) one contract in the nearest delivery month.
- Sell (buy) two contracts in the next month.
- Buy (sell) one contract in the following month.

Price is quoted as the difference between the price for the first month and the second month minus the difference between the price for the second and third month.

Serial options

Traditional exchange traded options (and futures) contracts expire every quarter in March, June, September and December. Serial options are expiry months during the year in addition to those every quarter.

On 10 May 1994 the Bund Serial Options were introduced, this enables four expiry months to be traded, two serial and two quarterly, including the three nearest calendar months. Thus, for example, in the trading period 27 March 95 to 21 Apr 95 listed option contracts expiring May 95, Jun 95, Jul 95, Sep 95 can be traded.

Also on 10 May 1994 serial options became available for the Euromark option. Here six listed option contracts are available for trading in any one trading period, two serial and four quarterly. Therefore as an example, during the trading period 18 Apr 95 to 15 May 95 the following listed contracts are tradable, May 95, Jun 95, Jul 95, Sep 95, Dec 95, Mar 96.

Purchasers of serial options will benefit from lower premiums applicable to short-dated options. Calendar spread strategies over one month periods become easier.

Single trade futures and option strategies

The following list gives LIFFE single trade futures and option strategies:

Futures strategies

Calendar Spread	Simultaneously buy one contract in the nearest delivery month and sell one contract in the next month.
Strip	Buying a four (or six) month strip involves simultaneously purchasing one contract in any four (or six) consecutive delivery months.
Butterfly	Simultaneously buy one contract in the nearest delivery month used in the strategy, sell two contracts in the next month and purchase one contract in the following month.

Option strategies

Butterfly	Buy put (or call), sell two puts (or calls) at higher strike,buy put (or call) at equally higher strike.
Call (put) spread	Buy call, sell call at higher strike (Buy put, sell put at lower strike).
Calendar spread	Sell near put (call), buy far put (call)
Diagonal calendar spread	Sell near put (or call), buy far put (or call) at different strike.
Guts	Buy call, buy put at higher strike.
Two by one ratio	Sell call, buy two calls at higher strike.
Call (put) spread	(Sell put, buy two puts at lower strike).
Iron butterfly	Buy straddle, sell strangle (e.g. sell put, buy put and call at higher strike, sell call at equally higher strike).
Combo	Sell call, buy put at lower strike.
Strangle	Buy put, buy call at higher strike.
Ladder	Buy call, sell call at higher strike, sell call at equally higher strike (sell put at higher strike, buy put at equally higher strike).
Straddle calendar spread	Sell straddle in near month, buy straddle in far month at same strike.
Diagonal straddle	Sell straddle in near month, buy straddle in far month at different strike.
Conversion/reversal	Conversion: sell call, buy put at same strike, buy future. Reversal: buy call, sell put at same strike, sell future.
Straddle	Buy put, buy call at same strike.
Volatility trade	Buy put, buy future to give zero net delta. Buy call, sell future to give zero net delta.

Condor	Buy put (or call), sell put (or call) at two equally higher strikes, buy put (or call) at yet higher strike.
Box	Buy call and sell put, buy put and sell call at higher strike.

Note: the above strategies are all buying strategies.

To achieve delta neutrality the appropriate number of futures should be sold or bought in each case.

Volume and open interest records for LIFFE contracts as at 31 August 1994

Exchange (all contacts)

Volume records

Record day:
1,615,165 on 2 March 1994.
Record week:
5,397,207 during week ending 4 March 1994.
Record month:
17,823,319 at February 1994.

Open interest records

Exchange record open interest:
  5,172,610 at 18 February 1994.

Futures

Volume records

Record day (all futures contracts):
1,364,417 on 2 March 1994.
Record week (all futures contracts):
4,641,264 during week ending 4 March 1994.
Record month:
14,420,463 at February 1994.

Individual daily contract records

Contract	Number of contracts traded	Date
Three-month sterling	226,921	16 Sep 92
Three-month Eurodollar	34,189	16 Oct 89
Long gilt	235,759	24 Feb 94
Japanese Govt Bond	7,924	21 Jan 94
German Govt Bond	419,329	2 Mar 94

Three-month Eurodeutschmark	383,108	2 Mar 94
Three-month ECU	8,927	21 Oct 93
Three-month Euro Swiss	29,873	21 Oct 93
BTP Italian Govt Bond	152,062	2 Mar 94
Eurolira	65,986	11 May 94
Bobl	15,912	30 Jul 93

Individual monthly contract records

Contract	Number of contracts traded	Month
Three-month sterling	1,815,491	Sep 92
Three-month Eurodollar	251,084	Oct 87
Long gilt	2,733,630	Feb 94
Japanese Govt Bond	74,854	Jun 94
German Govt Bond	4,382,715	Feb 94
Three-month Eurodeutschmark	3,234,518	May 94
Three-month ECU	99,334	Jul 93
BTP Italian Govt Bond	1,527,702	Feb 94
Eurolira	395,437	Jun 94
Bobl	137,473	Mar 93

Open interest records

Record open interest (all futures contracts):
2,444,959 on 2 March 1994.

Record open interest positions (individual contracts)

Contract	Number of open positions	Date
Three-month Sterling	555,081	29 Jul 94
Three-month Eurodollar	67,527	19 Jun 89
Long gilt	197,658	2 Mar 94
Japanese Govt Bond*	2,471	17 Jul 87
German Govt bond	300,834	3 Mar 94
German Bobl	28,152	30 Jul 93
Three-month Eurodeutschmark	1,057,287	26 May 94
Three-month ECU	39,746	1 Mar 94
Three-month Euro Swiss	67,688	28 Feb 94
BTP Italian Govt Bond	136,978	2 Mar 94
Eurolira	159,683	17 May 94

*New JGB launched 3 April 1991 – no open interest positions held.

Options on futures

Volume records

Record day (all financial option contracts):
206,039 on 25 Feb 94.

Record week (all financial option contracts):
717,301 during week ending 11 Feb 94.

Record month (all financial option contracts):
2,423,076 at Feb 94.

Individual daily contract records

Contract	Number of contracts traded	Date
Three-month Eurodollar	6,850	21 Feb 92
Long gilt	52,882	13 Apr 92
Three-month Sterling	71,357	29 Jul 94
German Govt Bond	108,444	7 Feb 94
Three-month Eurodeutschmark	51,054	2 Mar 94
BTP Italian Govt Bond	37,542	25 Feb 94
Three-month Euro Swiss	1,505	16 Feb 93

Individual monthly contract records

Contract	Number of contracts traded	Month
Three-month Eurodollar	19,801	Feb 92
Long gilt	415,060	Feb 94
Three-month Sterling	441,536	Aug 94
German Govt Bond	1,179,059	Feb 94
Three-month Eurodeutschmark	343,017	Oct 93
BTP Italian Govt Bond	192,772	Feb 94
Three-month Euro Swiss	9,841	Nov 92

Open interest records

Record open interest position (options on futures contracts):
1,730,055 on 20 May 1994.

Record open interest positions (individual contracts)

Contract	Number of open positions	Date
Three-month Eurodollar	20,583	21 Feb 92
Long gilt	177,002	15 Apr 92
Three-month Sterling	631,939	31 Aug 94
German Govt Bond	642,333	29 Apr 94
Three-month Eurodeutschmark	516,476	14 Mar 94
BTP Italian Govt Bond	165,341	29 Apr 94
Three-month Euro Swiss	9,460	14 Dec 92

Source: LIFFE Market Statistics.

Questions and further study

You might like to consider the answers to some of the following questions as further areas of study.

20.1 A number of exchange traded futures and option contracts fail when introduced. What are the conditions/specifications necessary for the success of individual exchange traded futures and options contracts?

20.2 Does the use of derivatives cause greater volatility in underlying than would otherwise be the case?

20.3 Why do exchanges continue to use open outcry rather than say systems like APT at LIFFE? Or alternatively, why is volume on APT so low in comparison with that for open outcry at LIFFE?

20.4 There are generally two recognised ways of corporate hedgers accounting for derivatives in their profit and loss accounts. They are hedge accounting and marking to market values of the derivatives used.

- Hedge accounting – match gains and losses on the derivative with the asset or liability it hedges. Profits/losses on the derivative are deferred and off-set against corresponding losses/gains on the underlying.

- Marked to market – derivatives are marked to market at the end of each accounting period and gains and losses are put through the profit and loss account. As a separate issue gains/losses on sale/purchase of the underlying are treated as if no use of derivatives had been made.

Which gives a true and fair view?

20.5 The marking to market method described in Question 20.4 produces volatile quarterly earnings. Why should this be so?

20.6 Why might 'after hours trading' (i.e. trading after pit trading has ceased each day) become important?

20.7 Does widespread hedging of interest rate risk alter the outcome of domestic monetary policy?

20.8 Many banks conduct their derivatives dealing in 'special purpose vehicles' or subsidiaries. How does this affect the jurisdiction of regulatory bodies?

Further reading

Shaleen, K. H. (1990) *Volume and Open Interest: Cutting edge strategies in the futures market*, McGraw Hill.

Bernstein, J. (1991) *Timing Signals in the Futures Market; The Trader's Definitive Guide to Buy/Sell Indicators*, McGraw Hill.

21 ▷ Postscript – Barings Bank

Barings Futures Singapore (BFS), the subsidiary of Barings Bank, at the end of 1994 was awarded the title 'Clearing Firm of the Year' at SIMEX. A matter of a few weeks later, on Sunday 26 February 1995, the whole Barings Group went into voluntary liquidation with losses estimated at £860m. It was eventually acquired by Internationale Nederlanden Group (ING) for a nominal sum of £1 in return for taking over Barings' assets and liabilities. Only liabilities were taken over whose value could be ascertained and be fixed for certain. Losses completely wiped out the entire capital of the bank which stood at £541m. How could it come about that a triple A rated bank could fail so quickly as the result of the alleged actions of a single individual, Nick Leeson?

As is usual in such matters, the situation had been developing for some time before the actual collapse and had been building during much of 1994 and 1995. The actual collapse was precipitated by BFS finding itself unable to meet variation margin payments of £7m due on the morning of Monday 27 February related to futures contracts it held at SIMEX. Accumulated losses to February 24 seemed to have amounted to £384m.

BFS was empowered to trade on clients' behalf at SIMEX and naturally there was no market risk attached to this for the bank. Price movements resulting in losses to clients would be fully covered by clients and be backed up by the margin system.

BFS also implemented five allowable, identified trading strategies on its own behalf – proprietary trading – but these too should not have introduced a lot of risk. Nevertheless BFS were not always running a totally matched book. The main strategy used was to exploit small but frequent price differences between the Nikkei 225 Index futures contract in Singapore and Osaka in Japan. By going long on one exchange and short on the other, obligations cancel each other out and losses on one position match gains on the other, except for the arbitrage profit.

Large positions in the Nikkei 225 contract at SIMEX were questioned by exchange officials, but they were reassured when they were told of the strategy and the off setting positions in Osaka. Unfortunately they did not check the information. Had they done so they would have found that they did not exist. As a result the positions at SIMEX were highly speculative and not at all safe. Positions taken at Osaka were in fact long, as at SIMEX, and therefore doubled the risk. Reassurances as to the illusory Osaka positions were given during a visit to Singapore by a Barings London official, demonstrating that they did not have the correct information either.

Earliest written evidence of SIMEX's concern is dated 30 December 1994 when they began to become alarmed at the increase in BFS' trading activity. A letter was sent to Barings London on 27 January 1995 giving full details of open positions at SIMEX.

SIMEX stated that they did not question BFS' positions earlier because 'they relied upon Barings' credit rating and good name'. In addition they had always met their variation margin payments. (Of course, otherwise they would be in default, as on February 27!) From SIMEX's point of view 'the best evidence the situation was in order was that Barings met margin calls, in amounts of millions of dollars, right up to Monday February 27, when the bank went into administration'.

Although SIMEX has position limits, they always granted requests by BFS to increase their limit, again for the reasons already identified. The fact that towards the end BFS held 15% of open positions on the Nikkei 225 contract was not an issue for them because 'manipulation of the market is not an issue... the contract is cash settled'.

Instead of off setting positions at SIMEX related to positions in Osaka, it appears therefore that long futures positions were taken only in the Nikkei 225 Index at both locations. Such positions lose value and require margin payments should the index fall. Indeed the index did fall requiring the index to be bought at a high price. Margin losses accumulated.

The Nikkei 225 was beginning to fall as the long futures positions were being taken. Leeson appears to have been betting that the fall would be reversed. The earthquake centred around Kobe sent the index downward still further. However, there was a view that the necessary reconstruction of the damaged infrastructure would provide a boost to the Japanese economy and thus push the index upwards. Perhaps Leeson held this view. It was not to be. Damage was greater than originally thought and caused a lot of economic dislocation. An appreciating Yen against the US dollar created further problems for Japanese exporters who were able to keep production lines going despite damage to their suppliers' production lines in the Kobe region. This also caused the index to fall.

A Barings London monitoring committee (Alco – asset and liability committee) was told at one stage, erroneously of course, that the futures positions, although not off set, were in fact short. Therefore there was no cause for concern as such positions would accumulate margin receipts.

The question arises, how was it possible to conceal such losses? Or indeed, were the aforementioned strategies condoned? At least the question is, what kind of control systems, if any, did Barings have in place? Were they effective? Could they be easily circumvented?

Price Waterhouse, appointed to investigate when Barings went into administration, were reported on March 15 as saying that they were investigating 'a pervasive climate of concealment'. Cooper & Lybrand, BFS auditors since August 1994, had not signed off BFS year end accounts.

The 'pervasive climate of concealment' mainly centred around two hidden trading books, Error Account 88888 (a Chinese lucky number) and Error Account 92000. The former was used for SIMEX trades and the latter for Osaka. The use of error accounts is not uncommon in organizations that trade futures; they are designed to record errors, i.e. when trades cannot be reconciled. In this instance however they appear to have been used for concealment. It is alleged that they were used to hide exposures in futures and options where there was no intention of taking an off setting hedge, contrary to the apparent authorities held by BFS. They were also used to conceal actual losses incurred. These hidden losses were discovered by Barings London on 23 February 1994 after Leeson had left Singapore and his note of regret to his employer.

The losses concealed in Error Account no. 88888 on 21 February amounted to over £50m. Leeson was subsequently accused by the Singapore authorities of forging documents which showed a Yen 7.7bn (£50.65m) payment to his trading unit made by the US investment firm Spears Leeds and Kellogg for alleged execution of a call option on the Nikkei 225. In this way the losses accumulated in the account were camouflaged and the accounts balanced. It was further alleged that these forged documents were handed on Leeson's instructions to the auditors Cooper & Lybrand on 3 February 1995 so that provisional audit clearance could be obtained for BFS' financial statement for 1994.

The loss of ¥7.7bn was then transferred to a customer account so that the loss did not appear to be that of BFS. It was further alleged that the transfer was supported by a message on the counterparty's notepaper sent from a personal fax machine. In addition a further alleged forged document designed to conceal the losses was a confirmation from Barings' bankers, Citibank in Singapore, that BFS actually received the ¥7.7bn in payment.

On 2 February 1994 the losses in Error Account 88888 were shown to have increased to ¥59.2bn (£386m). The account had been used for just over a year. The first entries were made in January 1994.

At close of business on 24 February 1995 the account had:

- 61,039 long futures contracts on the Nikkei 225;
- 26,079 short futures contracts in Japanese Government Bonds;
- 6,845 short futures contracts in Euroyen.

Margin payments on Monday 2 February 1994 would have amounted to the Yen equivalent of £7m.

Leeson allegedly also built up the very long position in the Nikkei 225 by purchasing contracts from BFS' main account which held hedged positions. On January 26, 16,000 March contracts were bought in this way. On the same day 26,000 contracts were sold from the Error Account at the end of the trading day. Such a pattern fitted BFS' rules not to hold overnight unhedged positions.

All the unauthorized proprietary trading in loss making positions naturally required very large variation payments. Between the end of January 1995 and the collapse on February 26, BFS borrowed up to $850m (£538m). This in turn was converted to Yen and made over as margin payments at Osaka and SIMEX. ¥70–80bn (£454m) was paid over in this way. About ¥60bn was lent by Japanese banks.

Therefore large numbers of contracts were bought, far in excess of client requirements and held as open, unhedged positions. There is also the question of Yen exposure. Some margin payments had been made financed by Yen borrowing, creating Yen exposure which was presumably itself unhedged. Because the Yen was actually appreciating against the US dollar and sterling, this would also have created currency exposure losses.

Reports to Barings' London monitoring committee (Alco) showed trading positions as matched and therefore risk free. The report for 27 February 1994 shows matched long and short positions with underlying values of $3.1bn on the Nikkei 225, $10.3bn on Japanese Government Bonds and $51m on Euroyen. Daily reports show the arbitrage 'switching book' was making significant profits in February 1995. In the month to February 21, income of £4.5m was recorded for arbitraging the Nikkei 225.

Daily 'value at risk' figures for all global trading operations were reported. The figures show how much of the Group's capital is at risk following market price movements. Throughout February 1995 the Singapore results showed 'nil'. This was largely possible due to Leeson's alleged misuse of the Error Accounts and the fact that he was able to do so quite freely as a result of being in control of trading and the back office in Singapore. He was General Manager and Chief Trader. As a result he could override any awkward questions in Singapore. There is thus evidence of weak management controls within the Barings Group and lack of effective operational controls. Although apparently fairly common in Singapore until then, to be in charge of trading (executing and agreeing trades and at the same time being in charge of settlement), recording, monitoring and payments would be regarded as a basic error of control. It is allowing someone to be their own policeman. Barings' own internal auditors reported in August 1994 that Leeson could override controls, yet little seemed to have changed. Nothing had been done.

Barings' eight person Alco met on 26 January 1995 and were still expressing concern over Leeson's trading activity. Nothing had been done either to investigate the truthfulness of reports from Singapore or to put in place a more effective control system at management and operational levels. Minutes of the 26 January meeting state that the futures positions 'should not be increased, and where possible be reduced'. Despite this Leeson increased positions substantially in February. As previously described, on 26 January itself, Leeson allegedly bought 16,000 March contracts on the Nikkei 225 for the hidden trading account no. 88888.

Barings' controls were such that Leeson had no gross position limits placed upon his proprietary trading. In theory it meant he could have limitless covered and uncovered positions, provided in the case of the latter he could conceal their true nature. His only restraint with regard to the number of positions he could hold was the capacity of central treasury in London to fund him. An internal auditor's report states 'no gross limits [are] set for arbitrage positions... [the] only constraint is that group treasury will eventually inform BFS that they will cease funding requirements if they grow too large'. It is not clear that even such funding limits were set, let alone followed. Indeed in August 1994 Barings London took steps to make funding Singapore easier. It increased its credit lines so that between January 1995 and its collapse it was able to draw $850m (£535m).

A further internal auditor's report states that Barings had 'no trades booked in its own name and consequently received funds from clients...to fund margin deposits... [but it was] often short of funding on a day to day basis'.

It was also reported that up until late 1994 Leeson could sign off the daily review of positions at SIMEX, along with its reconciliation. To be able to do both is a fundamental control error. There is no independent cross check.

Reports were apparently believed and very large sums of money were also remitted from Barings London to meet margin payments. Movement of such large sums would normally have required authorization at a very senior level indeed. Barings treasury in London during January and February 1995 allegedly remitted $1.3bn (£550m) to Leeson's unit in Singapore.

Perhaps there is the feeling of wanting to believe; that people are just being negative and of course large profits were apparently being generated – why stop such a good thing? Warning voices might spoil it. Leeson's unit in Singapore was making a very large contribution to group profits. In the first seven months of 1994 group pre-tax profits were £54.8m; Singapore had contributed £18.8m. It is perhaps difficult to stop someone apparently so successful.

Risks do seem to have been identified up to a point but little seems to have been done about them, either at managerial or operational level. Leeson's dual role in Singapore, with its inherent dangers, was identified but not acted upon. Funding risks were noted but it does not seem to be the case that their weakness as a control mechanism was appreciated. That concealment of such large positions could occur is evidence of a lack of control which was compounded by the willingness to fund the consequences of such positions, both in the payment of necessary initial margins and the subsequent variation payments needed to cover losses from the positions.

It may be of interest to note that to generate some income to meet the variation payments on the futures positions, option straddles were sold (options not traded futures style at SIMEX; therefore the short is paid the premium 'up front'). You can see from Figure 14.19 (p. 178) that a top straddle has a positive pay off if the underlying is not very volatile. However movements in the price of the underlying create losses once the break even points are breached. Top straddles were sold on the Nikkei 225, which of course fell 'a lot' and created further losses when the longs on the option legs started to become in-the-money. It is all evidence of an 'it will all come right in the end' attitude.

The full story of the Barings collapse has still to emerge at the time of writing. To date it seems that risk management controls were so weak that they could be easily overridden. The trading strategies adopted were not so complicated that risks could not be assessed easily. Long open futures positions are not difficult to understand and manage; their pay off risk profiles are straightforward.

An important message is that the financial integrity of the clearing house at SIMEX remained intact. The initial margin and variation margin systems worked. No original counterparty to the BFS trades lost out. Indeed if they kept their short positions it is they who will have received the margin payments. It is they who have gained from Barings' loss, as is expected in a futures market. It is a zero sum game after all.

Following the collapse there is now a perceived need to collate and co-ordinate information on individual firms trading across a number of exchanges so that the whole picture can be seen. Better communications are necessary with more uniform regulatory standards and practices. Lack of uniformity might in different circumstances pose a systemic risk. In this case the chief impact was arguably on the Nikkei 225 itself, which fell 3.8% on the news of the collapse. This posed a small threat to Japanese banks' capital due to their large holdings of Japanese equities.

It is a final salutary reminder that no matter how well conceived the high level managerial controls and no matter how well the controls are implemented at operational level to ensure that the high level controls are carried out, 'when a dealer is on the phone he can sell the bank'. It is only later, within hours or at the end of the day, that with good systems you can find out what a dealer has done. With poor controls you merely find out when it is really too late.

Index